# 新手学

# 外贸函电

## 一本通

朱菲菲◎编著

全新版

# Foreign
# Trade

中国铁道出版社有限公司
CHINA RAILWAY PUBLISHING HOUSE CO., LTD.

# 内 容 简 介

这是一本全面介绍外贸业务各流程中需要用到的英文函电的书籍。全书共10章，主要包括三个部分，第一部分介绍一些外贸函电常用术语；第二部分介绍外贸业务各流程需要用到的函电，包括签订单函电、议价函电和索赔函电等；第三部分介绍从事外贸活动还需要用到的其他外贸函电，包括祝贺函电和问候函电等。

针对具体的外贸业务编写，从实际出发，通过大量常用词汇和情境实例，真实展示在外贸实战中专业的英文函电。帮助外贸人员在短时间内学会得体的英文商务信函表达，从而更好地与客户沟通。

**图书在版编目（CIP）数据**

新手学外贸函电一本通:全新版/朱菲菲编著.—2版.—北京：中国铁道出版社有限公司，2021.4（2024.3重印）

ISBN 978-7-113-27303-3

Ⅰ.①新⋯ Ⅱ.①朱⋯ Ⅲ.①对外贸易-英语-电报信函-写作 Ⅳ.①F75

中国版本图书馆CIP数据核字（2020）第185091号

书　　名：**新手学外贸函电一本通**（全新版）
XINSHOU XUE WAIMAO HANDIAN YIBENTONG（QUANXIN BAN）

作　　者：朱菲菲

责任编辑：张亚慧　　编辑部电话：(010) 51873035　　邮箱：lampard@vip.163.com
编辑助理：张秀文
封面设计：宿　萌
责任校对：苗　丹
责任印制：赵星辰

出版发行：中国铁道出版社有限公司（100054，北京市西城区右安门西街8号）
印　　刷：北京铭成印刷有限公司
版　　次：2018年6月第1版　　2021年4月第2版　　2024年3月第6次印刷
开　　本：710 mm×1 000 mm　1/16　印张：19.75　字数：280千
书　　号：ISBN 978-7-113-27303-3
定　　价：55.00元

# 前　言

邮件是外贸企业常用的业务沟通方式之一，无论是传统的信函还是电子邮件，都因其可以存档、便于查询且能够在深思熟虑后再进行回复的特点，受到商务人士的青睐。

对于从事外贸工作的人员来说，最基本的要求就是能够利用邮件与客户顺畅地交流，不仅要明白对方想要表达的内容，而且能在邮件中得体地表达自己想要说明的意思。

在实际工作中，外贸人员在书写邮件时可能会面临无从下笔的情况，导致这种情况的原因可能是不知道该如何表达自己的意思，或是不懂专业的表达方式，甚至出现"中式英语"的表达……

那么，外贸人员如何才能克服这些问题，使自己写出的英文邮件具备专业水准？此时，外贸人员就需要研读专业的函电书籍，了解大量专业和准确的英文邮件的表达方式，充实自己的"模板库"。这样在实际工作中就可以拿来即用，不必苦苦思索词语，把精力集中于最重要的事项，从而使得自己的贸易工作越来越顺手。

为了帮助外贸从业人员或即将进入外贸行业的人员能够在短时间内迅速提高书写专业英文函电的能力，更好地从事国际贸易工作，笔者特意编写了本书。

本书分为三个部分，包括 10 章内容，具体章节内容如下。

◎ 第一部分：第 1 章

主要介绍外贸函电相关的基础知识，包括外贸相关知识、外贸函电的常用术语及外贸函电的写法和格式。是相对比较基础的外贸函电入门知识。

◎ 第二部分：第 2 章~第 9 章

主要介绍外贸业务具体流程需要用到的函电，包括开发客户的函电、询价函电、报价函电、还价函电、生产和装运函电、支付结算函电、保险和售后服务说明函电以及投诉和索赔函电等。通过对这部分内容的学习，从事外贸工作的人员可以充分且熟练地掌握日常工作中常见的英文函电格式和表达方式。

◎ 第三部分：第 10 章

主要介绍从事外贸活动需要用到的其他外贸函电，包括日常通知、节日问候、生病慰问和升职祝贺等。这些函电看似不与工作直接相关，但对于维护新老客户关系具有十分重要的作用。

本书针对具体的外贸业务编写，从实际出发，通过各种词汇和情境实例，展示在外贸实战中专业的英文函电，帮助外贸人员在短时间内学会得体的英文商务信函表达，从而更好地与客户沟通。除此之外，还将书中涉及的大量情景交流内容制作成语音音频，使读者能够轻松地掌握学习内容，并同时练习英语口语。

最后，希望所有读者都能够从本书中获益，在平时的工作中与客户顺利地沟通、交流。由于笔者能力有限，对于本书内容不完善的地方希望得到广大读者的批评指正。

编 者
2020 年 12 月

# 目 录

## CHAPTER 01　外贸函电基础知识
### Basic Knowledge of Foreign Trade Letters

在学习外贸业务流程之前，我们首先要掌握外贸函电的基础知识，包括外贸相关知识、外贸函电的常用术语及外贸函电的写法和格式。

# CHAPTER 02 发展客户拉业务
## Develop Customer and Service

做外贸业务，本质上依旧是一个产品卖出去的过程，因此只有找到合适的客户，维系意向客户，发展潜在客户，最终手上握有较多客户资源，才能将外贸业务做得风生水起。

# CHAPTER 03　开发信与促销信
## Sales Letters and Promotion Letters

　　在外贸业务员的日常工作中，需要经常发送拓展新客户的开发信和维护老客户关系的促销信，但这类函件不能千篇一律，需要根据不同情况进行调整。此外，代理函电也会在本章进行介绍。

# CHAPTER 04  订单操作函电
**Order Operation Letters**

对于外贸业务员来说，询盘、发盘与还盘的订单操作流程是在双方正式签约之前最重要的工作之一，直接影响合同的签订及履行，关系双方的经济利益，需要谨慎处理。

# CHAPTER 05　接受与签约函电
Acceptance and Contract Letters

在大致确定订单事项后，对外贸易的双方就可以展开实质性合作了。除了通过来往函电确认成交并签约，外贸公司在签约后还要准备生产前样品和向供应商下单，为正式生产做准备。

# CHAPTER 06　生产与装运函电
### Production and Shipment Letters

对于外贸公司来说，价格、质量和交货期是最重要的经营要素。而质量和交货期又与生产和装运息息相关，因此在客户下了订单之后，外贸业务员要密切关注订单的行踪，并及时与客户沟通。

# CHAPTER 07　支付结算和信用证
### Payment, Settlement and Letter of Credit

在国际贸易中，买卖双方签订销售合同后，最重要的就是货款的结算，对于货款支付时间和支付方式等都需要企业倍加小心。而信用证是国际贸易中使用最广泛的结算方式，需要重点把握。

# CHAPTER
## 08　保险与售后函电
### Insurance and After-sale Letters

在订单操作过程中，外贸业务员需要处理好保险问题，以免在发生意外后，双方因保险索赔问题产生纠纷。在售出产品后，应及时跟进，询问产品和市场情况，改进产品和推荐相关产品，以维系客户关系。

## PART 1　与保险有关的函电 Insurance Letter　/212

## PART 2　往来商议保险条款 Insurance Terms Negotiation　/217

# CHAPTER 09　投诉与索赔函电
## Complaints and Claims Letters

客户投诉或客户索赔是很多外贸业务员常常遇到的问题，不管是货物迟交、少交、损坏还是其他品质问题，都可能造成外贸双方合作关系出现裂痕。对此，外贸业务员要积极沟通，第一时间处理并给出答复。

# CHAPTER 10　其他外贸函电
## Other Foreign Trade Letters

外贸业务员平时还需要处理一些不一定直接与工作相关的函电，如日常通知、节日问候、生病慰问和升职祝贺等。这些函电尽管不与生意直接挂钩，但对于维护新老客户关系具有十分重要的作用。

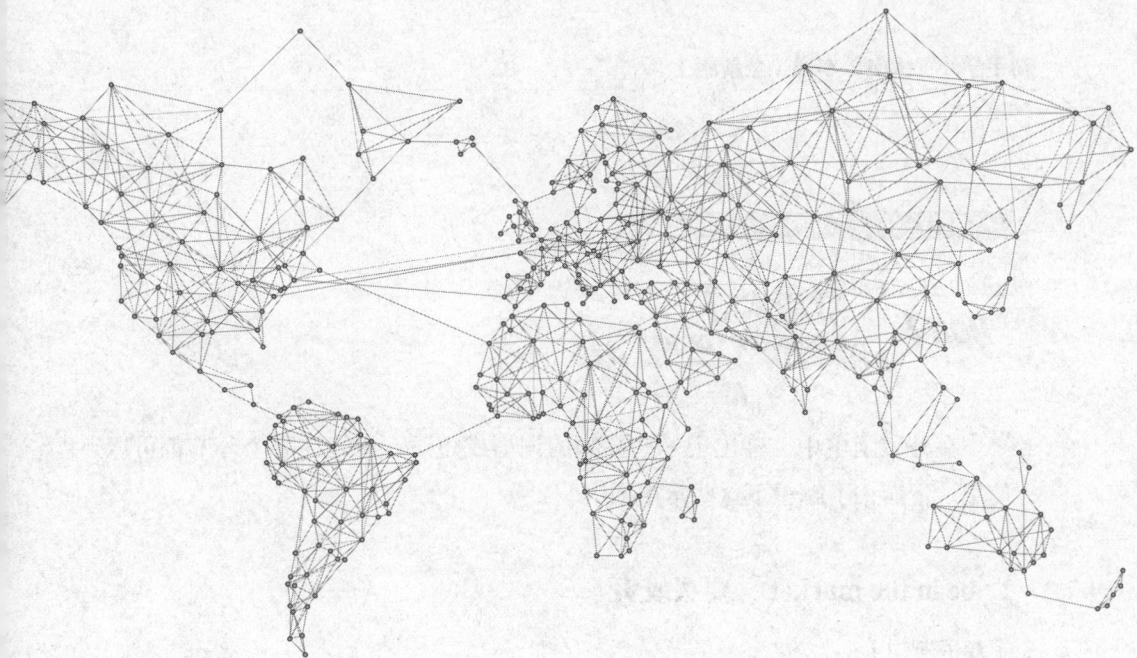

# CHAPTER01 外贸函电基础知识

## *Basic Knowledge of Foreign Trade Letters*

在学习外贸业务流程之前，我们首先要掌握外贸函电
的基础知识，包括外贸相关知识、外贸函电的常用术
语及外贸函电的写法和格式。

**PART 1 外贸 *Foreign Trade***

**PART 2 外贸函电常用术语 *Terms of Foreign Trade Letters***

**PART 3 外贸函电 *Foreign Trade Letters***

## PART 1 外贸 Foreign Trade

# Unit 1 常用术语 Common Terms

在外贸函电中，会出现一些高频的词语或短语，不管在哪个环节都可以使用。下面来了解一下这些常用术语。

## 1. be in the market 要买或卖

【双语例句】

Please advise us when you are in the market.

如果你有意做生意，请通知我们。

【用法解析】

"be in the market for … "是指"想要购买……"。在外贸函电往来中，如果对方暂时不感兴趣，这个短语可委婉表示"我们有机会再合作"。

## 2. for your information 供你参考

【双语例句】

For your information, we are sending you the sample and catalogue.

我们寄上样品和目录供你方参考。

【用法解析】

需要了解的是，在邮件末尾可以使用"for your information"的缩写"FYI"，表示邮件中包含的信息对于收信方是有价值的。

## 3. as soon as possible（ASAP） 尽快

【双语例句】

Please revise and resend the letter to us ASAP, thanks!

请将信尽快修改后重新发给我们，谢谢！

【用法解析】

"ASAP"的意思是尽快，在邮件中使用时，它的隐藏含义是要求收信方迅速执行邮件中的请求或命令。

## 4. on receipt of  一经收到（即刻）

【双语例句】

On receipt of your check,we shall ship the goods immediately.

收到贵方支票后，货物将会立即装运。

【用法解析】

"on receipt of"强调的是如果收到的话，将会采取什么行动。因此常用于督促对方采取行动的函电中。而表示已收到时，使用"in receipt of"，例如"We are in receipt of your letter of the 15th.（我方已收到你方 15 日的来函）"。

## 5. comply with  依照；符合

【双语例句】

I'm sorry, I can't comply with your request.

很抱歉，我不能答应你的请求。

【用法解析】

"comply with"有两种适用情景：一是表示接受或拒绝对方的要求时，二是表示是否与要求或规定相符。

PART 1 外贸 Foreign Trade

## Unit 2　成本加运费 Cost and Freight

　　成本加运费（Cost and Freight），缩写为 C&F、CFR 或者 CNF，是指国际贸易中，卖方将货物装上运输工具并支付起运港至目的港运费。按 CFR 条件成交时，卖方须负责租订运输工具、支付运费、办理货物的出口相关手续、向买方提供货运单据并及时将运输工具的名称和起航时间通知买方，由买方自行办理保险。

但卖方只要在装运港把货物装上开往指定目的港的船只，就认为是履行了交货义务，货物的风险从装运港越过船舷时起即由卖方转移给买方。一切货物灭失、损坏及发生事故后造成的额外开支，在货物越过指定港的船舷后，就由卖方转移至买方负担。

CFR 条件的价格构成为"成本＋国内费用＋出口运费＋预期利润"，与 CIF 的区别只有不包括保险费。在按 CFR 条件订立合同时，需要特别注意及时向买方提供装船通知，以便买方向保险公司办妥保险，否则卖方要承担违约责任。

在外贸函电往来的各个环节中，都有可能出现这个术语。

【询价邮件示例】
Many of customers are interested in your Seagull brand household scissors and we wish to have your CFR Shanghai quotations.
许多客户对你们海鸥牌的家用剪刀很感兴趣，期待你的报价（CFR 上海）。

【报价邮件示例】
We quote this article at $250 per M/T CFR.
我方的成本加运费报价为每吨 250 美元。

【合同邮件示例】
This contract is for 250 metric tons of groundnuts at RMB1, 800 per M/T CFR Copenhagen.
本合同项下为 250 公吨花生，每公吨 1 800 元，成本加运费至哥本哈根。

【运输邮件示例】
CFR to Berlin $14 per pair including 3% commission.
成本加运费至柏林每双 14 美元，包括 3% 佣金。

PART 1 外贸 Foreign Trade

# Unit 3 外贸一般流程
## General Process of Foreign Trade

出口货物流程主要包括：报价、订货、付款方式、备货、包装、通关手续、装船、运输保险、提单和结汇。

1. 外贸流程中的报价（offer）环节由产品的询价（inquiry）、报价（offer）和还价（counteroffer）组成。该环节一般涉及价格（price）、折扣（discount）、佣金（commission）、质量（quality）、数量（quantity）、规格（specification）、包装（package）和交货期（duedate）等内容。

【询价邮件示例】
Please quote us your best price CIF New York, inclusive of our 3% commission.
请报你方最优惠的纽约到岸价，包括我方 3% 佣金。

【报价邮件示例】
We are making you a firm offer, USD 5, 600/unit CIF Sydney, is Subject to reply by 14th May.
现提供稳固报价，CIF 价到悉尼每部 5 600 美元，但以 5 月 14 日前回复作为实施该价格的条件。

【还价邮件示例】
Good quality always deserves good price. You'd better consider its production efficiency as well as the price.
一分钱一分货。你不能只看它的价格，还要看它的生产效率。

How about we each give in half?
我们各让一半如何？

2. 订货（order）主要是对价格达成一致后，就其他相关事项进行协商确认，然后签订销售合同的过程。

【订货邮件示例】

Please confirm the order and E-mail a shipping schedule.

请确认订货，用电子邮件告知装运时间表。

3. 付款方式（payment methods）常见的有三种，信用证（L/C）、电汇（T/T）和直接付款方式（西联汇款和 paypal 等）。

【催款邮件示例】

We'll make the shipment as soon as your L/C is on hand.

一收到你方信用证，我们立即安排装运。

4. 备货（production）是整个贸易流程中最重要的部分。除了货物的品质和数量，生产进度也要关注。如有延误，要通知客户，请求谅解。

【通知交期推迟邮件示例】

We are sorry to inform you that we are not able to finish the No. × × × until Aug 20th.

很抱歉通知你方，我方在 8 月 20 日之前不能完成 × × × 号订单。

5. 包装（package）包括商品的包装和运输时采取的包装，不同商品的包装要求不同，通常有纸箱（carton）、木箱（wooden case）和编织袋（woven bag）形式。

【协商包装邮件示例】

We can use wooden cases for packing if you insist.

如果你方坚持，我们可以使用木箱包装。

6. 通关手续（customs formalities）也称为报关手续，包括报检和报关，对于前者，目前绝大多数商品都不再需要。而对于报关，绝大多数商品需要申报并提供相应单据。

7. 装船（shipment）的方式通常由买家决定，在装船后，卖家要及时通知买方装船信息。

【通知装船邮件示例】

Please be informed that the shipment of the cargo was sent yesterday, airway bill No. ×××.

特此通知这批货物昨天已装运，航空货物的领取号码是 ×××。

8. 运输保险（transportation insurance）包括基本险（basic risks）和特别险（special risks）。具体投保内容由买卖双方协商决定。

【协商保险邮件示例】

The compensation of damaged goods is covered in the insurance of risk of breakage. If you claim, the additional risk will be added.

货物破损的赔偿属于破损险的责任范围，如果贵方要求的话，可以加保这项附加险。

9. 提单（B/L）是出口商办理完出口通关手续且海关放行后，由外运公司签出、供进口商提货的结汇所用单据。

【寄送提单邮件示例】

Enclose that we hand you an official invoice in triplicate amount to £100.55 and insurance policy.

同函奉寄面额为 100.55 英镑的正式发票一式三份及保险单。

10. 结汇（settle the exchange）是外贸公司按照信用证规定，向银行提交相关单据，从而获得款项的手续。

---

**PART 2** 外贸函电常用术语 *Terms of Foreign Trade Letters*

**Unit 1** 　**共同海损**
　　*General Average*

共同海损（General Average），缩写为 G.A.，是指为了使船舶或船上货物避免共同危险，而有意地、合理地做出的特殊牺牲或支付的特殊费用。共同海损损失应由船、货（包括不同的货主）各方共同负担。所采取的共同海损措施称为共同海损行为。共同海损货物分摊额，以 "Cargo's Proportion of General Average" 表示。

【合同邮件示例】

In the adjustment of general average, the following Rules shall apply to the exclusion of any Law and Practice inconsistent therewith.

共同海损理算应适用下列规则，凡与这些规则相抵触的法律和惯例都不适用。

The contributory value in general average by the ship, goods and freight shall be determined as follows.

船舶、货物和运费的共同海损分摊价值，分别依照下列规定确定。

Abandoned goods should not be made as general average, unless such cargo is carried in accordance with the recognized custom of the trade.

被抛弃的货物，除非按照公认的海运习惯运送，否则不得作为共同海损给予补偿。

## PART 2 外贸函电常用术语 Terms of Foreign Trade Letters

### Unit 2　水渍险　With Particular Average

　　水渍险（With Particular Average），缩写为 WPA 或 WA，又称 "单独海损险"，英文原意是指单独海损负责赔偿，是海洋运输货物保险的主要险种之一。这里的 "海损" 是自然灾害及意外事故，导致货物被水淹没，引起货物的损失。如果浸渍是引起货物损害的间接原因，保险公司也不会进行赔付。

【协商邮件示例】

In the absence of your definite instructions, we will cover insurance WPA according to usual practice.

如果没有你的明确指示，我们将按一般惯例投保水渍险。

WPA plus Risk of Breakage suit your consignment.
贵方货物适合投保水渍险及破碎险进行托运。

Who will pay the premium for WPA?
水渍险费用由谁负担?

We shall cover WPA for 110% of the invoiced value.
我们按发票总金额的 110% 投保水渍险。

## Unit 3 付款交单
### Documents Against Payments

　　付款交单（Documents against Payments），缩写为 D/P，是指出口方在委托银行收款时，指示银行只有在付款人（进口方）付清货款时，才能向其交出货运单据，即交单以付款为条件，称为付款交单。按付款时间的不同，又可分为即期付款交单（D/P at sight）和远期付款交单（D/P after sight），区别是前者要求进口方见票即付，后者可在汇票到期日前付清货款。

【协商邮件示例】
We hope you will accept D/P payment terms.
我们希望贵方能接受付款交单的付款方式。

We can do the business on D/P at sight basis.
我们可以按即期付款交单的方式进行交易。

How about 50% by L/C and the rest by D/P?
货价的 50% 用信用证付款，其余的款项采取付款交单方式怎么样?

We agree to draw 30 days D/P.
我们同意开立期限为 30 天的付款交单汇票。

## Unit 4　即期汇票 Demand Draft

即期汇票即见票即付的汇票，包括载明即期付款、见票即付或提示付款及未载明付款日的汇票。逾期后再经承兑或背书的汇票，对该种承兑人或背书人而言，应视为即期汇票。即期汇票的持票人可以随时行使自己的票据权利，在此之前无须提前通知付款人准备履行义务。

【协商邮件示例】

We shall offset the price difference by a demand draft payable to your order.

我方将开出即期汇票支付你方订单以补偿差价。

Commission will be paid by demand draft usually after we receive the full payment.

佣金通常在我公司收到全部货款后以即期汇票支付。

## Unit 5　装货单 Shipping Order

装货单（Shipping Order），缩写为 S/O，是指船公司或其代理人在接受托运人提出托运申请后，发给托运人的单证，装货单一经签订，运输合同即告成立，同时也是承运人确认货物的证明，船长可将单上货物装船。此外装货单还是海关对出口货物进行监管的单证，但目前由于海关管理方式有所变化，出口企业一般难以取得海关签章的"出口货物装货单"，"出口货物装货单"也可不需要海关签章。

【协商邮件示例】

Prepayment is required before shipping orders.

签订装货单之前需要先付款。

We will advise you of the shipping order number and the intended vessel by email.

我们会邮件通知你装货单编号和预定船只。

【通知装货邮件示例】

Please read the attached S/O and relevant docs for your information.

请见附件装货单及相关文件，供你方参考。

## PART 2 外贸函电常用术语 *Terms of Foreign Trade Letters*

### *Unit 6* 其他外贸函电术语
*Other Foreign Trade Terms*

结算及单证类的常用术语如下。

| 术语 | 含 义 | 术语 | 含 义 |
|------|-------|------|-------|
| B/E | bill of exchange，汇票 | T/T | telegraphic transfer，电汇 |
| D/A | document against acceptance，承兑交单 | S/C | sales contract，销售合同；sales confirmation，销售确认书 |
| COD | cash on delivery，交货付款 | P/O | purchase order，采购订单 |
| CWO | cash with order，订货付款 | P/I | proforma invoice，形式发票 |
| MTD | multimodal transport document，多式联运单据 | C/O | certificate of origin，一般原产地证书 |
| B/L | bill of lading，提单，是货物的物权凭证 | P/L | packing list，装箱单，出口商提供的记载装货情况的单据 |
| D/O | delivery order，提货单，是目的港口提取货物需要出示的凭证 | B/N | booking note，订舱单（托单），向船公司订舱的书面单据 |

运输及价格类的常用术语如下。

| 术语 | 含义 | 术语 | 含义 |
|---|---|---|---|
| FCL | full container load，整箱货 | LCL | less than container load，拼箱货 |
| HQ | high cube，高柜 | GP | general purpose，普柜 |
| CTN | carton，箱 | PCS | pieces，件 |
| DOZ | dozen，打 | F.T. | freight ton，运费吨 |
| N.W. | net weight，净重 | G.W. | gross weight，毛重 |
| FOB | free on board，装运港船上交货 | CIF | cost, insurance and freight，成本、运费加保费 |
| DES | delivered ex ship，目的地船上交货 | DEQ | delivered ex quay，目的港码头交货 |
| DDU | delivered duty unpaid，未完税交货 | DDP | delivered duty paid，完税交货 |

## PART 3 外贸函电 Foreign Trade Letters

# Unit 1 信封和信头
## Envelope and Header

## 1. 信封的写法

正式的商业信封通常在左上角都已经印刷好寄信人的名称和地址，只需在信封中间偏下的位置填写收信人的姓名、地址即可。收信人的姓名、地址填写要规范，第一行写收信人姓名；第二行写门牌号码，街道名称；第三行写县市城镇、省州名称；第四行写国家名称。收信人名称、地址填写的示例如下。

Real Inc.

No. 43, 8th Ave

Brooklyn, New York

U.S.A

## 2. 信头的写法

信头包含寄信人的公司名称、地址、电话、传真和电子邮件地址，统称为"联系信息"，填写地址时要加上邮编。信头的规范写法可参考如下示例。

Guangzhou Trading Co., Ltd.

No. 12, Xingang East Road, Guangzhou City,

Guangdong Province 510308, China

Telephone: 86–000–000–0000

Fax: 86–00–0000–0000

Email: gztrading@gzt.org

**PART 3 外贸函电 Foreign Trade Letters**

**Unit 2** 存盘号、日期和封内地址
**Reference, Date and Inside Address**

## 1. 存盘号的写法

存盘号即"reference"，给信函编号便于来往书信的存盘和查阅，一般用"Our ref."（写信），或者"Your ref."（回信）。写信时只需注明"Our ref. ×××"，"Your ref."项不填。在回信时，由于来函有一个存盘号，因此应该注明"Our ref. ×××"（己方存盘号）和"Your ref. ×××"（与收到的对方存盘号一致）。有关信件的示例如下。

Our ref.

Your ref.

## 2. 日期的写法

为了方便日后查询，还需要写上邮件发送的日期。美式日期通常写在信头和收信人名称、地址之间，而英式通常写在收信人名称、地址之下。

为了避免出现"4/10/2017"这种分不清是 10 月 4 日还是 4 月 10 日的情况，通常月份不使用数字表示。可以写成"May 1"或"May 1st"，后面加", 2017"即可。日期的示例如下。

Date: May 1st, 2017

## 3. 封内地址的写法

封内地址是收信人名称和地址，填写规范和书写信封上的收信人名称、地址的规范一致。不过此栏在非完全公事化的信函中可以省去，因为称呼已说明了收信人。封内地址的示例如下。

Real Inc.

No. 43, 8th Ave

Brooklyn, New York

U.S.A

### PART 3 外贸函电 Foreign Trade Letters

**Unit 3** 经办人、称呼和主题
*Operator, Salutation and Subject*

## 1. 经办人的写法

经办人是指承办信件的具体个人或部门，是信件的具体收信人。书写时要加下画线。经办人的书写示例如下。

Attention: Mr. Brown Douglas, Export Manager

Attention of Mr. Douglas

To the attention of Mr. Brown Douglas

## 2. 称呼的写法

称呼是对收信人的称呼，一般以"Dear"开头，中间使用敬称 + 全名，有来往可称对方的姓，只有十分熟悉才可以称名，最后以逗号结尾。称呼女士时，统一使用"Ms."，因为你无法确定对方是否结婚，错用"Miss"或"Mrs."可能冒犯对方。称呼的书写示例如下。

Dear Sir or Madam,

Dear Mr. John Douglas,

Dear Mr. Douglas,

Dear John,

此外，还有一种特殊情况，即没有特定的收信人时，可以使用以下写法，注意结尾标点为冒号。

To whom it may concern:

## 3. 主题的写法

主题是对全文重点的提炼。在电子邮件中，主题会直接显示在邮件主题栏中，而在信封中，主题位置在称呼之后。书写时要加下画线。主题的书写示例如下。

RE: Counter offer for socks

Aquatic Products

**Unit 4** 正文和结尾
The Body and The Ending

## 1. 正文的写法

书写正文的基本要求是主题明确、内容简洁明了、语言精练及表述完整。一般来说，在正文开头直接表达写信的目的，然后对目的进行具体说明即可。如果是回信，要先将收到对方来信的日期和主题加以综合说明，并单独成段，以便对方一目了然。

回信时第一句的示例如下。

Thank you for your email of 29th February regarding the ...

With reference to our telephone conversation on Friday, I would like to let you know that ...

I am glad to inform you that ...

I am writing with regard to the complaint that you made on 29th February.

正文是外贸函电中最重要的部分，阐述的是具体的情况，我们将在后面通过具体的例子来探讨外贸函电中正文部分的书写技巧。

## 2. 结尾的写法

正文结束后，要另起一段表达歉意、希望或祝愿，或者提出请求。一般以希望合作愉快和希望尽快回复为结尾。结尾的示例如下。

Many apology again for the problem you have experienced.

We hope this will be a good start for a long and profitable business relationship.

We are anticipating your early reply.

Thank you in advance for your reply.

**PART 3 外贸函电 *Foreign Trade Letters***

*Unit 5* 敬语和落款
**Honeritics and Sign**

## 1. 敬语的写法

根据发信人与收信人之间的关系或熟悉程度的不同,敬语可分为以下3类。

1. 家人亲戚:Your loving mother; Yours lovingly; With love。

2. 一般朋友:Yours respectfully/sincerely/truly。

3. 机关团体:Yours faithfully; Best regards。

在外贸函电中,最常用的敬语是"Best regards",末尾用逗号。敬语的示例如下。

Best regards,

同时,敬语和称呼还存在对应关系。如果是以"Dear Sir"或"Dear Sir or Madam"开头,一般用"Yours faithfully";如果是以具体名字开头,一般用"Yours sincerely"或"Best regards";如果没有具体对象,一般用"Yours truly"。

## 2. 落款的写法

在电子邮件中,落款为写信人名称 + 公司名称。落款的示例如下。

Li Yi

Guangzhou Trading Co., Ltd.

传统函件中，先书写公司名称，再以 "Sig."（signature 的缩写）注明签名位置，手写签名。落款的格式如下。

Guangzhou Trading Co., Ltd.

Sig. _____

PART 3 外贸函电 Foreign Trade Letters

## Unit 6　抄送、附件和附言
### Carbon Copy, Attachment and Postscript

## 1. 抄送的写法

抄送（Carbon Copy）即 CC，在传统函件中，如需让收信人知道信函复印件发送的单位，则需要在落款后注明。抄送的示例如下。

CC our Shanghai Branch Office

## 2. 附件的写法

信内有附件时，常用 "Encl." 或 "Enc." 在信末左下角注明，提醒收信人查看。附件的示例如下。

Encl.: 2 invoices

说明信内含有附件的表达方式有如下几种。

① "Please see the file attached/enclosed.（请查看所附文件）" 或 "Please find attached/enclosed the file you requested.（随函附上你所要求的文件）"。

通常是正文有内容时，为了提醒收件人查看附件，在信件结尾使用。

②"I am attaching/enclosing the file for your consideration.（随函附上文件，供参考）"。通常是己方主动附上附件供对方参阅。

③"I am sending you the file as an attachment/enclosure.（把文件发给你，请在附件中查看）"，其中"as an attachment/enclosure"可以替换为"in enclosure/attachment"。

④"Attached/Enclosed is the file you requested.（附件是你要求的文件）"，直接说明附件内容。

⑤"Please affix your signature to the attached/enclosed form and return it to us at once.（请在附件上签名后立即送还我处）"，只单纯提及附件。

## 3. 附言的写法

信写完后，如果还有重要的话需要补充，可以在信末加"P.S."引出要补充的内容。出现附言一般表明发信人思维不够周密，应该尽量避免。附言的示例如下。

P.S. We require payment by L/C.

### PART 3 外贸函电 Foreign Trade Letters

**Unit 7　外贸函电的格式**
**Format of Foreign Trade Letter**

在前面 6 节中，我们了解了外贸函电各个部分的书写方法，下面来具体学习这些部分在信件中的格式。

## 1. 信封的格式

信封正面的左下角会注明信件类别：航空（By Air Mail）、挂号（Registered）、印刷品（Printed Matter）、快件（Express）和内有照片（Photo Enclosed）。

书写信封时，名称与地址均左端对齐，为齐头式，具体如下。

```
Guangzhou Trading Co., Ltd.
No. 12, Xingang East Road
Guangzhou City, Guangdong
China                                              ┌──────────┐
                                                   │          │
                                                   │   stamp  │
                        Real Inc.                  │          │
                        No. 43, 8th Ave            └──────────┘
                        Brooklyn, New York
                        U.S.A

By Air Mail
```

信封还可以写成缩格式，名称与地址逐行右缩，具体如下。

```
Guangzhou Trading Co., Ltd.
   No. 12, Xingang East Road
      Guangzhou City, Guangdong
         China                                     ┌──────────┐
                                                   │          │
                                                   │   stamp  │
                        Real Inc.                  │          │
                           No. 43, 8th Ave         └──────────┘
                              Brooklyn, New York
                                 U.S.A

By Air Mail
```

## 2. 信件的格式

在英文商业信函中，有 3 种格式，分别为齐头式、改进齐头式和缩格式。

齐头式（Block Form）即除信头居中外，全部左对齐。因为简单直观，便于使用，是最受欢迎的格式，具体如下。

```
                        Heading（信头）
Our ref.（存盘号）
Your ref.
Date（日期，美式）


Inside Address（封内地址）


Date（英式，后文均采用美式）


Attention（经办人）


Salutation（称呼）


Subject（主题）


Body（正文）
（正文的段落间需空一行）
Ending（结尾）


Complimentary closing（敬语）
Signature（落款）


Carbon Copy（抄送）
Enclosure（附件）


Postscript（附言）
```

改进齐头式（Modified Block Form）与齐头式的区别在于存盘号和日期靠右，与封内地址在同一行，落款偏右，节省空间，一目了然。在此列出不同部分，具体如下。

```
                    Heading（信头）
Inside Address（封内地址）              Our ref.（存盘号）
                                      Your ref.
                                      Date（日期，美式）

Inside Address（封内地址）

...
Complimentary closing（敬语）
                              Signature（落款）
```

缩格式（Indented Form）保留了改进齐头式的特点，同时更近一步，经办人和主题要居中，正文的段首向右缩进。在此列出不同部分，具体如下。

Attention（经办人）

Salutation（称呼）

Subject（主题）

Body（正文）＿＿＿＿＿＿＿＿＿＿＿＿＿
＿＿＿＿＿＿＿＿＿＿＿

Ending（结尾）

## 3. 电子邮件的格式

电子邮件是即刻发送，许多格式和传统信函不同，但以上所述信件格式仍然适用。在此列出不同部分，具体如下。

**To**     （收信人的电子邮件地址）
**From**    （发信人的电子邮件地址）
**Date**    Friday, August 4, 2017
**Time**    15:27:02 GMT
**Subject**   RE: Counter offer for socks

（称呼、正文、结尾和敬语等格式与上述相同）

Signature（落款）
Contact Information（联系信息，与上述信头格式相同）

（抄送、附件和附言等格式与上述相同）

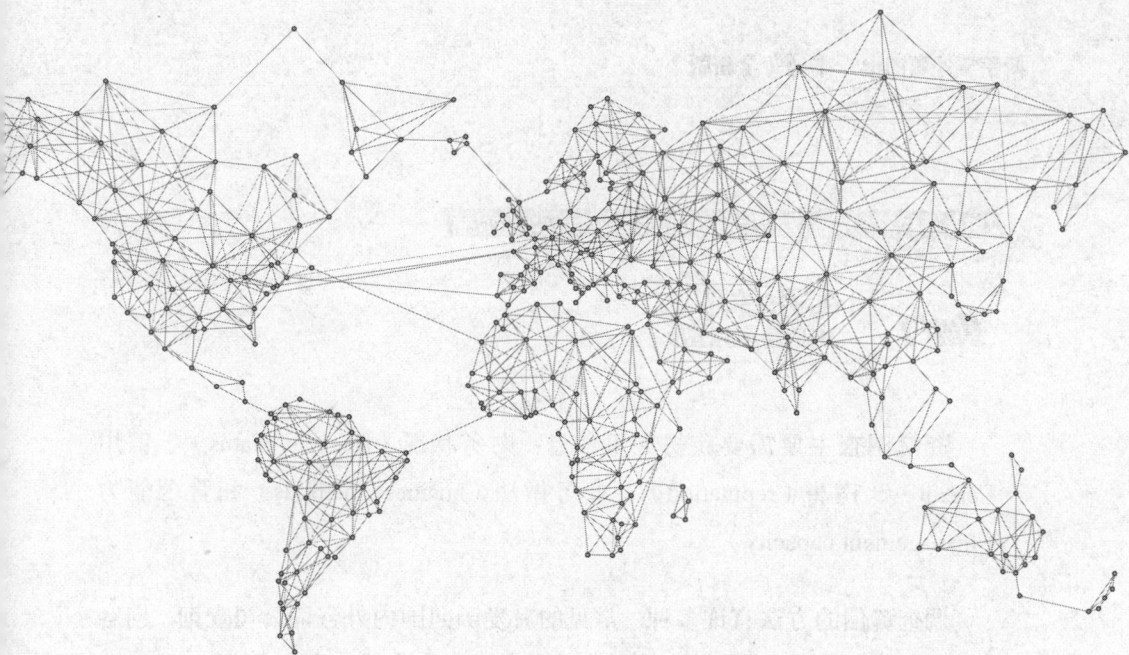

# CHAPTER02 发展客户拉业务

## Develop Customer and Service

做外贸业务，本质上依旧是一个产品卖出去的过程，因此只有找到合适的客户，维系意向客户，发展潜在客户，最终手上握有较多客户资源，才能将外贸业务做得风生水起。

PART 1 资信调查函电 Credit Investigation Letter

PART 2 预约会面函电 Appointment Letter

PART 3 会面后的跟进工作 Follow Up after Meeting

## Unit 1 写作技巧 Writing Skills

资信调查主要需要获得如下信息：财务状况（financial status）、信用（credit）、声誉（reputation）、业务做法（business methods）和管理能力（management capacity）。

调查资信的方法有许多种，常见的有发函向国内外咨询公司查询、向客户合作的其他公司咨询、向银行查询资信状况及向自己的客户查询。

发函查询的一方，应该明确表明要求并对提供的资信状况表示感谢，同时要保证对此进行保密。

【发函查询邮件示例】
We can assure you that any information you may give us will be treated in absolute confidence. Thank you in advance for your cooperation.
对你方提供的任何信息我方会严格保密，提前对你方的合作表示感谢。

回复查询信函的一方，应及时回信，并如实提供情况和提出建议，信内要包括"对所提供情况不负任何责任"这类句子，以避免可能出现的麻烦。即使无可奉告，也要说明情况并表示遗憾。

【回复查询邮件示例】
The information is confidential and without taking any responsibility on our part.
上述信息保密并且我方不为此承担任何责任。

在获得调查信息后，调查者要对被调查者进行客观的分析。分析时，应遵循"3C"原则，即分析被调查者的品行（conduct）、能力（capacity）及资本（capital）情况。

## *Unit 2* 资信调查函
### *Credit Survey Letter*

资信即履约能力和可信任程度，简单地说，就是公司是否可信。

## 常用词汇 *Vocabulary*

### 1. standing  n. 身份；名声

【双语例句】

For our credit standing, please refer to the Bank of China, Xi'an Branch.

关于我方的资信情况，请向中国银行西安分行查询。

【用法解析】

在资信调查函中，可以表示资信的短语有"credit standing（信用状况）""trade reputation（贸易声誉）"和"financial status（财务状况）"。

### 2. prospective  adj. 预期的；未来的

【双语例句】

Is she a prospective buyer?

她可能成为我们的顾客吗？

【用法解析】

"prospective"后加各种名词可以表示"prospective clients（潜在客户）"
"prospective investigation（远景调查）""prospective damage（预计损失）"
和"prospective earnings（预期收益）"等。

### 3. reference　n. 参考；证明人　　v. 注明出处

【双语例句】

The headmaster supplied him with a reference.

校长给他提供证明人。

【用法解析】

在回复商业信函时，开头常用"With reference to your letter"，但这种用法应避免在一般通信里出现。

## 基本词汇　*Basic Words*

| | |
|---|---|
| **state** [steɪt]　v. 陈述；说明 | **status** ['steɪtəs]　n. 状态；地位 |
| **firm** [fɜːrm]　n. 公司 | **strict** [strɪkt]　adj. 严格的 |
| **entail** [ɪn'teɪl]　v. 牵涉；需要 | **courtesy** ['kɜːrtəsi]　n. 礼貌；谦恭 |
| **furnish** ['fɜːrnɪʃ]　v. 供应；提供 | **reciprocate** [rɪ'sɪprəkeɪt]　v. 回应 |

## 情景实例　*Scene Example*

### 1. 写作步骤和表达方式

①说明咨询的目的。

Our prospective customers ×××　has given us your name as a banking reference.

我们的潜在客户×××把你定为他们的银行证明人。

We have received an important order from ×××, who have referred us to you for information concerning their standing.

我方收到了一个重要订单，来自×××公司，他们向我方介绍了贵方，目的是让我们了解他们的资信状况。

They state that they have done business with you for the past two years and have given us the name of your company as a reference.

他们向我方表示，他们在过去的两年中与你方有过生意来往，并且指定贵公司作为他们的证明人。

②表示感谢。

We should be grateful if you would let us know what level you consider
their safety.
如果你能告知我们你对该公司可信任程度的意见，我们将不胜感激。

It will be greatly appreciated if you could provide us some information about
the financial and business standing of the firm above.
若能提供有关上述公司财务及业务状况的资料，我们将不胜感激。

We would be much grateful if you could give us some information
concerning their business status.
如果贵公司能提供一些有关他们业务状况的资料，我们将不胜感激。

Since it is our first transaction with this firm, we should greatly appreciate
your advice.
由于这是我们与该公司所做的首笔生意，我们非常感谢你的建议。

③保证保守秘密。

Any information sent to us will be held in strict confidentiality by the
company and I won't entail any obligation on your part.
任何寄给我们的信息都将由公司严格保密，且你方不负任何责任。

Any information you give will be highly appreciated and kept in strict
confidence. We shall be pleased to do the same if you should need our
services at this end.
你方所提供的任何信息，我们都将感激不尽并严格保密。如果你方需要我们提供
信息，我们也会同样乐意。

We thank you for your courtesy and assure you of strict confidentiality.
我们很感谢你的好意，并向你保证严守秘密。

We can assure you that any information you may give us will be treated in
absolute confidence.
我们可以向你保证，你方给我们的任何信息都将绝对保密。

## 2. 邮件示范

（注：上一章介绍了外贸函电的正式格式，为便于介绍主要知识，自本章起，仅展示正文和结尾部分，其余部分不再展示。但应注意，平时书写时不能省去，即使是熟悉的客户，也至少要书写称呼、敬语和落款。）

某公司欲与纽约真实公司合作，但担心对方不可靠，于是发函给银行，咨询纽约真实公司的资信情况。

**英**

Recently we have received a letter from Real Inc. who has given your name and address as a bank reference. Since it is our first transaction with this firm, we should be obliged if you could furnish us with a detailed report on the financial position, credit standing, business lines, and general management of the Real Inc. of New York.

Any information sent to us will be held in strict confidence by the company and will entail no obligation on your part.

We thank you for your courtesy and would be pleased to offer reciprocate service at anytime in the future.

**中**

最近我们收到了纽约真实公司的来信，在信中该公司告知了我方贵银行的名称和地址，并说明贵银行作为该公司的担保银行。由于这是我们与该公司所做的首笔生意，若贵银行能向我方提供纽约真实公司的财务状况、资信状况、业务路线和一般管理等方面的详细报告，我们将不胜感激。

任何发送给我们的信息都将由公司严格保密，且你方不负任何责任。

感谢你的好意，今后我们将随时为责方服务。

## Unit 3 | 资信调查回函
### Letter of Credit Information

在贸易往来中，也可能收到其他公司的资信调查函，这时可以如实回复，并声明免责。

## 常用词汇 | Vocabulary

### 1. liability  n. 责任；债务

【双语例句】

The company has had to undertake heavy liability.

这家公司已经不得不承担沉重的债务。

【用法解析】

"liability"的意思是"责任，义务，倾向"，常与介词"for"连用，表示"对…负有责任"。与介词"to"连用时，作"有…的倾向"或"对…是不利条件"解。

### 2. confidential  adj. 秘密的；机密的

【双语例句】

The information of course will be strictly confidential.

我们自然会对信件中提到的信息严格保密。

【用法解析】

"confidential"指双方互有高度信任，能互通秘密，强调对别人的力量和能力等有信心。"confidential"无比较级和最高级形式。

### 3. obligation   n. 义务；责任

【双语例句】

I don't have any obligation to let out the secret.

我有责任不泄密。

【用法解析】

"obligation"指"义务"时，与"duty"的区别是，"duty"多指"永远的义务"，而"obligation"指临时性或一次性的义务；指"责任"时，"obligation"仅指对他人应尽的职责和义务，而"responsibility"则指一个人必须对后果负有职责或义务。

## 基本词汇 / *Basic Words*

**report** [rɪˈpɔːrt]  v. 汇报；报告          **relation** [rɪˈleɪʃn]  n. 关系；联系

**punctually** [ˈpʌŋktʃuəli]  adv. 准时地   **supplier** [səˈplaɪər]  n. 供货商

**settlement** [ˈsetlmənt]  n. 协议；解决   **recognize** [ˈrekəɡnaɪz]  v. 意识到

## 情景实例 / *Scene Example*

## 1. 写作步骤和表达方式

①表达意愿

Thank you for your inquiry about the business standing of ×××, we are pleased to share the following information with you.

感谢你查询有关×××的资信情况，我们愿意给你以下信息。

We have received your letter of May 10 th, and we are sending you the information you inquired.

我们已经收到你方5月10日的来信，现发送你方所询信息。

We are honored to have the opportunity to report favorably on ×××.

我们很荣幸有这次机会来报告有关×××的实际情况。

②提供详细信息

In all these years our relations with them have been consistently and entirely satisfactory.
这些年，我们与他们的业务联系一直非常令人满意。

After experiencing some difficulty during the first year, the firm has met its liabilities regularly and punctually.
度过开头一年的困境之后，公司运行正常，而且按时履行义务。

Our own experience with them has not been satisfactory.
我们与其打交道的经历并不令人满意。

The company mentioned is known to be inexperienced in business. Many suppliers will have lots of trouble in settlement of their accounts.
你们所提到的这家企业，从业经验尚浅。很多供应商在与他们进行结账时都会遇到麻烦。

It seems to us that the company's difficulties are due to bad management and in particular to overtrading.
在我们看来，公司的困难是由于管理不善和贸易过量。

③希望对方保密

There is a condition of this letter that the name of this Bank will not be disclosed in our report being passed on to your clients.
本函有一个条件，即在把我们的报告转交你们的客户时，请勿泄露本行的名称。

please be assured that our reply will be kept strictly confidential.
请确信我们会对给出的答复严格保密。

Please consider keeping the reply strictly confidential and we assume no responsibility for this.
请你对此答复严格保密，我们对此不承担责任。

We hope that we have been of assistance to you, and that you will recognize the importance of keeping this communication strictly private.
希望这些对你方有用，也望你方理解保守此秘密的重要性。

However, there is no obligation on my part.
但是，我方不承担任何责任。

## 2.邮件示范

　　某公司收到咨询水晶公司资信情况的函件，于是回信告知对方水晶公司商誉良好，可以放心合作。

**英**

In reply to your inquiry of 10 April, concerning the credit standing of Crystal Inc., we are pleased to say that it is one of the largest companies in that area. They are enjoying a good reputation in the business world.

They have a number of branches at home and abroad. Available information indicates that they have always provided in-time delivery, moderate prices and superior quality in all their transactions. therefore, We would like very much to recommend this company to you.

The information above must be treated to be strictly private and confidential and we shall have no responsibility for any irregularity therein.

**中**

对于贵公司 4 月 10 日关于水晶公司资信状况的询问，我们很高兴地说，该公司是该地区最大的公司之一。他们在商界享有良好的声誉。

他们在国内外有一大批分支机构。现有资料表明，他们在所有交易中总是按时交货，价格适中，质量上乘。因此，我们非常愿意向贵公司推荐这家公司。

以上资料必须严格保密，对任何不规范之处不负任何责任。

### PART 2 预约会面函电 Appointment Letter

### Unit 1　邀请客户会面
### Inviting Business Appointment

　　对于已经有一定联系的客户，要及时邀请对方进行看厂和会面，通过实际的参观和交谈巩固双方的关系。

## 常用词汇 *Vocabulary*

### 1. overview  n. 概观；总结

【双语例句】

This page gives an overview about the company.

这一页将向客户介绍公司的大致情况。

【用法解析】

"overview"和"review"的词根"view"都是"用眼审视"，不同点在于前缀"over-"是"从头到尾"，而前缀"re-"则表示"重新"。所以，"overview"是指"总的看法，全面见解"，而"review"是指"回顾，简单评述"。

### 2. mutual  adj. 共同的；相互的

【双语例句】

It will be to our mutual advantage to work closely.

密切合作将使我们在交易中互利互惠。

【用法解析】

"mutual"通常用在正式文体或技术术语中。常用短语有"mutual benefit（共同利益）""mutual friend（共同伙伴）""mutual concern（共同关心）"和"mutual understanding（相互了解）"等。

### 3. delegate  n. 代表  v. 委派；授权

【双语例句】

You can't do all the jobs yourself, you can delegate a task to your subordinate.

你不能包揽所有的工作，你可以把任务委派给下属。

【用法解析】

"delegate"的意思是"代表他人"，指受托被派去办理某事，尤指受团体或组织委托去参加会议。引申义为把某事托付给某人去办理。

## 基本词汇 *Basic Words*

**invite** [ɪnˈvaɪt] v. 邀请

**ability** [əˈbɪləti] n. 能力

**designate** [ˈdezɪgneɪt] v. 指定；选定

**opportunity** [ˌɑːpərˈtuːnəti] n. 机会

**suitable** [ˈsuːtəbl] adj. 合适的

**positive** [ˈpɑːzətɪv] adj. 积极的

## 情景实例 *Scene Example*

### 1. 邀请参观工厂

在广交会上，有客户对广东贸易有限公司的产品很感兴趣，因此一天的展会结束后，外贸业务员立即发函给该客户，并询问对方是否方便来看厂，以增加双方合作的可能性。

**英**

It was great to meet you at the Canton Fair today, and we'd like to thank you for your interest in our products.

We would like to invite you to visit our company in No. 12, Xingang East Road. This would be a good opportunity for you to get an overview of our ability, as well as to meet Li Yi to discuss our further cooperation.

In terms of possible dates, we were hoping that we could arrange something at June 4. Please let me know whether this would be available for you or not. I do hope your schedule will allow you to accept our invitation. I am look forward to your positive reply.

**中**

很高兴今天在广交会上见到你，并感谢你对我们公司的产品感兴趣。

我们想邀请你到新港东路 12 号参观我们的公司。这将是一个很好的机会，让你了解我们公司的能力，以及会见李宜，讨论我们进一步的合作。

关于日期，我们希望安排在 6 月 4 日，请告诉我是否方便。希望你的日程安排能让你接受我们的邀请。我期待你的肯定答复。

## 2. 邀请私人会面

广东贸易有限公司外贸业务员李宜在纽约出差，借此机会，公司销售主管给纽约真实公司负责人布朗发去邀约，询问他是否有时间与李宜会面。

**英**

I am the Sales Director of Guangzhou Trading Co., Ltd., and I met you at the Canton Fair last month. A representative of our sales team, Li Yi, will be in New York between April 5 and April 20 and would like to meet you on any of those days for 2 hours from 9 a.m. to 12 p.m.

He has done research on your company and believes that he has a mutually beneficial business proposition. He would like to discuss with you.

Would it be convenient for you, or someone you designate, to meet Li Yi on one of these days? I will call you in a few days to discuss any details or questions you may have and arrange an alternative time if required.

We look forward to receiving a positive reply from you.

**中**

我是广州贸易有限公司的销售总监，上个月在广交会上我们见过。4 月 5 日至 4 月 20 日，我们销售团队的代表李宜将在纽约，如果可能的话，我们想在这段时间内任意一天的上午 9 点到下午 12 点间与你谈论两个小时。

他对贵公司做了调查，他有一个互利的业务计划想和你讨论。

你这几天去见李宜或其他指定的人，方便吗？我会在几天内给你打电话，回答你想了解的任意细节或问题。如果需要的话，安排别的时间。

我们期待收到你的肯定答复。

**PART 2 预约会面函电 Appointment Letter**

*Unit 2* **确定时间地点**
*Determining the Time and Place*

如果受邀人能够出席会面，那么可以回复确认时间、地点。而邀请方在会面之前，也要提前 3 天再次确定时间、地点，以保证会面顺利。

## 常用词汇 *Vocabulary*

### 1. reconfirm   v. 再确认

【双语例句】

Could you reconfirm the shipping date for me?

您能替我再确定一下运送日期吗？

### 2. alternative   adj. 二择一；供选择的 n. 二择一；供替代的选择

【双语例句】

I had no alternative but to accept the offer.

我除了接受该项提议之外，别无选择。

【用法解析】

"alternative"作"选择"含义解时，强调必须从两个或多个选择中选择一个。相关短语有"find an alternative（找到可供选择的办法）""other alternatives（其他办法）"和"practicable alternatives（可行的选择）"等。

## 基本词汇 *Basic Words*

**appointment** [əˈpɔɪntmənt]  n. 约会

**date** [deɪt]  n. 日期

**arrange** [əˈreɪndʒ]  v. 安排

**participate** [pɑːrˈɪsɪpeɪt]  v. 参加

**March** [mɑːrtʃ]  n. 三月

**Monday** [ˈmʌndeɪ]  n. 星期一

**情景实例** *Scene Example*

## 1. 受邀方确认会面

　　纽约真实公司的负责人布朗收到与李宜会面的邀约后，回信表示同意，并确定了会面的时间、地点。

**英**

Thank you for your letter on April 1. I am glad to participate the appointment that you have arranged with me, I will be at my office on April 5 to meet Li Yi at 10 a.m.

If there is any problem concerning about the date, please do not hesitate to contact me through my telephone. And my phone number is ××××. I look forward to seeing you in this meeting.

**中**

感谢你 4 月 1 日的来信。我很高兴接受你方安排的此次会面，我将于 4 月 5 日上午 10 点在办公室会见李宜。

关于上述日期，如果有任何问题，请不要犹豫，打电话联系我，我的电话号码是 ××××。我期待这次会面。

## 2. 邀请方确认会面

　　某公司邀请客户参加会议，在会议正式开始前 3 天，该公司再次向受邀方发函确认时间、地点及是否能够到场。

**英**

I am writing to reconfirm our meeting schedule.

As agreed, we will meet at the office in the Bond street at 9:30 a.m. on Monday 20 March. I have scheduled the meeting for the whole day. If for any reason you are unable to attend, please phone me so that we can make alternative arrangements. Please let me know if you would like to arrange accommodation by us.

I look forward with great pleasure to our meeting.

**中**

我写信是想再次确认我们的会议日程。

根据约定，我们将于 3 月 20 日星期一上午 9:30 在邦德街的办公室会面，我已经安排了全天的会议。如果你不能出席，请打电话给予通知，以便我们另行安排。如果你希望我们代为安排酒店住宿，请告知。

谨在此预祝会谈成功。

## PART 2 预约会面函电 Appointment Letter

### Unit 3　取消会面　Cancelling a Meeting

　　如果因为某些原因不得不取消会面，在得知消息后即刻发送邮件通知对方是比较礼貌的行为。

### 常用词汇　Vocabulary

**1. cancellation　n. 取消；撤销；废除**

【双语例句】

The cancellation of the plan puts him in a bad mood.
取消计划使他很不开心。

【用法解析】

可以用于指代被取消的事物，例如，"We have a cancellation in the stalls.
（我们有一张正厅前座的退票）"。

## 2. adjustment　n. 调整；调节

【双语例句】

I've made a few adjustments to the seating plan.

我对座次表做了小小的调整。

【用法解析】

作"调整"解时，短语为"adjustments in the exchange rates（汇率的调整）"。
还可以作"调解"，如"the adjustment of conflicts（冲突的调解）"。

### 基本词汇　*Basic Words*

inform [ɪnˈfɔːrm]　v. 知会；通知

anticipation [ænˌtɪsɪˈpeɪʃn]　n. 预料

basis [ˈbeɪsɪs]　n. 原因

partnership [ˈpɑːrtnərʃɪp]　n. 伙伴关系

project [prəˈdʒekt]　n. 项目；方案

schedule [ˈskedʒuːl]　n. 工作计划

### 情景实例　*Scene Example*

　　广东贸易有限公司外贸业务员李宜遇到紧急事宜，不得不取消与纽约真实公司负责人布朗的会面。得知情况后，公司的销售经理立即发函给布朗说明情况。

**英**

With apology, I am writing this to inform you about the cancellation of the meeting that was fixed on April 5.

Within this meeting, the partnership and some business projects were to be discussed. But unfortunately, Mr. Li Yi has to leave New York suddenly for another important meeting. This is why he has cancelled the meeting on an emergency basis.

The meeting will be rescheduled sometime next month after the arrival of Mr. Li Yi. We will contact you to discuss an available date for you. Sorry again for the inconvenience.

Your kind understanding is much anticipated. We hope that you will make the required adjustments. Thanks for your cooperation in anticipation.

**中**

抱歉，我写此信是为了通知你取消 4 月 5 日的会面。

此次会面将讨论合作关系和一些商业项目。遗憾的是，李宜先生不得不突然离开纽约参加另一个重要会议。这就是他为什么紧急取消会面的原因。

会面将安排到下个月的某个时间，在李宜先生回到纽约之后。我们联系你看能否再安排一个方便的日期。我们对此次造成的不便再次表示歉意。

你的体贴关怀令人期待。我们希望你们能做出必要的调整。感谢你的支持。

---

### PART 3 会面后的跟进工作 Follow Up After Meeting

## Unit 1 跟进合作伙伴的意愿 Follow Up Partners' Will

在与合作伙伴会面之后，适当的跟进是很重要的。可以将会面时谈到的内容进行梳理，或者补充相关信息。总之，让对方知道你们做事的效率，从而对你们产生好感。

### 常用词汇 Vocabulary

**1. contribute  vt. 捐助；投稿 vi. 投稿；贡献**

【双语例句】

Honesty and hard work contribute to success and happiness.

诚实加苦干有助于成功和收获幸福。

【用法解析】

"contribute"作不及物动词时，其后常加介词"to"。"contribute"作"有助于，促使（发生某情况）"解时，主语一般是事物。

## 2. encounter　n. 邂逅；遭遇　v. 遭遇；偶然碰到

【双语例句】

Otherwise, we will encounter grave difficulties.

否则我们将遇到极大的困难。

【用法解析】

"encounter"用作动词的基本意思是"遇到，遭遇"，通常指遭遇困难或麻烦等，还可指未曾想到会遇见但却遇见了，即"偶然碰到"。

### 基本词汇　*Basic Words*

chat [tʃæt]　v. 闲聊；闲谈

improve [ɪm'pruːv]　v. 改进；改善

mention ['menʃn]　v. 提到；写到

issue ['ɪʃuː]　n. 重要议题

volume ['vɑːljuːm]　n. 量；额

attach [ə'tætʃ]　v. 把…附在…上

### 情景实例　*Scene Example*

　　李宜与布朗在会面中讨论了两家公司各自所面临的机遇和调整。在会面后，李宜整理出有效信息，给布朗发了一封跟进邮件。

**英**

I really enjoyed chatting with you earlier today and learning more about the contribution your made to your company. I understand the issues you're encountering and its negative impact on sales growth.

As mentioned, I've attached more information about our company and how we can help you to increase sales and solve your business problem.

Just let me know if you have any questions and I'd be more than happy to chat again.

**中**

我很高兴能在今天早些时候和你聊天，并且了解了更多你的工作对你所在公司的贡献。我理解你遇到的问题，以及其对销售量增长的不良影响。

如我所说，我在附件中附上了更多关于我们公司的信息，以及我们如何能帮助你提高销售量，解决业务问题。

如果你有任何问题，请告诉我，我很乐意再次与你聊天。

## PART 3 会面后的跟进工作 Follow up After Meeting

### Unit 2 展会邀请 Fairs' Invitation

对于打过交道，但还不太熟悉的客户来说，邀请对方参加展会是一个展示公司实力，促成双方交易的好机会。

### 常用词汇 Vocabulary

**1. booth    n. 货摊；电话亭；小间**

【双语例句】

There're many booths at the exhibition.

展览会上有许多摊位。

【用法解析】

相关短语有"telephone booth（电话亭）"和"ticket booth（售票亭）"等。而"booth number（摊位号）"是参展必备，在向客户说明己方摊位号时，可以采用"Our Booth No. ××× is ..."的句式。

## 2. layout  n. 安排；布局；设计

### 【双语例句】

What is the layout of this house like?

房子的格局如何？

### 【用法解析】

layout 近义单词有 "arrangement（布置）" "blueprint（蓝图）" 和 "format（版式）" 等。

## 基本词汇 *Basic Words*

**pleasure** [ˈpleʒər]  n. 荣幸

**below** [bɪˈloʊ]  adv. 在（或到）下面

**benefit** [ˈbenɪfɪt]  n. 优势；益处

**discuss** [dɪˈskʌs]  v. 讨论

**exhibition** [ˌeksɪˈbɪʃn]  n. 展览

## 情景实例 *Scene Example*

　　为了更好地推广公司的产品，李宜向外贸合作公司去函邀请对方前来参加广交会，并随函附上了地址和地图。

## 英

It is a pleasure for us to invite you to the 122nd Canton fair. You are sincerely welcome to visit our booth.

This visit will provide an opportunity for you to make a better understanding of our products, and discuss our future business cooperation in details. For your information, the event details are provided below.

Location: No.382 Yuejiang Middle Road, Haizhu District, Guangzhou City, Guangdong Province, China

Date:  Oct.13–Oct.16, 2017

Booth Number: 13-4-012

Also the enclosed is a map of the Canton fair's layout. If you have any questions or concerns, please do not hesitate to contact me.

We will be pleased to see you in the exhibition. We believe that this visit will be of great benefit for our future business cooperation.

**中**

能够有机会邀请您参加第 122 届广交会是我方的荣幸。欢迎你方届时光临我们的展位。

这次访问是一个契机，能让你方更好地了解我们的产品，还能就以后的商业合作进行详谈。以下是展会详细信息，仅供您参考。

地点：中国广东省广州市海珠区阅江中路 382 号

日期：2017 年 10 月 13 日至 10 月 16 日

展位号：13-4-012

随函附上一张广交会布局的地图。如果你方有任何问题或顾虑，请随时与我联系。

我们将很高兴看到你方出席展会。我们相信，这次访问将对我们今后的业务合作大有裨益。

---

**Tips 什么是广交会**

中国进出口商品交易会，简称广交会，每年春秋两季在广州举办，由商务部和广东省人民政府联合主办，中国对外贸易中心承办。广交会是中国目前历史最长、层次最高、规模最大、商品种类最全、到会采购商最多且分布国家和地区最广、成交效果最好的综合性国际贸易盛会。

广交会贸易方式灵活多样，以出口贸易为主，还可以开展多种形式的经济技术合作与交流，以及商检、保险、运输、广告、咨询等业务活动。

## Unit 3　展会后的联络往来
### Contacting after Fairs

在展会结束后，外贸业务员也要继续跟进客户。在邮件中，要提示对方相关信息，唤起对方记忆。然后附上丰富的资料，引起对方兴趣。

## 常用词汇　*Vocabulary*

### 1. stall　n. 小隔间；货摊

【双语例句】

The opening of a market stall is governed by municipal fiat.

市场摊位的开设受市政法令限制。

【用法解析】

"stall" 作动词是 "拖延" 的意思，如 "Quit stalling!（不要拖延时间）"。在展销会上的摊位也可称为 "booth"。

### 2. pity　n. 怜悯；同情；遗憾；可惜　v. 同情；怜悯

【双语例句】

It's a pity that I have to back to work.

遗憾的是我不得不回去工作。

【用法解析】

"pity" 作 "可惜的事，令人遗憾的事" 解时，为可数名词，但往往只用于单数形式，常用于 "It is/was a pity…" 结构，有时还可以把 "it is" 省去，直接用 "pity" 作为句子的开头。

## 3. for your reference　供你（你们）参考

**【双语例句】**

I am enclosing my resume for your reference.

谨附上履历表一份，以作为参考。

**【用法解析】**

在邮件中，除了"for your reference"，常用的表达"供参考"的短语还有"for your information"，常缩写为"FYI"，放在邮件正文末尾。

### 基本词汇　*Basic Words*

**feedback** [ˈfiːdbæk] n. 反馈的意见

**memory** [ˈmeməri] n. 回忆；记忆

**memo** [ˈmeموʊ] n. 备忘录

**refresh** [rɪˈfreʃ] v. 使想起

**catalog** [ˈkætəlɔːg] n. 目录

**sample** [ˈsæmpl] n. 样品

### 情景实例　*Scene Example*

### 1. 针对未详谈的客户

在展会后，李宜整理收到的名片，向没有详谈的客户发送了一封通用邮件，以期唤起对方的记忆。

**英**

Thank you for stopping by our stall at the Canton Fair on Jan. 8. I wanted to take a feedback whether all of your questions about our product were answered at the stall.

We deal in Chinese textiles which you may have seen at Booth No. ×××. In order to refresh your memory, I've attached our catalog and price list.

If you would like further information or if I can answer any of your queries, please contact us. I would reply to you immediately.

**中**

谢谢你于 1 月 8 日在广交会上参观我们的展位。我想得到一个反馈，了解你关于我们产品的所有问题在展位上是否都得到了回答。

我们公司是经营中国纺织品的，你在 ××× 号展位上已经看到了。为了唤起你的记忆，在此附上我们的产品目录和价目表。

如果你想了解更多的信息，或如果我能回答你的任何疑问，请与我们联系。我会立即答复你。

## 2. 针对详谈的客户

对于已经在展会上交流了很多，有下单意向的客户，李宜整理了交谈中的信息，并进一步询问对方的下一步计划。

**英**

It was nice to meet you at the Canton Fair on Jan. 8. Thanks for your kind visit to our stall. It's a little pity that your schedule is so tight. If possible, we'd like to invite you to our office next time and show you around about our three factories.

The follows are our meeting memo for your reference.

D–591, USD $27.3 per unit, add USD $1 per unit

V–192, USD $31.5 per unit, add USD $0.5 per unit

We'll arrange D–591 and V–192 sample for your test.

I do hope you could share some of your proposals of our next step cooperation. Looking forward to hearing from you.

**中**

很高兴于 1 月 8 日在广交会上见到你。谢谢你对我们展位的友好参观。真遗憾你的日程安排得这么紧。如果可能的话，我们想邀请你下次到我们公司，带你参观我们的三家工厂。

以下是我们的交谈备忘录，供你参考。

D-591，每台 27.3 美元，上浮 1 美元。

V-192，每台 31.5 美元，上浮 0.5 美元。

我们会安排 D-591 和 V-192 样品供你方检验。

希望你可以分享对下一步合作的建议。期待你的回复。

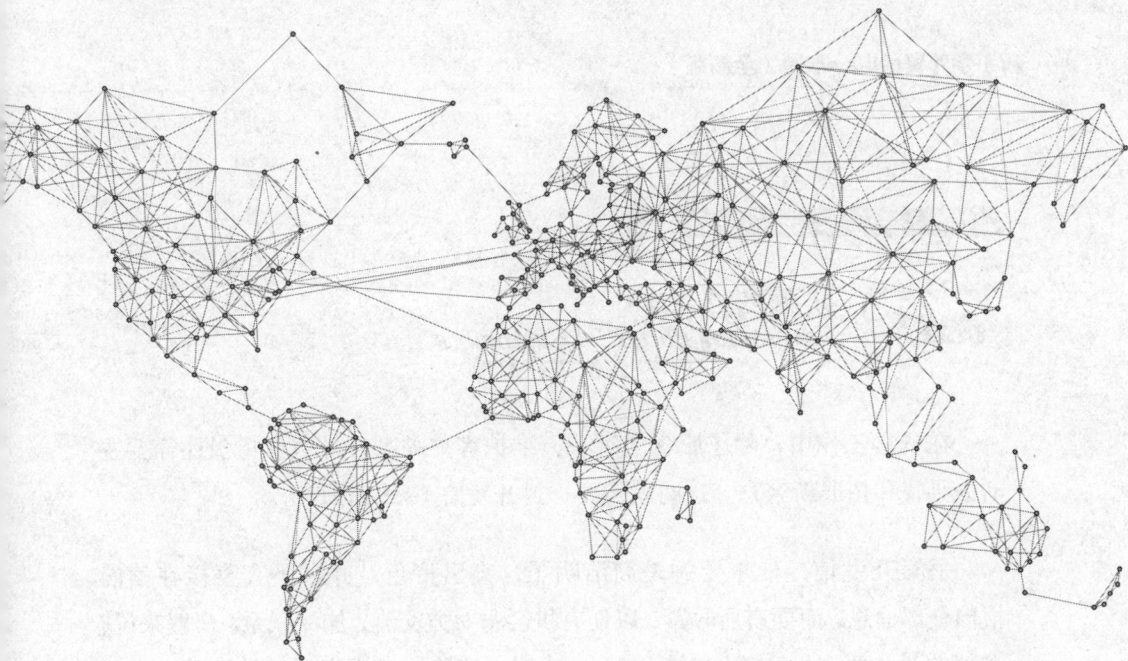

# CHAPTER 03

开发信与促销信

*Sales Letters and Promotion Letters*

在外贸业务员的日常工作中，需要经常发送拓展新客户的开发信和维护老客户关系的促销信，但这类函件不能千篇一律，需要根据不同情况进行调整。此外，代理函电也会在本章进行介绍。

*PART 1* 开发信 *Sales Letter*

*PART 2* 促销信 *Promotion Letter*

*PART 3* 代理函电 *Agent Letter*

# Unit 1 拓展潜在客户
## Developing Potential Customers

　　在日常工作中，除了服务老客户，维护客户关系，外贸业务员还需要主动去寻找和拓展新客户。这时就需要一封开发信（sales mail）。

　　书写开发信，最重要的是简洁明了，突出特色，并且不宜直接在信内报出全部信息，而要有所收紧，以便有机会与对方交流，加深联系。一般来说，在邮件开头要问候和感谢对方查看，体现出礼貌，然后表示发件的针对性，不是随便发送的，最后具体展开。

## 常用词汇 Vocabulary

### 1. field　n. 田地；领域

【双语例句】

He has become famous in his own field.

他在自己的领域里已经出名了。

【用法解析】

"field"的基本含义是"场地"，引申可表示"领域，方面，界"。相关短语有"hold the field（保持优势）""open a field for trade（开辟商业市场）"等。

### 2. capacity　n. 容量；能力；职位；资格

【双语例句】

China's grain production capacity has increased.

中国的粮食生产能力提高了。

【用法解析】

相关短语有"capacity for（…的能力）""capacity of（具有…容量）""at full capacity（全力以赴）""beyond the capacity of（出乎能力之外）"和"draw out capacity（发挥能力），等等。

## 基本词汇 *Basic Words*

serve [sɜːrv]  v.（给某人）提供

experience [ɪkˈspɪriəns]  n. 经验

information [ˌɪnfəˈmeɪʃn]  n. 信息

professional [prəˈfeʃənl]  adj. 专业的

introduce [ˌɪntrəˈduːs]  v. 把…介绍（给）；引见

factory [ˈfæktri]  n. 工厂

## 情景实例 *Scene Example*

广州贸易有限公司的李宜通过网络查找到与自己公司同领域的潜在客户，向对方发送了一封有针对性的开发信。

## 英

Good morning, my friend. Thanks for your time to read my email.

Glad to know you are in the market of air-conditioning.

This is Li Yi from Guangzhou Trading Co., Ltd. I've been working in air-conditioning field for more than five years. I wish I could serve you with my professional experience from now on.

I'd like to introduce you some information about our factory, GT Co., Ltd. is a professional manufacturer in producing air-conditioning, and we got the supports as below.

Staff number: over 300.

Production lines: four lines.

Monthly capacity: 6,000 units.

Samples and more information are available for your study anytime. We appreciate your kind reply soon.

**中**

早上好，朋友。感谢你阅读我的电子邮件。

很高兴知道你们从事空调领域。

我是广州贸易有限公司的李宜，我在空调领域有超过五年的行业经验。希望以后能以我的专业经验为你服务。

我想向你们介绍一下我们工厂的情况。广州贸易有限公司是一家专业生产精密空调的公司，我们公司规模如下。

员工人数：300 人以上。

生产线：4 条生产线。

月产量：6,000 台。

我们可随时提供样品和更多的信息供你参考。希望收到你的回复。

---

### PART 1 开发信 Sales Letter

## Unit 2 介绍优势 Introducing Advantages

在开发信中，最重要的一点是要突出自己公司或产品的优势，让对方觉得和你合作能够获得利益，简单来说就是展现"卖点"。

### 常用词汇 Vocabulary

### 1. specialize v. 专攻

【双语例句】

I specialize in the sale of cotton goods. May I act as your agent?

我专营棉布买卖，我可以成为你们的代理吗？

【用法解析】

在英式英语中，"specialize"也可写作"specialise"。

## 2. expressly　adv. 清楚地；特意地；专门地

【双语例句】

He has expressly forbidden her to go out on her own.
他已经明确禁止她独自外出。

【用法解析】

相关短语有"expressly for（专门为）"和"were expressly（已经明确地）"。
同样表达"明白地说"的单词还有"plainly（清晰地）""explicitly（明白地）"
和"clearly（清楚地）"等。

## 3. competitive　adj. 竞争的；有竞争力的；胜过或超过他人的

【双语例句】

Because of the high exchange rate, our products have lost their competitive
advantage.
由于汇率很高，我们的产品失去了竞争优势。

【用法解析】

相关短语有"competitive nature（天性好强）""competitive price（有竞争力的
价格）""competitive spirit（竞争精神）"和"highly competitive（很有竞争精
神）"等。

### 基本词汇　*Basic Words*

**address** [əˈdres]　n. 住址；地址　　　**export** [ˈekspɔ:t]　v. 出口

**profuse** [prəˈfju:s]　adj. 大量的　　　**series** [ˈsɪri:z]　n. 一系列

**manufacture** [ˌmænjuˈfæktʃər]　v. 制造　　　**profile** [ˈprovfaɪl]　n. 简介

## 情景实例 *Scene Example*

　　某公司生产圆珠笔多年，利用网络寻找到同领域的潜在客户，于是发函介绍己方优势，期望得到对方订单。

**英**

Good morning, my friend. Thanks for your time of reading my email.

We get your name and email address from http://www.×××.com and we know that you are in the market for ball pen. We would like to introduce our company and products, and hope that we may build business cooperation in the future.

Our factory specializing in the manufacture and export of ball pen for more than six years. We have profuse designs with a series of quality grade, and expressly, our price is very competitive because we are manufactory, we own the source.

You are welcome to visit our website http://www.×××.com which includes our company profiles, history and some latest designs. If any of these items be of interest to you, please let us know. We will be happy to give you details.

As a very active manufacturer, we develop new designs nearly every month. If you have the interest in it, it's my pleasure to offer news to you regularly.

If you have any inquiry and need our help, please don't hesitate to contact me.

**中**

早上好，朋友。感谢你阅读我的电子邮件。

我们从 http://www.×××.com 得知了你的名字和电子邮件地址，了解到你是做圆珠笔生意的。我们想介绍我们公司和产品，希望以后能建立业务合作。

我们是一家专业生产和出口圆珠笔六年以上的工厂。我们有丰富的设计与一系列的质量等级。明确地说，我们的价格是非常有竞争力的，因为我们是制造商，我们掌握第一手资源。

欢迎你访问我们的网站 http://www.×××.com，上面有公司概况、历史和一些最新的设计。如果你对这些产品感兴趣，请告诉我们，我们将乐意为你提供详细信息。

作为一个非常活跃的制造商，我们几乎每个月都会开发新的设计，如果你有兴趣的话，我很乐意定期为你提供信息。

如果你有任何疑问并需要我们的帮助，请随时与我联系。

**Tips 开发信的书写技巧**

开发信的开头和结尾内容可以参考范例，但主体需要自己写。如果售卖的是日用消费品或时尚产品，文字风格可以稍微轻松活泼一些。如果售卖的是工业产品，还是严谨专业一些比较好。针对己方特点写好开发信后，也不代表一劳永逸，还应该根据客户的规模、国籍不同略作调整。

**PART 1 开发信 Sales Letter**

## Unit 3 突出专业素养
### Highlighting Specialty

在与客户的前期接触中，不仅要及时回复对方的询问，更要注意突出自身的专业素养，让对方感到是和专业人士打交道，从而增强信心，最终更有效地达成双方的合作。

**常用词汇 Vocabulary**

## 1. regarding　prep. 关于；至于

【双语例句】

She said nothing regarding your request.
她对你的要求只字不提。

**【用法解析】**

在邮件中，"regarding"是"with reference to sb./sth."的简洁版本，也可以用
"concerning"代替。

## 2. acquire  vt. 获得；学到；取得

**【双语例句】**

We should acquire more firsthand information.

我们应当取得更多的第一手资料。

**【用法解析】**

"acquire"所接的宾语多为知识、技能和方法等，强调通过努力而获得，是
一个逐渐获得的过程。相关短语有"acquire an education（受教育）""acquire
an understanding（取得谅解）"及"acquire assiduously（持之以恒地积累）"等。

## 3. deposit  v. 付（订金等）n. 订金

**【双语例句】**

You must pay a deposit if you want to reserve the room.

你要预订房间，就得先付订金。

**【用法解析】**

相关短语有"deposit some money（存些钱）""give deposit（付保证金）"和
"demand deposit（定期存款）"等。

## 4. lead time  n. 间隔时间；交付周期；研制周期

**【双语例句】**

Please advise your sample and product lead time.

请提供你们的样品并告知产品的交货时间。

**【用法解析】**

"lead time"是前置时间，即生产周期或者研制周期，是指从订购到供应商交
货所间隔的时间，通常以天数或小时计算。

## 基本词汇 *Basic Words*

**inquiry** ['ɪnkwəri]　n. 询问；询盘

**reply** [rɪ'plaɪ]　n. 回答；答复

**steady** ['stedi]　adj. 稳固的

**healthy** ['helθi]　adj. 健康的

**mattress** ['mætrəs]　n. 床垫

**backbone** ['bækboʊn]　n. 脊梁骨

**balance** ['bæləns]　n. 余额

**shipment** ['ʃɪpmənt]　n. 运输

## 情景实例 *Scene Example*

在发出开发信后，生产床垫的某公司收到希望进一步了解企业的客户邮件，该公司业务员立即回复了一封邮件，从专业角度介绍了己方的优势。

**英**

Thank you very much for your kind inquiry to us. Regarding your inquiry, please find our reply as below.

1.Our products are fast sales in EU countries and America. Especially we already had steady partners in those places. And the cooperation has been lasting more than 5 years.

2.Regarding American market, our customers prefer healthy sleeping, so they would like to buy the mattress to protect their backbones. Please refer to the attachments, I would like to introduce some suitable items for your market.

3.Currently, our products have acquired the CFR1633 Certification. We think you might require it. Please refer to the certification as attached.

4.Payment term:

A.30% deposit T/T in advance, 70% balance T/T before shipment.

B.50% deposit T/T in advance, 50% balance by irrevocable L/C at sight.

5.Lead time: 15 days upon deposit received

6.MOQ: 1*20GP, FOB Shenzhen

**中**

非常感谢您对我们的友好询盘。关于你方的疑问，请查看如下回复。

1. 我们的产品在欧盟国家和美国销售很好。特别是我们已经在这些地方有稳定的、持续 5 年以上的合作伙伴。

2. 在美国市场，顾客更喜欢健康的睡眠方式，所以他们买床垫考虑的是对脊椎有保护作用。请参考附件，我介绍了一些适合你们市场的商品。

3. 目前，我们的产品已获得 CFR1633 认证。我们认为你可能需要它。请参考附件中的证明书。

4. 付款条件。

A. 电汇预付 30% 订金，余额在装运前付清。

B. 电汇预付 50% 订金，余款以不可撤销的即期信用证付清。

5. 交付日期：收到订金后 15 天。

6. 最小起订量：1 个 20 英尺的小柜，深圳离岸价。

---

**Tips 展现公司优势**

行业内的客户一般会比较关心产品的质量，工厂产品的市场销售情况、质量认证书等方面。所以范例在回复客户问题的时候，着重突出了优势和实力。

①有稳定的客源，是公司实力和产品质量的保证；
②分析最终消费者的实际要求和特点，体现个人的专业水准；
③分析客户市场对质量的要求，展示公司的实力；
④最后向客户说明公司其他方面的操作程序，让客户进行深入了解。

---

**PART 2 促销信 Promotion Letter**

## Unit 1　促销注意事项 Promotional Notes

　　相对于开发信，促销信发送的对象通常是已有合作的客户，在写作时要更注重对促销产品的介绍，主要是为了激发客户需求，吸引客户合作。

撰写一封有效的促销信，必须具有以下 4 个特征：吸引注意（attention），激发兴趣（interest），产生购买欲望（desire），进而导致购买行动（action）。具体来说，促销信中应注意以下 5 点。

①强调利益而不是产品或服务的特性。

【邮件示例】

By integrating this revolutionary new machine into your manufacturing system, we are sure your production volume can be substantially increased.
通过把这台革命性的新机器集成到你的制造系统中，我们确信你的生产量可以大幅度增加。

②描述产品或服务的使用或性能时，使用主动语态，使得读者可以更好地沉浸其中。

【邮件示例】

HubSpot serves 18,118 companies around the world, 74% of which see a sales revenue increase within seven months of starting to use our software.
HubSpot 为世界各地的 18 118 家公司服务，其中 74% 的公司在使用我们的软件后 7 个月内增加了销售收入。

③专注于一个主要的诉求。

【邮件示例】

Welcome new and old customers visit our website to know more about our products.
欢迎新老客户光临我们的网站了解我们的产品。

④在谈及所有好处之后，再谈价格，除非确实是明显的降价。

【邮件示例】

Starting in June, a special discount is offered on the WA line.

从六月开始，我们将对 WA 产品提供特别折扣。

⑤使用宣传手册（如随函附上的小册子）来说明产品或服务的细节。

【邮件示例】

Enclosed please find the detailed specifications.

随函附上详细规格说明书。

【邮件示例】

Please check the brief video about our company in the attachment.

请在附件中查看有关我们公司的短片。

## *PART 2* 促销信 *Promotion Letter*

### *Unit 2* 写作技巧 *Writing Skills*

促销信应以诱人的开头来吸引对方的注意力，然后通过介绍产品或服务的特征（feature）、优势（advantage）和利益（benefit）来引起对方的兴趣和欲望，并最终导致对方采取购买行为。具体的写作技巧如下。

①有力的标题。一般以"产品＋卖点"的形式展现，最后附上公司名称，与广告邮件区分开。

【邮件示例】

BIG DISCOUNT for Halloween—Crystal Inc.

万圣节大优惠——水晶公司

②吸引注意力的开头。在邮件的开头，就要让人明白能够从产品中获得好处，突出重点。

【邮件示例】

Would you like to reduce your rising fuel costs?

你想要减少日益增长的燃油花费吗?

Just imagine how comfortable you are when you stretch out those tired limbs on our newly developed White Cloud water bed.

想象一下你在我们新开发的"白云水床"上伸展疲惫的四肢时,你是多么舒服。

③进一步介绍。在吸引注意力后,就要围绕产品的特性、质量、原材料、与行相比的优势进行介绍,以此让客户加深了解。

【邮件示例】

Our ladies' dresses are all made of selected fabrics and deliberately designed, cut, stitched and trimmed.

我们售卖的女装都是精心挑选的织物,经过精心设计、剪裁、缝制而成的。

Printed with high-grade technology, this keds sneaker will turn out dazzling with forbes1954's striped design.

这款科迪斯运动鞋采用高档技术打造,将使用福布斯1954年的条纹设计,令人眼花缭乱。

④许诺好处。通过产品介绍激发客户的购买欲望后,就可以通过承诺试用、退款或退货策略,进一步坚定客户购买的决心。

【邮件示例】

Our Fast Microwave Oven use for free for first two weeks.

我们快速微波炉前两个星期免费试用。

If you find the model machine unsuitable to your needs for any reasons, we will replace your order or refund your money.

无论出于何种原因,只要你认为样机不适合你方需要,即可换货或退款。

⑤促使行动。到了邮件最后,要促使客户采取行动,购买产品。这时语气要礼貌坚决,并提供给客户如何购买产品的指示,以方便客户购买。

【邮件示例】

Since a special discount of 15% will only be offered for a month, you may place your order as soon as possible.

由于 15% 的特殊折扣仅限本月，你可以尽快下订单。

## PART 2 促销信 Promotion Letter

### Unit 3 写促销信
### Writing a Promotion Letter

　　外贸业务员在正式书写促销信时，不必包含以上所有步骤和注意事项，而要根据己方需求灵活运用。

### 常用词汇 Vocabulary

### 1. token　n. 象征　adj. 象征性的

【双语例句】

We charge only a token fee for use of the facilities.

对这些设施的使用我们只收取象征性的费用。

【用法解析】

"token" 表示爱情、友谊等的纪念物或礼品等，比 "sign" 庄严文雅，通常用于严肃的场合，在一般情况下可以用 "sign" 代替。相关短语有 "by the same token（由于同样原因）" "in token of（表示，作为）" 和 "token payment（象征性付款）" 等。

### 2. patronage　n. 赞助；光顾

【双语例句】

We respectfully solicit your continuous patronage.

恭请继续光顾。

## 【用法解析】

常用于美式英语。相关短语有 "enjoy patronage of（获得…的资助）" "under the patronage of（在…赞助下）" 和 "political patronage（政治赞助）" 等。

## 基本词汇 *Basic Words*

reduce [rɪˈduːs] v. 减少

usage [ˈjuːsɪdʒ] n. 用法

loyal [ˈlɔɪəl] adj. 忠实的

merchandise [ˈmɜːrtʃəndaɪz] n. 商品；货品

fuel [ˈfjuːəl] n. 燃料

heat [hiːt] n. 热；温度

discount [dɪsˈkaʊnt] n. 折扣

## 情景实例 *Scene Example*

### 1. 推荐新产品

某公司推出新款节约器，于是向客户发出促销信，详细介绍了产品性能及相关折扣信息。

**英**

Would you like to reduce your rising fuel costs?

Our recent researches and tests have showed that rooms with our newly developed Energy Savers stay warmer and require 20 percent less fuel than those rooms of the same size without the usage of the savers. The new savers are popular because they are able to store and reflect heat in a much more efficient way. Read the enclosed brochure, you will find that the self-stick backing makes them easy to install yourself.

As a token of appreciation of your kind patronage over these years, we offer a special discount of 10%. There is also another 5% discount on top of its 10% sale discount on its savers with purchases above 10,000 pieces.

If we can be of any further help, please feel free to let us know. Customers' inquiries always meet with our careful attention. Only by receiving your detailed requirements can we offer you more info.

**中**

想要减少日益增长的燃油花费吗?

我们最近的调查和测试显示：使用了我们新发明的能源节约器的空间，在保持温暖时，比同等空间下没有使用我们节约器的要省油20%。这个新节约器非常受欢迎，因为它可以更有效地存储和反射热量。阅读附赠的小册子，你将发现，产品自粘的背面能帮助你轻易安装。

为了感谢你方多年来的惠顾，我们给你方 10% 的特别折扣。另外，如购买 10 000 件以上商品，在 10% 折扣之外，还有 5% 的折扣。

如果需要任何进一步的帮助，请随时告诉我们。我们会认真对待客户的询盘。只有收到你的详细要求，我们才能给你更多的信息。

## 2. 清仓旧产品

　　某公司需要清仓旧产品，于是向客户发出促销信，简单介绍了基本情况，并告知库存有限，希望尽快订货。

**英**

As one of our most loyal customers, we are writing this letter to inform you that several items are going to have a special discount in June. Some of our merchandise will have up to 30% discount and we attached a list of all the items that will be on sale.

There will be limited stock of certain items, so do place your order early to get the best deals. We are looking forward to receive your first order soon.

**中**

作为我们最忠诚的客户之一，我们写信通知您，6 月有一些商品将提供特别折扣。一些商品将有 30% 的折扣，我们附上了所有打折商品的清单。

某些型号的库存很有限，所以请尽早订货以获得较好的交易。我们期待您的第一次订货。

## PART 3 代理函电 *Agent Letter*

### Unit 1 物色代理商
### Looking for Agents

代理商是厂家授权在某地区经销某种产品的一般代理人。在对外贸易中，如果出口企业需要在某地区开辟市场，而不便设立分支机构，物色代理商就显得十分重要。

## 常用词汇 *Vocabulary*

### 1. be conversant with   adj. 精通（通晓；和…有关）

【双语例句】

Our manager is conversant with account system.

我们的经理精通会计制度。

【用法解析】

"conversant" 的意思是"熟悉的，亲近的"，相关短语还有"keep someone conversant on something（使某人随时知道某事）"。

### 2. implement   n. 工具；器具  vt. 实施；向…提供工具（或手段）

【双语例句】

The government is implementing a new policy to help the unemployed.

政府正在实施一项新的帮助失业者的政策。

【用法解析】

"implement" 原属于苏格兰法律用语，指"实行"，现在则被广泛运用，可与

"carry out, fulfil"等词互换。相关短语有"implement one's purpose（实现个人的目的）"、"implement a contract（履行合同）"和"household implements（日用器具）"等。

## 基本词汇 *Basic Words*

**range** [reɪndʒ]  n. 一系列

**match** [mætʃ]  v. 相配；相一致

**Germany** [ˈdʒɜːrməni]  n. 德国

**technical** [ˈteknɪkl]  adj. 技术的

**agent** [ˈeɪdʒənt]  n. 代理人

**brief** [briːf]  adj. 简洁的

## 情景实例 *Scene Example*

### 1. 委托寻找

某公司希望用己方生产的印刷机开辟新的市场，于是找到该地区的公司，委托其寻找 3 ~ 4 个符合要求的代理商。

**英**

Our company manufactures a range of printing presses that are used successfully by companies in over 20 countries. A product specification brochure is enclosed.

We are considering expanding our products to new markets and we would appreciate your assistance. In particular, we would like to identify the best agents who are currently serving the printing industry in your region. We are looking for organizations which conduct their business in a truly professional manner. They must be fully conversant with the technical side of the printing industry and have a comprehensive understanding of all the features of the lines they represent.

We would be very grateful if you could take a minute to send us the names of three or four organizations that match our requirements. We shall then contact them to explore the possibility of establishing a mutually acceptable business relationship. Thank you very much for your time and consideration in this matter.

**中**

我公司生产的一系列印刷机，获得 20 多个国家的公司采用。随函附上产品规格说明书，以供参考。

我们正在考虑为产品开拓新的市场，希望能获得贵方帮助。具体来说，我们希望寻找到你方区域内印刷行业的最佳代理商。我们正在寻找用真正专业的方式开展业务地机构。他们必须完全熟悉印刷业的技术，并对他们所代理的产品线有一个全面地了解。

若能拨冗寄给我们 3 ~ 4 个符合要求的代理商商号，我们将感激不尽。我们将与他们联系，寻求建立互惠互利的业务关系的可能性。感谢你方为这件事所花费的时间和精力。

## 2. 广告寻找

某公司希望拓展美国市场，于是到相关网站发布招募代理商的信息，说明了己方情况、要求和联系方式。

**英**

### CHINESE MANUFACTURER SEEKS AGENT

It's our pleasure to introducing ourselves as the leading Packaging Machines producer in China.

We have been dealing with flexible printing and production of the packaging for 20 years. We mainly sell them to France, Britain, Germany, Switzerland, Netherlands, Poland, Russia, etc.

We are looking for agents at the U.S. market to implement our sales network on the commission basis.

Agents should have knowledge about related products, processing experience, and sales communication skills to win the order.

We are an ISO 9001:2008 Company. You can watch the brief video about the company and its facilities at www.abcd.com. If you are interested in looking for more information about this opportunity, please contact Mr. Li Yi at agent@abcd.com

【中】

中国制造商寻求代理商

我们是中国领先的包装机械生产商。

我们从事软包装印刷和生产已有 20 年，主要销往法国、英国、德国、瑞士、荷兰、波兰、俄罗斯等国家。

我们正在寻找美国市场的代理商，支付佣金并委托其建立销售网络。

代理商应具备相关产品知识、加工经验和销售沟通技巧，以赢得订单。

我们公司已获得 ISO 9001:2008 认证。你可以在 www.abcd.com 上观看短片，了解本公司及公司的设施。如果你想要了解更多关于这次招募代理商机会的信息，请通过 agent@abcd.com 联系李宜先生。

## PART 3 代理函电 Agent Letter

### Unit 2 代理邀约 Agents Offer

出口企业在寻找到某地区合适的代理商后，可以发函邀请其做己方产品的代理。通常来说，邀约函中要包括对己方公司及产品的介绍，选择对方公司的理由以及代理条件等。而是否接受邀约，决定权在代理商手中。

### 常用词汇 Vocabulary

**1. moderate　adj. 适度的；温和的　v. 节制；使…稳定**

【双语例句】

The hotel is moderate in its charges.

这家旅店收费适当。

【用法解析】

相关短语有"moderate in（在…方面有节制的）""show moderate（显得温和）"
"moderate speech（稳健的谈吐）"和"moderate price（适当的价格）"等。

## 2. durable　adj. 耐用持久的

【双语例句】

Our products have the quality of being durable.
我们的产品经久耐用。

【用法解析】

相关短语有"durable goods（耐久品）""durable cloth（耐磨的布料）"和"durable
material（耐穿的料子）"等。

### 基本词汇  *Basic Words*

| | |
|---|---|
| **flexible** ['fleksəbl]　adj. 柔韧的 | **Poland** ['poʊlənd]　n. 波兰 |
| **capable** ['keɪpəbl]　adj. 有能力 | **handle** ['hændl]　v. 处理；应付 |
| **sole** [soʊl]　adj. 仅有的 | **draft** [dræft]　n. 草案 |
| **market** ['mɑːrkɪt]　n. 市场 | **fit** [fɪt]　adj. 适合的 |

### 情景实例  *Scene Example*

## 1. 邀约函

广州贸易有限公司想要拓展白俄罗斯市场，于是发函给几个白俄罗斯的
代理商，在信中介绍了己方情况和代理要求，希望对方接受代理邀约。

**英**

My name is Li Yi, and I am the Sales Manager of Guangzhou Trading Co., Ltd., which is located in China. I am writing to you on behalf of my company, to invite you as our sales agent.

One of our friends at your end suggested several organizations that match our requirements. We have since been informed that you may be interested in acting as our agent in your country.

We have been dealing with flexible printing and production of the packaging for 20 years. I am enclosing a brochure detailing our various products for your reference. As you will see, the product is resistant to the toughest of conditions and moderately priced.

We currently export to France, Britain, Germany, Switzerland, Netherlands, Poland, Russia, etc., and would like to expand to Belarus market, there is an increasing demand for products such as those produced by our company.

The type of agency we are looking for will be capable of covering the whole of Belarus. We are offering a 10% commission on net list prices, plus advertising support.

We believe that this is a unique opportunity to develop an expanding market. If you believe that you have the resources to handle a sole agency covering Belarus, and feel that you can develop this market, please contact me as soon as possible.

Thank you in advance!

**中**

我是广州贸易有限公司的销售经理李宜，公司位于中国。我代表公司写信给你，邀请你方做我们的销售代理。

一位朋友向我们推荐了几个在贵方所在地符合我们要求的机构。我们由此获悉，你方可能有兴趣担任我方在贵国的代理。

我们从事软包装印刷和生产已有 20 年。随函寄上我公司各种产品的小册子，供你方参考。正如你将看到的，该产品能经受最恶劣的条件，价格也适中。

目前我们的产品出口到法国、英国、德国、瑞士、荷兰、波兰、俄罗斯等国家，希望拓展白俄罗斯市场，那里有着不断增长的对我公司这类产品的需求。

我们要找的代理机构类型将是能够覆盖整个白俄罗斯的机构。我们提供净价单10%的佣金，再加上对广告投入的支持。

我们相信，这是在不断扩大的市场中发展的独特机会。如果你认为你方有资源接下白俄罗斯的独家代理，并认为你方可以开发这个市场，请尽快与我联系。

提前感谢你!

## 2. 回复邀约函

收到邀约已方成为白俄罗斯独家代理的信函，代理商回函表示认同对方提出的邀约，但需要进一步确认代理合同的相关条款，表现出合作意向。

英

Thank you for your letter of June 22 in which you offered us a sole agency for your products in Belarus.

We can certainly handle an agency of the type you describe and agree that there is an increasing demand for inexpensive and durable packaging machine at our end. Before we can take your offer further, we would be grateful for the following information:

1. Payment of accounts. Would our customers pay your company directly, or would they pay us first and we in turn settle with your company after deducting our commission? How would payment be arranged? Bill of exchange, letter of credit or bank draft?

2. Delivery. Would we hold stock or would your company supply customers directly? In the case of the latter, how long would it take for an order to be made and shipped once it had been received?

3. Advertising. You mentioned that your company would help with advertising. Could you give us more details?

4. Length of the contract. How long would the initial contract run? In our view, three years would allow us to estimate the size of the market.

If you can send us this information, ideally enclosing a draft contract, we could give you our answer within fourteen days of receipt.

## 中

感谢贵方 6 月 22 日来信，邀约我方成为你方产品在白俄罗斯的独家代理。

我们当然可以经营你们所描述的那种类型的代理，并且认同在我方市场，对实惠并耐用的包装机械的需求越来越大。在我们进一步接受你方报价之前，如能提供以下信息我们将不胜感激。

1. 支付账户。我们的客户是直接支付给贵公司，还是先付给我们，我们扣除佣金后，再和贵公司结算？如何安排付款？汇票、信用证还是银行汇票？

2. 交货。是我们会持有一定的仓储量，还是你方直接向客户发货？如果是后者，在收到订单后，需要多长时间才能生产并发运？

3. 广告。你提到贵公司会帮忙做广告，你能告诉我们更多的细节吗？

4. 合同期限。初始合同持续多久？我们认为要试水市场规模，需要三年时间。

如果你方能将这些信息发给我方，最好附上一份合同草案，我们可以在收到后十四天内给你方答复。

收到邀约己方成为白俄罗斯独家代理的信函，代理商回函表示其目前不从事这方面经营，委婉地拒绝了提议。

## 英

With reference to your letter of June 22, offering us a sole agency for your products in Belarus. Thanks for reaching out to us. We appreciate the inquiry.

However, we are currently not in the market, but feel free to send us anything you think may be of interest. If we know any organization which would be a good fit, we'll happily send the names of them along to you.

**中**

关于贵方 6 月 22 日来信，邀约我方成为你方产品在白俄罗斯的独家代理。谢谢你方的主动接触。我们感谢你方的询问。

然而，我们目前不经营这一方面，但请随意给我们发送任何可能有用的信息。如果我们找到任何一个合适的机构，我们会很乐意把他们的名字发给你方。

*PART 3 代理函电 Agent Letter*

## Unit 3 代理申请 Agent Application

代理商在看到出口企业发布的招募代理商信息后，也会主动发函申请成为代理商，并充分阐述己方作为代理商的资格。而是否接受申请，决定权在出口企业手中。

## 常用词汇 *Vocabulary*

### 1. attribute vt. 把…归于 n. 属性；标志；象征；特征

【双语例句】

Organizing ability is an essential attribute for a good manager.
组织能力是优秀管理者的基本品质。

【用法解析】

"attribute"用作名词时的基本意思是"特性、属性"，指某人或某事所特有的性质或属性，如"best attribute（好品性）"。相关短语有"be an attribute of（是…的本性）"和"attribute to（把…归因于）"等。

### 2. enhance vt. 提高；增加；加强

【双语例句】

He made great efforts to enhance his reputation.

他做了许多努力来提高他的声誉。

Large paintings can enhance the feeling of space in small rooms.

大型油画可以增加小房间的宽敞感。

### 【用法解析】

"enhance"的基本意思是"提高、增强"，指在力量或数量等方面的"加强"或"增多"，更多用于在理想程度或吸引力方面增强其价值、魅力或声望，常可译为"使…看起来更好"。

## 3. distribute　v. 分配；散发；分布

### 【双语例句】

These books are distributed freely.

这些书免费分发。

### 【用法解析】

"distribute"的意思是"分散、分发、分类"，指将某物分成数份并配给适当的人或单位，也可指将其均衡地分散在某一地区。

## 4. turnover　n. 营业额；流动；成交量

### 【双语例句】

The firm has an annual turnover of 75 million pounds.

这家公司的年营业额为 7 500 万英镑。

Our turnover actually increased last year.

去年我们的营业额竟然增加了。

### 【用法解析】

相关短语有"import turnover（进口额）""annual turnover（年营业额）"和"turnover tax（营业税）"等。

## 基本词汇 / *Basic Words*

**technique** [tek'ni:k]　n. 技巧；技艺

**trend** [trend]　n. 趋势；趋向

**connection** [kə'nekʃn]　n. 联系；关联

**approval** [ə'pru:vl]　n. 赞成；同意

**support** [sə'pɔ:rt]　n. 支持；拥护

**pick** [pɪk]　v. 选择；挑选

## 情景实例 / *Scene Example*

### 1. 申请函

在看到广州贸易有限公司发布的招募包装机械代理商的广告后，代理商发函说明了己方优势，申请成为对方的销售代理。

**英**

Being knowledgeable of latest sales techniques and approaching trends in today's competitive market, we believe that our skills could come in very handy to enhance your sales.

Our experience as a sales agency with various companies has rendered us capable of selling any product effectively. We have built up a considerable number of well−established connections showing excellent business results. Especially, the following attributes will help us contribute to your sales team:

1.Specialized in finding new clients, obtaining orders and maintaining old clients.

2.Competent at monitoring competition by finding information on pricing and merchandising techniques.

3.Demonstrated ability to investigate customer problems and developing appropriate solutions.

Attached is a leaflet which completely details our qualifications as a Sales agency. We will be pleased to answer any questions you might have.

Thank you for your time and consideration. I am looking forward to hearing from you soon.

**中**

在当今竞争激烈的市场中，我们掌握着最新的销售技巧和流行趋势，相信我们的技术将极大提高你方的销售业绩。

我们为不同公司做销售代理的经验使我们能够有效地销售任何产品。我们已建立了相当多的良好关系，显示出良好的经营业绩。尤其是以下特性将有助于我们为你方的销售团队做出贡献。

1. 专业寻找新客户，获得订单，维护老客户。

2. 通过查找定价和经营技术信息，掌握竞争情况。

3. 具有调查客户问题和制定适当解决方案的能力。

附上一份宣传册，详述了我们作为销售代理的资格。我们会很乐意回答你的任何问题。

谢谢你能抽时间阅读和考虑。希望能早日收到你方的来信。

## 2. 回复申请函

收到某代理商申请成为白俄罗斯独家代理的信函，出口企业回函表示选择了对方企业，进一步说明了代理协议细则，并附上协议草案。

**英**

Thank you for your letter of 12 April, proposing a sole agency for our packaging machines.We've examined all the organizations and we have actually selected you to be our sole agency. We entrust your capacity of enhancing our sales in your market.

We have drawn up a draft agreement that is enclosed. As per the agreement, your task will be to pick the products from our warehouse and distribute them in your market.

For doing this, you will be allowed to take margin of 10% on the selling price of the products which will also be subject to incentives if would be able to cross the targets of $50,000 per month. You will be rewarded with 15% margin on the products for the over sales of our products. Additionally, We are also offering advertising support.

Please examine the detailed terms and conditions, let us know whether it meet with your approval.

中

感谢贵方 4 月 12 日来信，提出成为我方包装机械独家代理的建议。我们已经检验过所有的机构，实际上，我们已经选定你方作为我们的独家代理。我们相信你方能提高我方在你方市场的销售量。

在附件中，我们草拟了一份协议草案。根据协议，你方的任务将是从我方公司仓库挑选产品，并在你方市场分销。

为了做到这一点，你方可以基于产品的销售价格收取 10% 的佣金，如果能超过设定的每月 50 000 美元的目标，也会得到奖励。超额销售的产品，你们将得到 15% 的佣金。此外，我们还提供广告支持。

请检查详细的条款和条件，并让我方知道你方是否满意。

收到某代理商申请成为白俄罗斯独家代理的信函，出口企业回函表示对方营业额较低，拒绝此提议，但双方可以先展开试行合作。

英

Thank you for your letter of September 1. I am regret to say that we have to decline your proposal of acting as our sole agency.

We would, however, be willing to engage in a trial collaboration with your company to see how the arrangement works. You need to increase the turnover to prove the ability of sole agency.

We enclose price lists covering all the products you are interested in and look forward to hearing from you soon.

中

感谢贵方 9 月 1 日来信。很遗憾，我们不得不拒绝你方提出的，成为我方独家代理的建议。

不过，我们愿意与贵公司先试行合作，为今后合作打下基础。你方需要扩大营业额，以证明你方独家代理的能力。

随函附上贵公司所感兴趣产品的价目表，盼早日收到回复。

## PART 3 代理函电 Agent Letter

### Unit 4  欢迎新代理 Welcome New Agent

　　对于外贸公司来说，在某地区设置新代理商后，该地区的销售量和销售额无疑会呈倍数快速增长。因此可以发函告知该地区客户，并在己方网站上公示。既巩固和新代理商的关系，又从侧面展现了公司的实力。

### 常用词汇 Vocabulary

## 1. rapidly  adv. 迅速地；很快地

【双语例句】

The company developed rapidly under his administration.
在他的管理下，公司发展得很快。

Her gaze sweeps rapidly around the room.
她快速地扫视了一下这个房间。

【用法解析】

相关短语有"rapidly growing（迅速生长）""rapidly acting（快速反应）"和"rapidly recover（恢复得很快）"等。

## 2. appoint　v. 任命；委派；指定；约定

【双语例句】

The company decided to appoint a new treasurer.

公司决定任命一位新司库。

Why didn't you appoint Ron twelve months ago?

你为什么 12 个月前不任命罗恩呢?

【用法解析】

相关短语有 "appoint sb as（任命某人为）" "appoint sb to the position of（委派某人担任…职务）" 和 "appoint a day for（为某事确定日子）" 等。

### 基本词汇 *Basic Words*

**expand** [ɪkˈspænd]　v. 扩大；增加

**announce** [əˈnaʊns]　v. 宣布；宣告

**shred** [ʃred]　v. 切碎；撕碎

**period** [ˈpɪriəd]　n. 一段时间

**Belarus** [bɛˈlɑrəs]　n. 白俄罗斯

**wrap** [ræp]　v. 包；裹

### 情景实例 *Scene Example*

　　广州贸易有限公司最终选择了贝扎德公司作为己方产品在白俄罗斯的独家代理，于是发函告知白俄罗斯地区的客户并在网站上公示。

**英**

During a rapidly expanding period, we are pleased to announce that we have appointed Bezard as our sole agent for Belarus. Bezard is appointed on an exclusive basis, and as such no other companies represent the interests of Guangzhou Trading Co., Ltd. in this region.

The business line of Bezard involves in wrapping machines, cutting machines and shredding machines manufacture. They are keen to be our sole agency in Belarus due to our competitive price and our overall strength has been well-received by customers.

We are very pleased to have Bezard in our team.

中

在这个迅速发展的时期，我们很高兴地宣布，我们已经任命贝扎德作为我们在白俄罗斯的独家代理。贝扎德被任命为独家代理，即没有其他公司可以代表广州贸易有限公司在该地区的利益。

贝扎德的商业业务涉及包装机、切割机和粉碎机的制造。他们希望成为我们在白俄罗斯的独家代理，是由于我们具有竞争力的价格，以及我们的整体实力得到客户的认可。

很高兴贝扎德加入我们的团队。

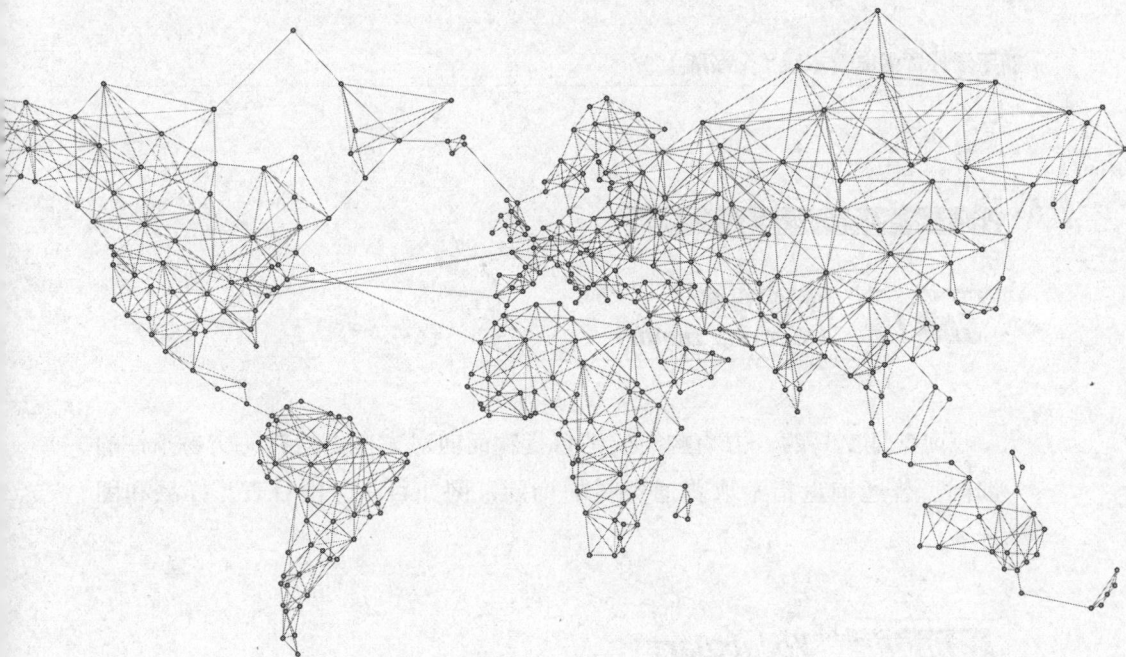

# CHAPTER04 订单操作函电

## *Order Operation Letters*

对于外贸业务员来说，询盘、发盘与还盘的订单操作
流程是在双方正式签约之前最重要的工作之一，直接
影响合同的签订及履行，关系双方的经济利益，需要
谨慎处理。

## Unit 1　普通询盘
### A General Inquiry

询盘是交易的一方为购买或销售货物而向对方提出的有关交易条件的询问。普通询盘指索取普通资料的询问，例如目录、价目表、样品和图片等。

## 常用词汇　Vocabulary

### 1. possession　n. 拥有；财产；所有

【双语例句】

A good job was a prized possession.

一个好的职业是一份珍贵的财富。

【用法解析】

表示"某人拥有某物"是"be in possession of"或"be in sb's possession"，"某物为某人所拥有"是"be in the possession of"。前者不用定冠词"the"，后者则必用定冠词"the"。

### 2. elaborate　adj. 详尽的；复杂的　v. 详细地说明

【双语例句】

He launched into an elaborate explanation of his theory.

他开始详尽地阐述他的理论。

【用法解析】

"elaborate"的基本意思是"注重细节"。对于尚未实现的事物，译为"详细制定，精心制作"。对于已存在的事物，则意在完全显现其细节，即"详尽说明，详细阐述"。

## 3. warranty　n. 保单；根据；保修期

### 【双语例句】

This product comes with one year warranty.

本产品有一年的保修期。

This warranty is good for one year after the date of the purchase of the product.

本保证书自购置此产品之日起有效期为一年。

### 【用法解析】

复数形式为 warranties，同义词有 security，engagement，insurance。用于法律行业，意为保证、担保、承诺；用于金融行业，意为保证书、担保地契、许可证。

## 基本词汇 *Basic Words*

**manager** [ˈmænɪdʒər]　n. 经理

**selection** [sɪˈlekʃn]　n. 挑选

**rubber** [ˈrʌbər]　n. 橡胶

**screw** [skruː]　n. 螺丝钉

**ally** [əˈlaɪ]　n. 盟友；支持者

**chappal** [tʃʌpəl]　n.（印）凉鞋

## 情景实例 *Scene Example*

## 1. 向产品供应商询盘

　　水晶公司得知某公司的螺丝钉质量可靠，但没有特定的购买意向，打算进行全面比较后再进行选择，因此公司负责人约翰发函要求对方提供各款产品的信息。

**英**

My name is John Green and I am the sales manager at Crystal Inc. I came to know from some trusted sources of your possession of some high quality screws. I would like to learn more about it. I would appreciate if you can send any information that could help me in my selection process.

Please elaborate on the various options along with the different prices, discounts and availability. I also need to know if you offer extended warranty. Please contact me immediately if you have any questions or need to know more about our requirements.

Looking forward to hearing from you.

## 中

我叫约翰·格林，是水晶公司的销售经理。我从可靠来源得知，贵公司生产高质量的螺丝钉。我非常想了解更多有关的信息。如果你能在我的选择过程中提供任何信息，我将不胜感激。

请详细说明各种产品型号，以及它们的价格、折扣和适用范围。我还需要知道，你方是否提供延长保修期。如果你方有任何问题或需要了解我们的需求，请立即联系我。

期待你方的来信。

## 2. 向原材料供应商询盘

WA 公司需要天然橡胶来生产产品，于是向原材料供应商发出询盘，并在信中详细介绍了己方公司信息，以期达成长期合作。

## 英

Hope you are doing well!

I am connecting to you as I have got your reference from one of my friends in the industry.

Firstly, I would like to introduce my business to you so that you can take a call on whether we can be business allies or not. We are a start-up company by the name of WA and we've captured a part of the market. We produce small rubber items like rubber bands, erasers and sandals. Thus, we require natural rubber in bulk supply.

If you can meet our requirements, please let us know your terms and conditions regarding prices, trade—discount, delivery schedule etc. as soon as possible I am looking forward to your reply.

**中**

希望你最近顺利！

一个工业界的朋友向我推荐了贵公司，所以我来联系你们。

首先，我想向你们介绍我公司的业务，以便你方决定我们是否能合作。我们是一家初创公司，叫 WA，我们已经占有了一部分市场。我们生产小型橡胶制品，例如橡皮筋、橡皮擦和凉鞋。因此，我们需要天然橡胶的批量供应。

如果你方能满足我们的要求，请尽早告知我方关于产品的价格、贸易折扣和交货期的条款和条件。期待你方的回复。

**PART 1 询盘函电 Inquiry Letter**

**Unit 2 具体询盘**
**A Specific Inquiry**

具体询盘，指具体询问商品名称、规格、数量、单价、交货期和付款方式等。具体询盘说明买方有具体的采购意向，容易达成合作，外贸业务员应高度重视。

**常用词汇 Vocabulary**

**1. inquire v. 询问；查究**

【双语例句】

I recommend that you inquire about the job.

我建议你打听一下这项工作。

【用法解析】

"inquire" 多用作书面语，比 "ask" 正式，常译作 "询问，调查"，指为得到某人或某物的真实确切情况而详细询问，但不一定要有被问者。

## 2. specification　n. 规格；详述；说明书

【双语例句】

Can you give me a price list with specification?

你能否给我一份有规格说明的价目单？

【用法解析】

相关短语有"order specification（订货说明书）""quality specification（质量标准）"和"test specification（试验规范）"等。

## 3. procurement　n. 采购；获得；促成

【双语例句】

He is in charge of the procurement of materials.

他负责物资的采购。

【用法解析】

与"purchase"相比，"procurement"的程序更多，规模更大，有经过整合分析，以更好地获得资源的意思。

### 基本词汇 *Basic Words*

behalf [bɪˈhæf]　n. 代表；利益

decision [dɪˈsɪʒn]　n. 决定；抉择

product [ˈprɑːdʌkt]　n. 产品；制品

trial [ˈtraɪəl]　n. 试用

sheet [ʃiːt]　n. 床单；一张

credit [ˈkredɪt]　n. 信用

### 情景实例 *Scene Example*

纽约真实公司需要买入某种特殊型号的螺丝钉，看到某公司网站上有这款产品，因此其负责人布朗向其发出了具体询盘。

## 英

My name is Brown Douglas and I'm contacting you on behalf of Real Inc. of New York. I would like to inquire about one of your products, WAFER. We would like to buy 2,000 pcs for a trial order. A full description of our requirements is given on the attached sheet.

Please quote us your best FOB Guangzhou price, giving a full specification of your products. We usually deal with new suppliers on the basis of payment in US dollar by confirmed irrevocable sight of credit. We also appreciate if you could offer me the discounts on bulk orders.

I have seen the product details on your website and I'm very interested in buying it. We appreciate if you can send us samples so we can test before making a decision. I have confidence in your commitment to me of quality but part of our procurement process is to have a test before any purchase.

I need to make a decision in the coming few days so it's really important that I receive this information as soon as possible. Awaiting your reply.

## 中

我叫布朗·道格拉斯，我代表纽约真实公司方面与你联系。我想询盘的产品是你们公司的 WAFER。我们想购买 2 000 件，作为试订单。附件中对我们的要求做了全面的说明。

请报广州离岸价的最优惠价格，并提供贵方产品的所有规格。与新供应商打交道时，我们通常开立美元付款的、保兑的且不可撤销的即期信用证。我们同样想了解大批量订单的折扣。

我已经在你们的网站上看到了产品细节，我非常有兴趣购买。如果你们能寄给我们样品，以便我们可以在做出决定前进行检测，我们将不胜感激。虽然我对贵公司的质量承诺充满信心，但我们采购的标准要求是在购买前要进行检测。

我需要在未来几天内做出决定，所以我要尽快收到相关信息。等待你的答复。

# Unit 3 回复无效的询盘
## *Response to an Invalid Inquiry*

如果客户所询盘的产品缺货，或者已经停止生产，不仅要告知基本信息，还要巧妙地建议对方作出其他选择。

## 常用词汇 *Vocabulary*

### 1. regret   v. 惋惜；为 … 感到遗憾  n. 遗憾；抱歉

【双语例句】

We regret that we have to place the entire shipment at your disposal.

很遗憾，我们只得将全部货品退回贵方自行处理。

【用法解析】

在英语语境中，"sorry" 是做错事的道歉，应注意不要滥用，而应使用 "regret" 来表示对无能为力的事感到懊悔。用于 "报告不开心的事" 时，表达方式有 "I regret that" "I regret to say that" "I regret to have to announce that" 等，语气的轻重有所不同。

### 2. substitute   n. 代用品  vt. 代替

【双语例句】

Water is not a proper substitute for wine.

水不是酒的适当代用品。

【用法解析】

"substitute" 的意思是 "代替"，指在需要时，把某事物用作代替者或用某事物替换某事物，常用短语为 "substitute sb/sth. for sb/sth."。

## 基本词汇 *Basic Words*

**item** [ˈaɪtəm]  n. 一件商品

**stock** [stɑːk]  v. 存货；储备

**notify** [ˈnoʊtɪfaɪ]  v.（正式）通知

**fulfill** [fʊlˈfɪl]  v. 履行；兑现

**website** [ˈwebsaɪt]  n. 网站

**longer** [ˈlɔŋɡər]  adv. 长期地

## 情景实例 *Scene Example*

### 1. 产品缺货

WA 公司收到缺货的产品询盘，于是回信向客户表示歉意，并说明会提供该产品的到货提醒。

### 英

Thank you for your recent inquiry about WA-2.

We regret to inform you that we will not be able to process this particular item. The product you ordered is not available with us at this time. We will have it back again in stock by May 1st with us.

We apologize for any inconvenience we may have caused and will notify you as soon as we can fulfill your order. Thank you for your patience. We hope to cooperate with you in near future.

### 中

谢谢你方近日对 WA-2 产品的询盘。

很遗憾地通知你方，我们无法供应这款特定产品。你方订购的产品此时缺货。我们将在 5 月 1 日前重新进货。

我方对可能造成的不便表示歉意，一旦我方能满足你方订单需求，我方将立即通知你方。谢谢你们的耐心。期待在不久的将来可以合作。

## 2. 停止生产

WA 公司收到已不再生产的产品询盘，于是回信向客户告知情况，并推荐其他产品。

**英**

Thank you for your recent inquiry about WA-1.

We regret to inform you that we no longer supply this particular item, but we can offer you a substitute.

We are enclosing our catalog for your review. Please have a look at some of our other products to see if there is anything we make that you may like. You can also visit our website to check them out: http://www. ×××.com.

If there's anything I can help, please feel free to contact us. We look forward to doing business with you.

**中**

谢谢你方近日对 WA-1 产品的询盘。

很遗憾地通知你方，我们已不再供应这款特定商品，但我们可以提供能够替代的产品。

随函附上产品目录供您参考。请看看我们的其他产品，是否有你感兴趣的。您也可以访问我们的网站查看：http://www. ×××.com。

有什么我可以帮忙的，请随时与我们联系。我们期待着与你方合作。

---

**PART 1** 询盘函电 *Inquiry Letter*

**Unit 4** 回复目的不明的询盘
*Response to an Unknown Inquiry*

如果询盘信息过于简单，目的不明，无法做出有效回复，外贸业务员就需要回信告知对方需要更多信息才能够为其服务。

## 常用词汇 *Vocabulary*

### 1. await　v. 等候；期待；将降临于

【双语例句】

We await your shipping instructions.

我们等候你们的装船指示。

【用法解析】

"await" 的意思是"等候某人／某物"，是正式用语，可引申表示为"做好准备，备妥以待"，多指被动地、急切地等待事情发生，也可表示"认为某事件将降临到某人身上"。

### 2. lack of　缺乏

【双语例句】

Her decision seems to show a lack of political judgment.

她的决定似乎显示出缺乏政治判断力。

【用法解析】

"lack of" 后通常接名词，表示缺乏或寻求的某物。"lack" 构成的短语还有："be lacking"，欠缺；"be lacking in"，缺乏（某种品质或特点等），不够；"lack for"，缺（多用于否定句），如 "She does not lack for friends.（她不缺朋友）"。

### 3. competent　adj. 有能力的；足够的；胜任的

【双语例句】

He is competent enough to fill that position.

他完全胜任那个职位。

【用法解析】

"competent" 的意思是"有能力的，能胜任的"，即指具备完成某一项工作所需要的能力，如专业知识和技术等；也可表示"令人满意的"；用作表语时，还可表示"有法定权力的"。

## 基本词汇 / *Basic Words*

**paper** [ˈpeɪpər]  n. 纸；纸张

**confident** [ˈkɑːnfɪdənt]  adj. 自信的

**lack** [læk]  n. 缺乏；匮乏

**material** [məˈtɪriəl]  n. 材料

**quantity** [ˈkwɑːntəti]  n. 数量；数额

**regard** [rɪˈgɑːrd]  n. 注意；关注

## 情景实例 / *Scene Example*

某公司收到墙纸询盘，但对方询问不具体，无法给出回应，于是回信要求对方给出详细信息。

### 英

Thank you for your inquiry of our WP–3 on Dec.10.

We are in wall paper filed for many years, so we are competent enough to meet your requirements. But the inquiry you made is lack of specifications, such as the material, quantity etc. I would like to know your requirements in more detail and explain to you how our products can help you in that regard.

So please send us the details. After we confirm, we are happy to provide you with our good–quality products and competitive price.

Await your earliest reply.

### 中

谢谢你方 12 月 10 日对 WP–3 产品的询盘。

我们经营墙纸业务多年，因此，我们确信我们有能力满足您的要求。但你方的询盘不太具体，比如没提到材料和数量等方面的问题。我们想更详细地了解你方的需求，并向你方说明我们的产品在这方面对你方有何帮助。

所以请给我们发送详细信息。待我们确认后，才能够向你方提供优质的产品和有竞争力的价格。

等待你方的回复。

**Unit 5**　*客户各种问题的解答*
*Answering Customers' Questions*

如果客户在询盘时还问到其他相关信息，也要有针对性地进行回复，解答客户的问题。

*常用词汇* *Vocabulary*

## 1. request　n. 请求；要求　vt. 请求；要求

【双语例句】

I will be obliged to any sincere request.

我将接受任何真诚的请求。

【用法解析】

"request"的意思是"请求"，指有礼貌地或正式地要求。相关短语有"request from（向……请求）""request of（请求……）""make a request（提出要求）"和"at sb's request（应某人的请求）"等。

"request"的宾语一般为物，为人时只能用于含动词不定式的复合结构，宾语后不可接介词"for"；如果接"that"后跟从句，谓语动词须用虚拟式。

## 2. clarification　n. 澄清；阐明

【双语例句】

After I read the clause, I feel it needs some clarification.

读过这一条款之后，我觉得这条需要说明一下。

【用法解析】

"clarification"指消除理解障碍的解释。

## 基本词汇 *Basic Words*

**literature** [ˈlɪtrətʃər]  n. 资料

**equipment** [ɪˈkwɪpmənt]  n. 设备

**device** [dɪˈvaɪs]  n. 装置；设备

**electronic** [ɪˌlekˈtrɑːnɪk]  adj. 电子的

**audio** [ˈɔːdioʊ]  adj. 录音的

**industry** [ˈɪndəstri]  n. 工业

## 情景实例 *Scene Example*

　　某公司收到客户发函询问公司情况，于是回信告知对方公司的基本信息，并在附件中进行详细介绍。

### 英

Thank you for inquiring our company. As you requested, I have attached a copy of our company literature to this email. We are one of China's largest exporters of electronic equipment. We specialize in audio and video devices. And we have over 20 years of experience in the electronics industry.

If you have further questions or need additional clarifications, please do not hesitate to contact me.

I look forward to doing business with you.

### 中

感谢您对我们公司的问询。根据您的要求，我在邮件中附加了一份有关我们公司的介绍。我们是中国最大的电子产品出口商之一。我们专注于视频和音频设备业务，在电子产品行业有 20 多年的经验。

如果您有进一步的问题想问或需要了解更多的说明，请随时与我联系。

我们期待着与贵公司合作。

**PART 2 发盘函电 Offer Letter**

**Unit 1 发盘术语 Terms of Offer**

在发盘阶段，常用术语如下。

| 术语 | 含义 | 术语 | 含义 |
|---|---|---|---|
| Offer | 发盘 | Quote | 报价 |
| Commodity | 商品品名 | Validity | 有效期限 |
| Quantity | 数量 | Container Size | 货柜尺寸 |
| Loading Port | 装货港 | CU.FT | 立方英尺 |
| Discharge Port | 卸货港 | Shipment Fee | 装运费 |
| Catalogue | 目录 | Certificate | 证书 |
| Packing Instruction | 包装说明 | Reference Price | 参考价格 |

通常来说，在说明具体交易条件时，可以每条另起一行，一一论述，示例如下。

Lead time: 15 days upon deposit received

MOQ: 1*20GP, FOB Shenzhen

或者以短句的形式说明，示例如下。

L–102 is 0.082$/pcs CIF Guangdong. 3,000 PCS/CTN. 30% T/T in advance.

也可以直接以句子的形式阐述重点信息，示例如下。

For this product, the best price is USD 79.00 per set FOB Guangdong, cash discounts are allowed only on accounts that are paid within the ten–day limit.

# Unit 2 发盘注意事项
## Notes of Offer

发盘因撰写情况或背景不同，在内容、要求上也有所不同。在回复新客户的询盘时，一定要慎之又慎，因为首次回复的内容会直接影响对方与己方后续合作。

在回复新客户的首次询盘时，需要注意以下几点：

①分析客户信息。收到询盘，不要急于回复，首先要确认客户公司信息真实性，然后从客户的邮件去鉴别是否专业，最后从客户的询问要求判断目标是否明确。

②回复询盘的时间以 24 小时之内为佳，最好能根据客户所在国时间设置定时发送，在当地时间 9:00 ~ 9:30 时回复邮件为最佳。

③首次回盘的目的是引起对方和你继续交流的愿望，而不是成交。所以，如果确认对方是有诚意的买家，在回复时不能直接报价，而要提供对方所需的详细信息，并突出公司产品优势、自身的业务能力或者专业度。

【突出公司优势示例】
We can assure that our MC173 is one of the most outstanding products on the market today, and our confidence is supported by our five-year guarantee.
我们可以保证我们的 MC173 是当前市场上最出色的产品，我们的信心源自五年的质量保证。

【突出业务能力优势示例】
For your kind information, we've got satisfied customers scattered all over Europe like Ireland, England, Germany, Italy ...

供你参考，我们的客户遍布欧洲各地，如爱尔兰，英国，德国，意大利……

【突出自身专业度示例】
There is a large variety of models. Can you please advise your budget and approximate order quantity? So we will recommend you some trendy designs based on your requirements.
产品种类丰富。能否告知你的预算和大致的订货量？我们可以根据你的要求推荐一些比较流行的款式。

在向老客户发盘，或者在与新客户进入切实的发盘阶段时，发盘信函的结构一般如下。

①感谢对方来函，明确答复对方来函询问事项。

【邮件示例】
Thank you for your inquiry of June 15, in which you asked about if we could provide 5,000 pcs of batteries.
感谢贵方 6 月 15 日的询价，询问我方能否提供 5 000 块电池。

②阐明交易的条件（品名、规格、数量、包装、价格、装运、支付和保险等）。

【邮件示例】
To comply with your request, we are offering you the followings:
为了满足贵方要求，我们报盘如下：

Commodity: Qingdao Superior White Crystal Sugar
品名：青岛上等白色冰糖

③声明发盘有效期或约束条件。

【邮件示例】
Period of validity:10 days
有效期：10 天

This offer will valid for 3 days.
发盘的有效期为 3 天。

④鼓励对方订货。

**【邮件示例】**

We hope that you place a trial order with us.

我们希望你方试订货。

**PART 2 发盘函电 *Offer Letter***

## Unit 3 实盘和虚盘
### *Firm Offer and Non-firm Offer*

发盘可以分成两类：实盘和虚盘。实盘是发盘人承诺在一定期限内，受发盘内容约束，非经接盘人同意，不得撤回和变更，若买方表示接受，则交易达成，双方就有了法律约束力的合同关系。虚盘是发盘人所做的非承诺性表示，通常使用"须经我方最后确认有效"等语以示保留。

**常用词汇 *Vocabulary***

## 1. receipt  n. 收到

**【双语例句】**

On receipt of your instructions he will send the goods.

一收到你的指令他就发货。

**【用法解析】**

"in receipt of"表示"收到了……的"，属于商业文件和公文用语。表示"一收到……立刻……"用"on/upon (the) receipt of"，"the"可省略。

## 2. subject to  adj. 受限于；服从于 adv. 在…条件下，依照…

**【双语例句】**

The price is subject to change without notice.

价格随时更改，不另行通知。

This can only be done subject to his consent.

只有在他同意的条件下才可以做这事。

【用法解析】

"subject to" 在英语中应用广泛，必须根据前后文才能确定意思。一般来说，在外贸英语中常用的意思为 "以……为准"。

## 3. valid    adj. 有效的；合法的

【双语例句】

The offer above valid for two week ending June 4th 5 p.m.

上述报价有效期为两周，至六月四日下午五时为止。

【用法解析】

"valid" 强调有效期，相关短语有 "valid from ... to ...（……至……期间有效）" "valid until（直到……失效）" 和 "be valid for ...（在……内有效）" 等。

## 4. quote    v. 报价

【双语例句】

Please quote your price in terms of pound.

请您报盘时用英镑报价。

【用法解析】

"quote" 表示报价时，相关短语有 "quote at（使定价为……）" "quote for（为……而定价）" 和 "quote sb for sth at（向某人报某物价格为……）" 等。

## 基本词汇  *Basic Words*

| | |
|---|---|
| **February** [ˈfebrueri]   n. 二月 | **ton** [tʌn]   n. 吨 |
| **walnut** [ˈwɔːlnʌt]   n. 核桃 | **carton** [ˈkɑːrtn]   n. 硬纸盒 |
| **until** [ənˈtɪl]   prep. 直到…为止 | **accept** [əˈksept]   v. 接受 |

## 情景实例 *Scene Example*

### 1. 报实盘

某公司收到客户询盘，要求对 250 吨的核桃仁报价，于是向其发出规定有效期的实盘。

**英**

Thank you for your inquiry of February 21, asking for 250 metric tons of quotation of our Walnut meat. We are pleased to offer as follows.

Price: USD $200 net per metric ton CIF any European Main Ports

Shipment: within two months after receipt of L/C at sight

Packing: Exporter Carton

Insurance: W.P.A. for 110% of CIF value

The above offer is firm until March 10. Please note that we have quoted our most favorable price and are unable to accept any counter offer. If you think our offer is satisfactory, please let us know. You can be assured of our best service.

We look forward to receiving your first order.

**中**

感谢你方 2 月 21 日的询盘，要求 250 吨的核桃仁报价。我们的报盘如下。

价格：每公吨净价 200 美元，欧洲主要港口 CIF 价格

装运：收到即期信用证后两个月内装运

包装：出口纸箱

保险：按 CIF 价的 110% 投保水渍险

上述报盘有效期至 3 月 10 日。请注意我们已经提供最优惠价格，不接受任何还盘。如果你方认为我们的报盘价令人满意，请联系我们。我们可以保证你方会得到最好的服务。

我们期待收到贵方的第一笔订单。

> **Tips 如何表达实盘有效期**
>
> 实盘有效期的表达方式，可归纳为以下3种。
>
> ①规定有效期的日期，如 "Our offer remains firm until April 4." 或 "Our offer is valid until April 4."。
>
> ②规定有效期的天数，如 "Our offer remains firm for 3 days." 或 "Our offer is valid for 3 days."。
>
> ③限定答复的有效期，如 "Our offer is firm, subject to your reply reaching us by Wednesday Nov. 17." 或 "We offer our firm the following, subject to your reply reaching us within two weeks from today."。

## 2. 报虚盘

某公司收到客户询盘，要求对 MC-5 产品进行报价，于是发出仅供参考的虚盘，注明"以我方最终确认为准"。

**英**

Thanks for your inquiry about MC-5 by email, dated back to April 5, 2020. Now we here kindly quote you our best price as follows.

Price：USD $0.071/pcs FOB Guangdong

Payment：T/T & L/C at sight

Delivery time: 20 days after getting 30% Deposit

The above offer is subject to our final confirmation. If you think our offer meets your requirements, please let us know at an earlier date. We would be glad to offer any additional information you need.

We look forward to receiving a trial order from you.

**中**

感谢你于 2020 年 4 月 5 日对 MC-5 产品的询价。现在我们在此向你方报最优惠价如下。

价格：每件 0.071 美元，广东离岸价

付款方式：电汇或即期信用证

交货时间：获得 30% 定金后 20 天

上述报盘以我方最终确认为准。如果你方认为我们的报盘符合你方要求，请尽早通知我们。我们很乐意提供你所需要的更多信息。

我们期待收到你方的试订单。

## PART 2 发盘函电 Offer Letter

### Unit 4  回复客户的询价
### Response to Customer Enquiry

　　针对不同的询盘，不同的买家，外贸业务员需要拿捏好不同的分寸，找到吸引买家的点，这是共通的法则。

## 常用词汇  Vocabulary

### 1. in compliance with　按照（要求，愿望等）；依从

【双语例句】

In compliance with your wishes, we have withdrawn our suggestion.
遵照你的要求我们已将建议撤销。

Our quotation is in compliance with the present level.
我们所报价格符合当前市场水平。

【用法解析】

表示"与…相符合"，还可以用"in line with"，而"与…不相符合"则是"out of line with"。

## 2. brochure　n. 小册子，资料手册

【双语例句】

The computer's features are detailed in our brochure.

该计算机的特征在我们的小册子中有详细介绍。

【用法解析】

多用于公司的介绍册或商品信息册。

## 3. specialize in　专门从事

【双语例句】

This shop specializes in chocolates.

这个商店专门出售巧克力。

【用法解析】

可以表达"专攻"某专业，但常用于表示公司业务领域。

### 基本词汇　*Basic Words*

edition [ɪˈdɪʃn]　n. 版本

hundreds [ˈhʌndrədz]　n. 成百上千

glove [glʌv]　n. 手套

vinyl [ˈvaɪnl]　n. 乙烯基

enclose [ɪnˈkloʊz]　v. 随函附上

assistance [əˈsɪstəns]　n. 帮助

vary [ˈveri]　v. 不同；有别

supermarket [ˈsuːpərmɑːkɪt]　n. 超市

### 情景实例　*Scene Example*

## 1. 针对一般询盘

某公司收到索取产品目录的询盘，于是简短回复，附上产品手册，并告知公司网站信息。

**英**

Thank you for your inquiry of 12 September asking for the latest edition of our catalog.

In compliance with your wishes, we are pleased to enclose our latest brochure. We would also like to inform you that it is possible to make purchases online at our website: http://www.×××.com

If there is additional information you would like to have regarding our products, please do not hesitate to contact us. We will be most happy to be of assistance.

We look forward to welcoming you as our customer.

**中**

感谢你方 9 月 12 日询价，索要我方最新版本的产品目录。

依照你方的要求，我们很高兴随函附上最新的产品手册。此外我们也想告知你方，可以在我们的网站上在线购买产品：http://www.×××.com。

如果你方希望获得更多我们的产品信息，请随时与我们联系。我们将非常乐意提供帮助。

期待与你方的合作。

　　某公司收到索取所有产品价目单的询盘，由于范围太宽泛，于是回复告知对方不能提供，希望对方确定具体目标再进行询盘。

**英**

Thanks for your inquiry of 12 September asking for our price list.

Since we have hundreds of products of different series, please tell me which series that you are interested in. Then we will quote according to your selection. If you do not have the catalogs of our products, please kindly refer to our website "http://www.×××.com". Thank you!

**中**

感谢你方 9 月 12 日询价，询问我方价格表。

由于我们有数百种不同系列的产品，请告诉我贵方感兴趣的系列产品。然后我们会根据你的选择报价。如果您没有我们产品的目录，请参考我们的网站"http://www.×××.com"。谢谢！

## 2. 针对具体询盘

波兰客户发来 50 箱 PE 手套的询盘，外贸业务员在研究对方市场后进行了详细回复，并建议对方考虑新型的包装和产品。

**英**

Thank you for your letter of June 4, inquiring about our PE gloves.

According to your requirement, the food grade of PE gloves we are supplying to European markets is mainly 1.1 gram/pc, 20 microns, 100 pcs/bag, 100 bags/ctn.

Under 50 CTNS quantity, prices vary from 15 USD to 16 USD per carton based on the different material.

Meanwhile, after a study of your company and sales channel, we found that you're supplying food packaging items for many chain-store and supermarket in Poland, so I think the regular packaging way is not suitable for these customers.

We have another packaging way specializing in supplying store and supermarkets. It's 50 pcs gloves per bag with a hole for hanging on, then 200 bags/carton. We believe this is more suitable for your demands.

What's more, if you have the plan to expand the product supplies, I think it will be very worthy to consider our vinyl gloves, which are hot sale on the Polish market. Vinyl glove now is more and more popular in the European market, it's more durable and flexible. It's one of our most competitive products so I'm sure that it will be helpful to expand your business.

If you have an interest in cooperating with us, we can provide both types of gloves for your evaluation. We look forward to your kindly reply and further discussion.

中

感谢你 6 月 4 日对 PE 手套的询盘。

根据你的要求，我们供应欧洲市场的食品级 PE 手套，主要规格是每件 1.1 克，20 微米，每袋 100 个，每箱 100 袋。

50 箱以下的订货量，根据材料不同，每箱价格从 15 美元到 16 美元不等，材料不同价格不同。

同时，经过对贵公司和销售渠道的研究，我们发现贵公司正在为波兰的许多连锁店和超市提供食品包装，所以我认为常规的包装方式不适合这些顾客。

我们有另一种专门供应商店和超市的包装方式，每袋 50 个手套，袋子上有用于悬挂的孔，每箱 200 袋。我们相信这款更适合你方的要求。

还有，如果你计划扩大销售范围，可以考虑我们的乙烯基手套，这款手套目前在波兰市场热销。乙烯基手套目前在欧洲市场越来越流行，它更耐用，更灵活。这是我们最具竞争力的产品之一，所以我相信这将有助于扩大您的业务范围。

如果您有兴趣与我们合作，我们可以提供两种手套供您评估。我们期待您的答复和进一步的讨论。

---

**PART 2 发盘函电 Offer Letter**

## Unit 5 主动给客户发盘
### Take the Initiative to Offer Customers

除了收到询盘时向客户发盘，还可以主动给客户发盘。与前述开发信不同的是，发盘对象通常是曾做过交易，但近期未联络的老客户。主动发盘是一种与对方保持联系的方式。

## 常用词汇 *Vocabulary*

### 1. discontinued  adj. 中断了的；已停止的

【双语例句】

If the money is not paid promptly, the service will be discontinued.

如果不立即付款的话，服务将会中止。

【用法解析】

相关短语有 "therapy discontinued（停止治疗）" "permanently discontinued（永久中断）" 和 "discontinued operations（非连续性经营活动）" 等。表达不再生产还可以说 "We've stopped doing that line.（我们已经不生产那种产品了）"。

### 2. occur to  想到；意识到

【双语例句】

A good idea suddenly occurred to me.

我忽然想起一个好主意。

【用法解析】

可以与 "awake to（意识，察觉，醒悟）" 互换。

## 基本词汇 *Basic Words*

**blanket** [ˈblæŋkɪt]  n. 毯子；毛毯

**descriptive** [dɪˈskrɪptɪv]  adj. 描写的

**prompt** [prɑːmpt]  adv. 立即

**similar** [ˈsɪmələr]  adj. 相像的

**leaflet** [ˈliːflət]  n. 小册子

**view** [vjuː]  n. 看法；意见

## 情景实例 *Scene Example*

由于过去合作过的老客户已一年未下订单，某生产毛毯的公司主动向其发去报价信息，以期收到回复。

### 英

At the same time of last year, you placed a bulk order for Type BS183 blanket. This is a discontinued line which we had on offer at the time. Now we have a similar product on offer Type BN254. It occurs to us that you might be interested.

A descriptive leaflet is enclosed. We have a stock of 590 of Type BN254 which we are selling off at USD $30 each. We can offer a discount of up to 15%, but we are prepared to give 20% discount for an offer to buy the complete stock.

We are confident that our new products can meet your needs in every way. We are giving you the first chance in view of your previous order, but we should appreciate a prompt reply so that we can put the offer out in the event of your not being interested.

### 中

去年的这个时候，你方下单订购了大批 BS183 型毛毯，而现在这款产品已经停产了。我们现在已经在供应一款类似的产品，BN254 型毛毯。我们认为你方可能会感兴趣。

附件是对这款产品的相关描述。我们有 590 条 BN254 型毛毯的库存，每条售价 30 美元。我们的折扣高达 15%，但如果购买全部库存，我们愿意提供 20% 的折扣。

相信我们的新产品能满足你方的各种需求。考虑到你方以前的订单，我们给你方首先选择的机会，但是我们希望你方迅速答复，以便万一你方没有兴趣，我们可以向其他客户普遍发盘。

**Unit 1** 受盘人提出新发盘
The Offeree Made a New Offer

在接到发盘之后，如果收盘人对发盘条件不满意，即可向发盘人提出新发盘提议，要求对发盘内容进行修改，这也被称为还盘。在交易磋商的过程中，通过不断的还盘，双方逐渐趋向一致，直到最后达成交易。

**常用词汇** *Vocabulary*

## 1. metric adj. 公制的；米制的；十进制的 n. 标准；度量

【双语例句】

We have set up a metric to grade your writing examinations.

我们设立了一个标准来评价你们的写作水平。

Most countries adopt metric system.

大多数国家采用米制。

【用法解析】

相关短语有"go metric（采用公制）""metric ton（公吨）"和"metric scale（米尺，公制尺）"。

## 2. bulk n. 大批 adj. 散装的；大量的

【双语例句】

The goods will be shipped in bulk.

此货将散装发运。

For bulk order, shipping cost will be separately quoted.

若大量订购，邮费可另行报价。

## 【用法解析】

"bulk"表示大量时，不指准确的度量，只表示相当大的量。在外贸语境中，多表示海运中的散装，如"bulk cargo（散装货）"和"load in bulk（散装入船）"；也可以表示大量，如"bulk order（大宗订购）"和"bulk production（大量生产）"，视具体情景而定。

## 基本词汇 | *Basic Words*

**polish** [ˈpɑːlɪʃ]  v. 润饰；润色

**immediately** [ɪˈmiːdiətli]  adv. 立即

**attractive** [əˈtræktɪv]  adj. 吸引人的

**per** [pər]  prep. 每；每一

**appear** [əˈpɪr]  v. 呈现；显现

## 情景实例 | *Scene Example*

某公司向供应商采购大米，在收到对方报价后，认为和该国其他供应商相比较明显偏高，于是发函向供应商还盘，要求降价 10%。

英

We are in receipt of your letter of June 19 offering us 300 metric tons of polished rice at US$300 per metric ton on the usual terms.

We regret to inform you that we can't accept your offer as we found that your prices appear to be on the high side. Other suppliers in your country offered us more attractive quotations in which prices are from 8% to 12% below yours.

Such being the case, we have to ask you to consider if you can make a reduction in your price, say 10%, other terms as per your letter of June 19. If you do so, we will immediately place you a bulk order.

We are looking forward to your favorable reply.

# 中

收到你方 6 月 19 日 300 公吨精米报价，按通常条款每吨 300 美元。

很遗憾地通知你方，我们无法接受你方的报价，因为我方发现你方价格偏高。你们国家的其他供应商向我方提供了更有吸引力的报价，价格比你方报价低 8%~12%。

既然如此，我们不得不要求你方考虑是否能降价 10%，其他条件按你方 6 月 19 日来函所述。如果你方同意，我们会立即下一个大批量订单。

我们期待你方的肯定答复。

## PART 3 还盘函电 Counter-offer Letter

### Unit 2 对还盘的答复
### Answer to a Counter-offer

在发盘人收到还盘后，如果对还盘条件不满意，则可选择再次还盘，这称作 "Counter-counter offer"。如无异议，则可接受还盘。

## 常用词汇 Vocabulary

## 1. margin  n. 盈余，毛利

【双语例句】

Our pricing policy aims at producing a 35% gross margin.
我们的定价政策目的在于赢得 35% 的毛利润。

【用法解析】

相关短语有 "a fair/large margin of profit（相当多 / 大量的利润）""a narrow margin of profit（微利）""retail/wholesale price margins（零售 / 批发价格极限）"和 "loss margin（亏损极限）"等。

## 2. speculation　n. 推测；投机；沉思

【双语例句】

He makes some unprofitable speculations.

他在做些无利可图的投机生意。

【用法解析】

在"speculation"前可加名词，构成专有名词，如"stock speculation（股票投机）""exchange speculation（外汇投机）"和"bull speculation（多头投机）"等。

## 3. at your end　在你那里

【双语例句】

Could you tell us about the supply position at your end?

请告诉我，你们那里的供应情况怎样？

【用法解析】

类似的短语有"at your fingertips（在你附近）""at your doorsteps（在跟前）"和"at your wit's end（智穷计尽）"等。

## 4. sales contract　销售合同

【双语例句】

We enclose our sales contract No.45 in duplicate.

附上我们第 45 号销售合同，一式两份。

【用法解析】

在外贸活动中，销售合同常缩写为"S/C"，此外，销售确认书（sales confirmation）的缩写也是"S/C"，两者除名词不同，没有什么区别。

### 基本词汇 *Basic Words*

calculate ['kælkjuleɪt]　v. 计算

profit ['prɑːfɪt]　n. 利润

wild [waɪld]　adj. 无法无天的

superior [suːˈpɪriər]　adj. 更好的

exception [ɪkˈsepʃn]　n. 例外

counter ['kaʊntər]　v. 反驳

## 情景实例 *Scene Example*

### 1. 再次还盘

　　某供应商销售大米，在发盘后，收到客户还盘要求降价 10%。由于对此条件不满意，该供应商再次发函还盘，表示若对方订购 500 吨大米，可以降价 3%。

**英**

Referring to your counter offer of June 20, asking for a 10% cut down of the price, we regret to tell you that it is difficult for us to accept your counter offer.

The price we set in our offer is carefully calculated. My offer was based on reasonable profit, not on wild speculations. As a matter of fact, we have had considerable business with many customers at your end. As you know, our products are far superior in quality compared to polished rice provided by most suppliers in the world. For long lasting trade relations between us, however, we decide as an exception to allow you a 3% discount if you order 500 metric tons.

If you think our proposal acceptable, please place an order on before June 30.

**中**

收到你方 6 月 20 日的还盘，要求降价 10%，我们很遗憾地告诉你方，我们很难接受你方的还盘。

我方报价是经过慎重计算的，基于合理的利润，并非漫天要价。事实上，我们已经和你方地区的许多客户做成了可观的生意。如你所知，我们的精米品质远远超过世界上大多数供应商提供的产品质量。不过，为了我们之间长期的贸易关系，如果你方订购 500 吨，我们决定破例给你方 3% 的折扣。

如果你方可以接受我们的提议，请在 6 月 30 日之前订货。

## 2. 接受还盘

　　某供应商销售毛衣，在收到客户还盘后，对客户还盘条件表示接受，并发函确认订单。

**英**

Thank you for your counter offer dated June 23.

Although your price is below our level, we accept, as an exception, your order with a view to initiating business with you. Our understanding of your proposal is as follows:

Product　Quantity　Catalogue　Price

sweaters　10,000 pcs　XL M　US ＄20 each

Once we receive your confirmation, we will immediately send S/C to you. We trust that the current business is only the beginning of a series of transactions in the future.

Await your earliest reply.

**中**

感谢你方 6 月 23 日的还盘。

尽管贵方的价格低于我们的价格水平，我们还是破例接受你们的订单，以期达成与贵公司的首笔业务。我们对你方的还盘作如下理解：

产品　　数量　　规格　　　价格

毛衣　10 000 件　XL M　　每件 20 美元

一旦我们收到你方的确认，我们会立即给你方发送销售确认书。我们相信，这笔交易只是未来一系列交易的开端。

期待你方尽早答复。

**Tips 讨价还价术语**

在讨价还价时，常用"level"这个单词。如"the prevailing/present market level"是指当前普遍价格；不符合市场水平，可以用"not on a level with"；希望降低价格，是"Business is hopeful if your reduce your level.（如果你方能够降低价格，成交有望）"；又如"at your/our level（按你方 / 我方价格）"。

在谈论价格高时，可用"a bit high（有点高）""on the high side（偏高）""excessive（过高）""rather high（相当高）"和"prohibitive（望而却步）"等术语表示高的程度。

此外，谈论价格的术语还有"competitive（有竞争力）""acceptable（可接受）""reasonable（合理）""attractive（有吸引力）""unworkable（行不通的）""impracticable（不切实际的）"和"infeasible（不可实行的）"等。

**PART 3 还盘函电 Counter-offer Letter**

**Unit 3　拒绝客户的要求**
**Rejecting Customers' Requests**

　　如果客户的还盘无法令人接受，或者客户提出了其他不能接受的要求，外贸业务员就需要在回电中明确地加以拒绝。

**常用词汇　Vocabulary**

**1. realistic　adj. 现实的**

【双语例句】

But I think our offer is reasonable and realistic.
不过我认为我们的报价是现实的、合理的。

【用法解析】

如果前加否定词缀为"unrealistic（不现实的）"，在这种情况下，既可以指价格高，又可以指价格低，需视情况而定。

## 2. substantial    adj. 大量的；可观的

【双语例句】

Substantial profits accrue when sales take off.

当销售额突飞猛进之后，可观的利润就开始自然累积。

【用法解析】

"substantial"和"substantially"在表示"大量的"和"大体上的"时，都属于公文英语，一般用在比较正式的场合。

## 3. hesitate    v.（对某事）犹豫；迟疑不决

【双语例句】

Don't hesitate to make comments or suggestions if you have any.

有意见尽管提好了。

【用法解析】

"hesitate"是普通用词，主要指由于不确定或紧张而在行动或说话之前出现较长的停顿。其后常接介词 about/over，常用习语为"he who hesitates is lost"，迟疑者必有失。

## 基本词汇　Basic Words

quite [kwaɪt]　adv. 相当

compete [kəmˈpiːt]　v. 竞争

security [sɪˈkjʊərəti]　n. 保护措施

squeeze [skwiːz]　v. 挤压

software [ˈsɔːftwer]　n. 软件

system [ˈsɪstəm]　n. 系统

## 情景实例　Scene Example

## 1. 拒绝折扣要求

　　某公司收到客户的还盘，要求提供折扣。该公司认为己方价格合理，且还有大量其他客户询盘，于是发函表示拒绝。

## 英

Thank you for your inquiry of August 24. We are pleased to hear from you as a valued customer.

It is with regret that I have to say that we cannot agree to your request for a discount as the price we have quoted is quite realistic. And if we go any lower, our profit margins will get squeezed far too much. The fact is that most of our competitors also try to compete with our prices but still cannot go any lower than us. Also, we would like to point out that we have received substantial orders from other sources at our level.

If you could improve your offer, please let us know. Since supplies of this product are limited at the moment, we would ask you to act quickly.

We assure you that any further inquiries from you will receive our prompt attention.

## 中

感谢你方 8 月 24 日的询价。我们非常高兴收到贵公司的来信。

很遗憾，我不得不说，我们不能同意你方的折扣要求，因为我方所报的价格是相当实在的。如果我们再降价，我们的利润将被挤压得太多。而事实是我们的大多数竞争对手也试图与我们进行价格竞争，但也无法低过我们的价格。此外，我们想说的是，在这个价格基础上，我们已经收到了来自其他客户的大量订单。

如果你方能提高报价，请告诉我们。由于目前该产品的供应有限，我们希望你方迅速采取行动。

我们保证你方的任何进一步询盘将得到我们的迅速关注。

## 2. 拒绝其他要求

某公司收到客户询问是否能够提供产品的技术资料，鉴于己方保密信息的需要，回函向其表示拒绝。

**英**

Thank you for your inquiry of August 24. We are always pleased to hear from a valued customer.

I regret to say that we cannot agree to your request for technical information regarding our software security systems. The fact is that most of our competitors also keep such information private and confidential.

I sincerely hope that this does not cause inconvenience to you in any way. If there is any other way in which we can help, do not hesitate to contact us again.

**中**

感谢贵公司 8 月 24 日的询价。谨此致谢。

很遗憾，我们不能同意你来信要求本公司提供有关软件保密系统的技术资料。事实是，我们的大多数竞争对手也将这些信息保密。

我真诚地希望这不会给贵公司带来任何不便。如果需要我们的其他帮助，请随时再联系我们。

## PART 4 其他函电 Other Letter

**Unit 1** 通知客户价格调整
*Informing Customer of Price Adjustment*

　　在发盘时，价格都有一定的有效期，在有效期之后就会重新报价，此时价格可能发生较大变动。外贸业务员需要发函进行解释，防止客户流失。

### 常用词汇 Vocabulary

1. **refrain** v. 抑制；避免；克制

【双语例句】

We refrain from reproducing them here.

我们不打算在这里重新复制它们。

【用法解析】

"refrain" 的意思是自觉地控制自己不做那些由于愿望或冲动而想做的事。通常用法是 "refrain from" 后加克制的行动。

## 2. subcontractor　n. 转包商；次承包商

【双语例句】

The manufacture of belts and buckles is distributed to subcontractor.

皮带和带扣的生产，交分包商承担制作。

【用法解析】

在合同上， "subcontractor" 是指转包合同的承包者。

## 3. effective　adj. 有效的；生效的

【双语例句】

Their efforts to improve the production have been very effective.

他们为提高生产力做出的努力已卓有成效。

When does the new system become effective?

新制度何时生效?

【用法解析】

"effective" 表示生效时，强调效用，可用于人或事物。

## 基本词汇　Basic Words

**model** [ˈmɑːdl]　n. 模型

**raw** [rɔː]　adj. 原始的

**slight** [slaɪt]　adj. 轻微的

**stem** [stem]　v. 起源于

**dare** [der]　v. 敢于

**twelve** [twelv]　num. 十二

## 情景实例 *Scene Example*

### 1. 涨价通知

由于原材料上涨，劳动力成本提高，某公司全面提高产品价格。该公司外贸业务员发函告知客户相关情况，并希望对方理解。

**英**

Enclosed is our new price list which will come into effect at the end of this month. You will see that we have increased our prices on most models. We have, however, refrained from going up in price on some models of which we hold large stocks. The explanation for our increased prices stems from the fact that we are now paying 10% more for our raw materials than we were paying last year, along with some of our subcontractors having raised their prices as much as 15%.

As you know, we take great pride in our product an dare proud of the reputation for quality and dependability we have built for over 15years. We will not compromise because of raising costs. We have, therefore, decided to raise the price of some of our products.

We hope you will understand our position and look forward to your cooperation.

**中**

随函附上我方最新价格表，将于本月底生效。你会发现我们大多数型号的产品都涨价了。但是，一些我们持有大量库存的型号，仍然没有涨价。对于涨价的解释，源于这样一个事实：相比去年，我们需要多付 10% 的原材料价格，还有一些转包商把价格提高了 15%。

正如贵方所知，我们建立了超过 15 年的良好声誉，以产品质量和可靠性闻名，我们为此感到非常自豪。我们不会因为成本的提高而采取折中方案。因此，我们决定提高一些产品的价格。

我们希望你方能理解我们的立场，并期待与你们的合作。

## 2. 提醒订货

因物价上涨，某公司的产品价格将有微涨，该公司外贸业务员将相关情况告知客户，并提醒对方在涨价前订货。

## 英

I hope you had a good weekend.

It's a friendly notification of a slight price increase, effective March 1. The new price should rise approximately 5%. The adjustment is a result of Consumer Price Index changes and increased transportation costs over the last twelve months.

Therefore, I suggest you place your order before new price effective. Please feel free to contact us if we can help you in any way.

## 中

希望周末过得愉快。

这是一个友好的提醒，3月1日后，价格会略有上涨。新的价格应该会上涨5%左右。这次调整是一年来物价上涨和运输成本增加的结果。

因此，我建议贵方在新价格生效前下订单。如果我们能以任何方式帮助到你方，请随时与我们联系。

### PART 4 其他函电 Other Letter

### Unit 2 商定佣金 Commission Discussion

在对外贸易中，常遇到负责介绍客户的中间商，作为采购代理协调买方事务，这时就会向外贸公司收取一定的佣金。

## 常用词汇 *Vocabulary*

### 1. commission　n. 佣金

【双语例句】

Do not deduct any commission from the consignment value.

不要从货物的价值中扣除佣金。

【用法解析】

相关短语有 "commission for（…佣金）" "on commission（佣金交易）" 和 "commission on a sale（销售佣金）" 等

### 2. remit　v. 汇款

【双语例句】

He remitted some money to his mother.

他给他母亲寄了一些钱。

【用法解析】

相关短语有 "remitting bank（汇出行）" "remit a debt（免债）" 和 "remit account（划账）" 等。

### 3. deduct　vt. 扣除；演绎

【双语例句】

The cost of the breakages will be deducted from your pay.

损坏东西的费用将从你的工资中扣除。

【用法解析】

"deduct" 的基本意思是 "扣除，减去"，其后常与介词 "from" 搭配，意为 "从…扣除…"。

## 基本词汇 *Basic Words*

**message** [ˈmesɪdʒ]  n. 信息；消息

**means** [miːnz]  v. 意思是

**avoid** [əˈvɔɪd]  v. 避免

**fax** [fæks]  v. 传真

**delay** [dɪˈleɪ]  v. 延迟

**further** [ˈfɜːrðər]  adv. 在更大范围内

## 情景实例 *Scene Example*

### 1. 要求佣金

　　某中间商是国际销售代理，收到某公司发盘后，有意与该公司合作，为其介绍客户并赚取佣金，于是发函告知对方情况。

### 英

Thank you very much for your message and your interest in doing business with us. Your listed products have been well accessed by our company.

I believe you understand that we are an International Sales Representative, which means we could provide you with a big customer base to sell your products in your country on a commission basis.

Therefore, your company will give us 1% commission of the total approved order once payment is confirmed in your account. Based on our good arrangement of the contract with your company, I will do my best to support you get the offer.

If you have any questions, please feel free to contact us or call us.

### 中

非常感谢你方的来信并表达与我方合作的意愿。我方已接受贵公司所列出的产品。

相信你方知道，我们是国际销售代理人，这意味着我们的工作建立在佣金的基础上，为你们向我国的客户群（超过 50 个）推荐你方产品。

因此，一旦贵公司确认取得订单，贵公司将给我方总值 1% 的佣金。基于我方与贵公司签订合同的良好安排，我将尽力支持贵公司取得订单。

如有疑问，请随时联系或打电话与我们沟通。

## 2. 提供佣金

在一笔订单基本完成之后，某公司发函感谢中间商的努力，并告知在收到信用证收益后，将立即支付佣金余款。

**英**

Referring to contract no. 645 for 500 pieces of printed cotton, we appreciate your efforts in marketing our products.

To avoid any further delay in shipping, we suggest that we arrange the necessary insurance cover. The premium will cost USD $140 and we could deduct it from the 2% commission payable to you. The balance of the commission will be remitted to you as soon as the proceeds from the letter of credit have been collected.

We believe that this arrangement will be acceptable. Please fax your confirmation as soon as possible.

**中**

关于 500 件印花棉布的第 645 号合同，我们非常感谢你方推销我们产品的努力。

为避免装船延误，我们建议安排必要的保险。保险费是 140 美元，我们可以从应付给你的 2% 佣金中扣除。一旦收到信用证的收益，佣金余款将立即汇给你方。

我们相信这种安排是可以接受的。请尽快传真确认。

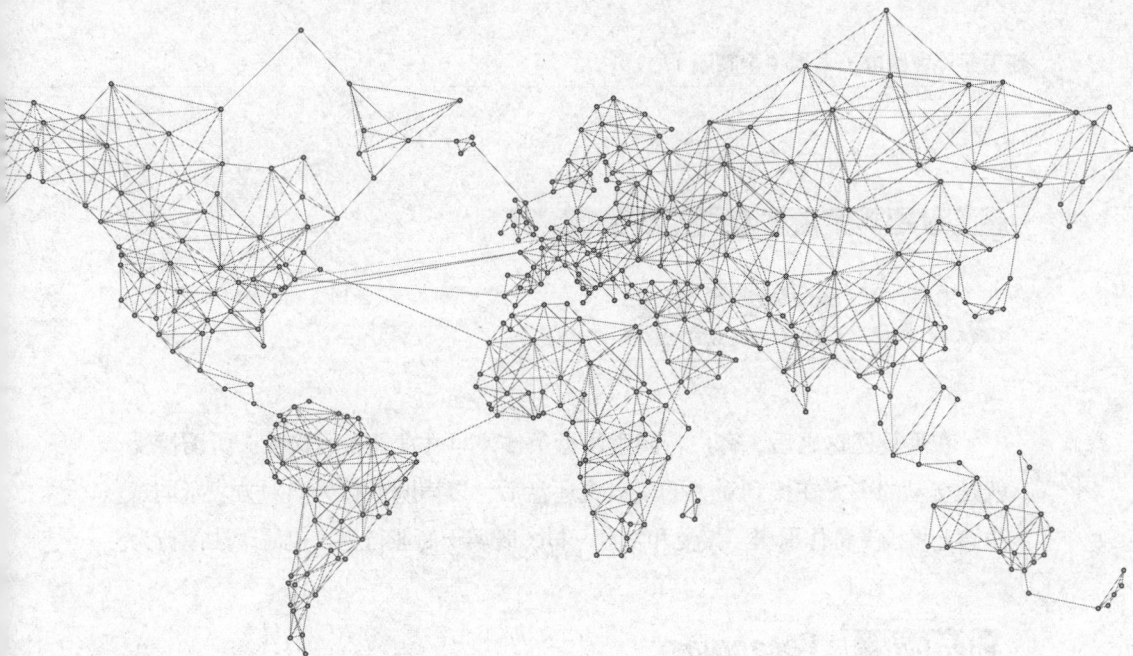

# 接受与签约函电

*Acceptance and Contract Letters*

在大致确定订单事项后，对外贸易的双方就可以展开
实质性合作了。除了通过来往函电确认成交并签约，
外贸公司在签约后还要准备生产前样品和向供应商下
单，为正式生产做准备。

PART 1 建立合作关系 *Create a Partnership*

PART 2 签约成交函 *Letter of Signing*

PART 3 生产前准备 *Pre-production preparation*

**PART 1 建立合作关系 Create a Partnership**

**Unit 1** 客户接受发盘
*Offer Acceptance*

在反复还盘之后，客户若同意还盘条件，即可发函表示接受。所谓接受，就是交易的一方在接到对方的发盘或还盘后，以声明或行为向对方表示同意。法律上将接受称作承诺。接受和发盘一样，既属于商业行为，也属于法律行为。

**常用词汇** *Vocabulary*

## 1. concession　n.让步；特许权；租界；妥协

【双语例句】

They made concessions to the workers in negotiations.

他们在与工人谈判中做出了让步。

【用法解析】

相关短语有"gain a concession（获得让步）""sell sth at remarkable concessions（以优惠价出售某物）""grant concessions（授予特权）"和"concession to reality（承认现实）"等。

## 2. revise　n.校订；修正；再校稿　v.校订；修正；校正

【双语例句】

The market turmoil has spurred economists to revise their forecasts.

当前的市场动荡已促使经济学家们重新修正自己的预测数据。

【用法解析】

"revise"后可加名词表示对某事物的修订，如"revise a contract（修改合同）"，也可以加抽象名词，如"revise one's opinion of（改变对…的看法）"。

## 3. article   n. 文章；物品；条款

**【双语例句】**

The clerk attached a price tag to each article.

店员给每一件商品贴上标价签。

**【用法解析】**

"article" 的基本意思是"物件，物品"，常指一套中之一。"article" 还可作 "文章"解释，指报纸、杂志上的短文。引申可表示"项目，条款"，指法律上的规定，也可指协议或合同上的契约。

## 基本词汇 *Basic Words*

**June** [dʒuːn]  n. 六月          **appreciate** [əˈpriːʃieɪt]  v. 感激

**wooden** [ˈwʊdn]  adj. 木制的          **send** [send]  v. 发送

**consideration** [kənˌsɪdəˈreɪʃn]  n. 仔细考虑；深思

## 情景实例 *Scene Example*

某采购商收到供应商还盘后，觉得还盘价格能够接受，于是发函告知对方，决定下订单。

**英**

We have received your E-Mail of June. 9.

After the consideration, we do appreciate your concession and want to accept your revised price. We have pleasure in confirming the following offer and accepting below:

Article No.  DR2010 USD19.00  CIFC5  Toronto per set

Article No.  DR2202 USD23.80  CIFC5  Toronto per set

Article No.  DR2211 USD30.00  CIFC5  Toronto per set

We decided to place an order for 3, 000 pieces of each article, if you can guarantee delivery on or before July 1. Please note that 12 pieces to a box and 100 boxes to a wooden case, 2% more or less in weight. Please send us your PI.

Look forward to more cooperation.

**中**

我们收到了您 6 月 9 日的电子邮件。

经过考虑，我们非常感谢你方的让步，并希望接受你方修改后的价格。我们很高兴确认并接受以下报价：

DR2010 型产品　19 美元　CIF 价含 5% 佣金　多伦多港　每件

DR2202 型产品　23.8 美元　CIF 价含 5% 佣金　多伦多港　每件

DR2211 型产品　30 美元　CIF 价含 5% 佣金　多伦多港　每件

我们决定订购每种型号的产品共 3 000 件，如果你方能保证在 7 月 1 日或之前交货。请注意，一箱 12 件，木箱 100 箱，重量误差在 ±2% 以内。请将你方的形式发票寄给我方。

期待更多的合作。

---

**PART 1 建立合作关系 Create a Partnership**

**Unit 2 开具形式发票 Issuing PI**

　　形式发票是一种非正式发票，采购商常常需要它作为申请进口和批准外汇之用，也可在进口报关而正式发票尚未到达时，供采购商报关使用。

## 常用词汇 *Vocabulary*

### 1. proforma invoice 形式发票

【双语例句】

This Proforma Invoice is subject to our last approval.

本形式发票有待我方最后同意。

【用法解析】

与形式发票相对的是商业发票，即"commercial invoice（CI）"，是出口贸易结算单据中最重要的单据之一，可供买方清关报税之用。

### 2. imply vt. 暗示；意指；含有 ... 的意义

【双语例句】

The fact that she was here implies a degree of interest.

她当时在场，这一事实就意味着她有一定程度的兴趣。

【用法解析】

"imply"通常指含蓄地、不明确地"暗示"。相关短语有"imply a lack of interest（缺乏兴趣）""imply vaguely（模糊地暗示）"和"imply by（用…暗示）"等。

### 3. license n. 许可证；执照；特许 vt. 发许可证给；特许

【双语例句】

This shop is licensed to sell tobacco.

这家商店被获准经销烟草商品。

【用法解析】

"license"的基本意思是批准某人以某种资格从事某种行动或经营某种业务，并授予正式的法律许可，引申则可表示"授权"。在英式英语中，"license"也可写作"licence"。

## 基本词汇　*Basic Words*

**shirt** [ʃɜːrt]　n. 衬衫

**import** [ɪmˈpɔːrt]　v. 进口

**expire** [ɪkˈspaɪər]　v. 失效

**apply** [əˈplaɪ]　v. 申请

**invoice** [ˈɪnvɔɪs]　n. 发票

**confirm** [kənˈfɜːrm]　v. 确认

## 情景实例　*Scene Example*

　　某供应商收到采购商的函电，要求寄送形式发票，以便申请进口许可证，于是附函附上形式发票，并说明仅供报关使用，不代表最终成交条款。

### 英

Thank you for your email of May 15.

As requested, we are sending you here with our Proforma Invoice No. 190 quadruplicate for shirts. As we know you will have to apply for an import license for your order, we have made up the invoice to expire on June 20.

The above–mentioned invoice, however, does not imply unreserved acceptance of your order as both prices and quantities must be further confirmed by us.

As soon as you have obtained the necessary import license, please let us know by email so we may confirm our offer. In the meantime, if there is any change in price or delivery, we shall contact you.

We look forward to receiving further news from you.

### 中

感谢您 5 月 15 日的电子邮件。

按照要求，我们随函寄上我方为衬衫销售开具的 190 号形式发票一式四份。我们知道，你方必须为你的订单申请进口许可证，因此我们已设定发票于 6 月 20 日到期。

上述发票并不意味着毫无保留地接受你的订单，订单的价格和数量必须由我方进一步确认。

一旦您获得了必要的进口许可证，请通过电子邮件告知我们，以便我们确认我们的报价。同时，如果价格或交货期有任何变化，我们将与您联系。

我们期待收到您的进一步消息。

**PART 1 建立合作关系 Create a Partnership**

## Unit 3 订单确认函
### Order Confirmation Letter

在双方对交易条件达成一致后，就进入了确认订单环节。订单确认函可以由交易的任意一方发出，作为对交易条款的最后确认。买方确认采购货物品名、数目和金额等无误，卖方确认可以供货。

## 常用词汇 *Vocabulary*

### 1. transaction　n. 交易；办理；处理；事务

【双语例句】

His failure in this transaction was due to nothing else than his own carelessness.
他在这笔交易中的失利完全是由于他自己的粗心大意。

【用法解析】

相关短语有"business transaction（业务交易）""cash transaction（现金交易）""block transaction（集团交易）""transaction price（成交价）"和"paper transaction（纸上交易）"等。

### 2. execution　n. 处决；执行；实施

【双语例句】

We should carry the new plan into execution as soon as possible.
我们应该尽快实行这项新计划。

【用法解析】

相关短语有"suspend execution（暂停执行）""put/carry sth into execution（投入实施）""compulsory execution（强制执行）"和"mass execution（批量执行）"等。

## 基本词汇　*Basic Words*

**metre** [ˈmiːtər]　n. 米；公尺

**polythene** [ˈpɑːlɪθiːn]　n. 聚乙烯

**conclusion** [kənˈkluːʒn]　n. 结论

**attention** [əˈtenʃn]　n. 注意

**waterproof** [ˈwɔːtərpruːf]　adj. 防水的

**cardboard** [ˈkɑːrdbɔːrd]　n. 硬纸板

**payroll** [ˈpeɪroʊl]　n. 工资名单

**tax** [tæks]　n. 税款

## 情景实例　*Scene Example*

### 1. 买方确认

某公司向供货商采购棉布，在经过一系列还盘之后，该公司向对方发出最后的订单确认函。

**英**

As a result of our recent exchange of information, we have a strong interest to work with your proposal. Please see the following terms and conditions as a confirmation of the start of our business relationship.

Product Name: Cotton Prints DY 78

Quantity: 1% more or less allowed; 3,000 metres

Price: USD $ 3.3 per metres; FOB

Packing: Package of 100 metres in a waterproof polythene bag; then in a cardboard box

Payment: T/T 100% WITHIN 30 DAYS AFTER SHIPMENT DATE

Shipment: Within 2 weeks of receiving L/C

We hope that this first transaction will come to a successful conclusion for both of us. We look forward to continuing a mutually beneficial trade between our companies.

## 中

由于我们最近的信息交流，我们对你方的建议很感兴趣。请参阅下列条款和条件，以确认我们业务关系的开始。

产品名称：78 号印花棉布

数量：允许 1% 的误差；3 000 米

价格：每米 3.3 美元；离岸价

包装：每 100 米用防水聚乙烯袋包装；然后用纸板箱包装

付款：装运日期后 30 天内电汇 100%

装运：收到信用证后两周内

我们希望这第一笔交易对我们双方都会有圆满的结果，期待继续进行我们之间的互利贸易。

## 2. 卖方确认

在收到采购商货款后，某供应商发函向对方确认订单内容，并说明将尽快生产并发货。

## 英

Welcome you as one of our customers. We want to say how pleased we were to receive your order dated July 14 for:

| | | |
|---|---|---|
| 250 No. OG–18 | payroll greeting cards | $102.50 |
| 250 No. OG–22 | payroll card envelopes | $21.95 |

100  No. OM–01  performance greeting cards      $80.00

Subtotal                                        $204.45

Our best attention has been paid to the execution of this order. And we have received your check for $242.76, including goods, tax, shipping. Your order will be delivered promptly. We ensure that your order must reach you before February 12, and will give you satisfaction.

We thank you again for the above order and hope that this will lead to a durable cooperation between us.

**中**

欢迎你方成为我们的客户。我们很高兴收到你方 7 月 14 日的订单：

250 件  OG–18 型  工资卡        102.50 美元

250 件  OG–22 型  工资卡信封    21.95 美元

100 件  OM–01 型  贺卡          80 美元

小计                           204.45 美元

我们已尽了最大的努力来执行该订单。我们已收到你方 242.76 美元的支票，包括货款、税金和运费，我们将迅速交货。我们保证，你方所订货物将在 2 月 12 日前到达你方，并使你方满意。

我们再次感谢上述订单，希望这笔交易能使我们之间保持长久的合作关系。

**PART 1  建立合作关系 *Create a Partnership***

**Unit 4** **感谢客户订货**
**_Thank You for Letter of Order_**

在订单确认之后，一笔交易虽未完成，但已经没有大的变数了。这时，外贸业务员可以发函感谢客户订货，并告知售后信息等。

## 常用词汇 *Vocabulary*

### 1. console　vt. 安慰；慰藉　n. 仪表盘；操控台

【双语例句】

There are many lights and electrical instruments on the computer console.

电脑控制板上有许多小灯和电子设备。

【用法解析】

在计算机用语中，"console"还指控制台功能。

### 2. query　n. 疑问；质问；疑问号　vt. 质问；表示疑虑

【双语例句】

I send all my income tax query to my accountant.

我把所有有关所得税的疑问送交会计师。

I query the validity of his statement.

我对他的说法的正确性提出质疑。

【用法解析】

"query"的基本意思是"对…表示怀疑，询问"，表示对事物提出疑问，并要求得到可靠的信息或明确的解释。

## 基本词汇 *Basic Words*

**trust** [trʌst]　n. 相信；信任　　　　　　**deep** [di:p]　adj. 深的；厚的

**represent** [ˌreprɪˈzent]　v. 代表　　　　**increase** [ˈɪŋkri:s]　v. 增长；增多

**productivity** [ˌprɑ:dʌkˈtɪvəti]　n. 生产率

## 情景实例 *Scene Example*

　　某公司收到采购商的确认订单，于是回函向对方表示感谢，并告知对方保修期和售后服务信息。

**英**

Thank you for your order No. 56 of May 5.

We value your trust in our company and we will do our best to meet your service expectations. We assure you that our product will help to increase the productivity of your company.

Your purchase also includes a twelve–month warranty. Should you experience a technical problem with your console, you can contact one of our specialists on × × × × – × × × × who will advise you on a solution.

Thanks again for your order. If you have any queries, please contact and do not hesitate to call me. We hope that this order represents the beginning of a long and deep–going relationship between our companies.

**中**

感谢贵方 5 月 5 日的第 56 号订单。

我们珍视你方对我们公司的信任，我们将尽力满足你方的服务期望。我们向你方保证，我们的产品将有助于提高贵公司的生产率。

你方的订单还包括十二个月的保修期。如果你方在操作中遇到技术问题，可以联系我们的技术人员，电话是 × × × × – × × × ×，他会告知你如何解决问题。

再次感谢你方的订货，如果你有任何疑问，请联系并立即致电我。希望这一订单是我们之间长期深入合作关系的开始。

## PART 2 签约成交函 Letter of Signing

### Unit 1 邀请签约 Invitation to Sign Up

在确认订单之后，双方通常会签订一份合同（采购确认书或销售确认书）。

在准备好合同并寄送给对方之后，通常会附上一封信告知对方，这就是邀请签约函。

## 常用词汇 *Vocabulary*

### 1. execute    vt. 执行；实行；处决；完成

【双语例句】

Deliberate slowly, execute promptly.

慢慢酌量，快快行动。

【用法解析】

"execute" 的基本意思是"执行，实现"，指某人使计划好的事得以实现或执行，也指完成某个需要高度技巧的过程。

### 2. duplicate    n. 副本

【双语例句】

This form should be filled out in duplicate.

这种表格要填写一式两份。

【用法解析】

"duplicate" 用作及物动词，其基本意思是"复制"，即做一份与原件完全一致的复制品，引申可表示"复印，重复"。

### 3. instruct    v. 命令；指示

【双语例句】

The customer can instruct the computer to perform financial services.

顾客可指示计算机进行金融服务。

I will instruct you when to start.

我会告诉你我们该何时动身。

【用法解析】

"instruct"的基本意思是"命令，指示"，多指上级对下级发号施令，也可指"教，讲授"，引申可指"通知"。

## 基本词汇 *Basic Words*

**airmail** ['ermeɪl]  v. 航空邮寄

**sign** [saɪn]  v. 签字；签署

**copy** ['kɑ:pi]  n. 复印件

**file** [faɪl]  n. 文件；档案

**speed** [spi:d]  v. 快；迅速

## 情景实例 *Scene Example*

### 1. 采购方邀约

某采购商与供应商谈妥交易条件之后，向对方寄送了购货合同，并发函告知对方，希望予以会签，并表示信用证将尽快开立。

**英**

As a result of our recent exchange of emails, our Purchase Contract No. W3KF in two originals were airmailed to you. Please sign and return one copy of them for our file.

We are taking all necessary steps to open the letter of credit, which we hope will reach you within 10 days. We would be grateful if you would execute the order as speedily as possible. Any delay could lead to future problems with our clients.

We are pleased that this first transaction with your company has come to a successful result. We look forward to a continuing and mutually beneficial trade between our companies.

**中**

经过我们最近的电邮交流，我们将编号 W3KF 的两份原件购货合同空邮给你。请会签并退回一份副本，供我方存档。

我们正在采取一切必要措施来开立信用证，希望 10 天内到达贵方。贵方如能尽快执行订单，我们将不胜感激。任何的延误，都可能导致以后我方客户的不便。

我们很高兴与贵公司的首次交易取得圆满成功，期待着双方公司之间持续互利的贸易。

## 2. 销售方邀约

某供应商与采购商谈妥交易条件之后，向对方寄送了销售确认书，并发函告知对方，希望予以会签，并催促对方尽快开立信用证。

**英**

We are glad that we have reached an agreement through our mutual effort finally. We are sending you our Sales Confirmation No. 3897 in duplicate. Please sign it and return one copy for our file.

Please instruct your bank to issue the letter of credit as early as possible in order that we may process with the goods immediately. You may rest assured that we shall effect shipment strictly as contracted.

May we take this opportunity to express our appreciation for the accomplishment of this transaction and assure you that we shall do our best to cooperate with you in the future.

**中**

我们很高兴通过我们的共同努力终于达成了协议，现寄上第 3897 号销售确认书一式两份，请签字并寄回一份以便存档。

请通知你方银行尽早开具信用证，以便我方立即处理货物。请放心，我们将按合同规定严格装运。

请允许我们借此机会对这笔交易的完成表示感谢，并向你保证，我们将尽最大努力与你合作。

## Unit 2 确认收到合同
### Contract Received Confirmation

　　交易的一方在收到对方寄来的合同之后，应回函确认收到合同并表示感谢，告知对方合同已经会签确认并寄回一份，并表明对未来的期待。

## 常用词汇 *Vocabulary*

**1. duly　adv. 的确；当然地；适当地**

【双语例句】

The deeds which conveyed the title under that patent were duly recorded.

转让该专利下所有权的契约已妥当记录。

【用法解析】

与"duly"相关的短语还有"duly authorized（正式授权）""duly endorsed（经适当背书）"和"duly honoured（及时付款）"等。

**2. bridge　n. 桥梁；纽带 vt. 架桥；渡过；缩短差距**

【双语例句】

The price gap is too wide to bridge.

价格差距太大，无法弥合。

【用法解析】

"bridge"的基本意思是"桥"，引申指借以相互联系或接触的事物。表示弥合差距的短语是"bridge the gap"。

**3. peak season　旺季**

【双语例句】

Now is the peak season for wheat.

现在这个季节正是小麦生长的盛期。

## 【用法解析】

"high season" 也指旺季。与 "peak" 相关的短语还有 "peak time（高峰期）" "at the peak（处在最高峰）" 和 "peak value（峰值）" 等。

## 基本词汇 *Basic Words*

**gap** [gæp]  n. 隔阂；差距

**London** [ˈlʌndən]  n. 伦敦

**harmful** [ˈhɑːrmfl]  adj. 有害的

**establish** [ɪˈstæblɪʃ]  v. 建立；创立

**course** [kɔːrs]  n. 进展；进程

**step** [step]  n. 步伐；步态

## 情景实例 *Scene Example*

某公司收到供应商的销售合同，在签署并寄回一份副本后，向对方发函表示确认并已开立信用证，并催促尽快安排装运。

## 英

We have duly received your Sales Contract No. 216 covering 3,000 dozen Silk Blouses we have booked with you. The duplicate with our signature has been airmailed to you. Thanks to mutual efforts, we were able to bridge the price gap and put the deal through.

The relative L/C has been established with the Bank of Barclays, London, in your favor. It will reach you in due course.

As the peak season is drawing near, and our customer is badly in need of the goods. Any delay in delivering our order will be harmful to our future dealings.

We trust that this order will be the first step of a series of deals to come between us.

**中**

我们已收到贵公司第 216 号销售合同，涉及我们已订购的 3 000 打丝绸衬衫。我们签约的副本已经航空邮寄给你。感谢双方的共同努力，让我们能够弥合价格差距，使交易得以成功。

以你方为受益人的有关信用证已由伦敦的巴克莱银行开出，将如期抵达你处。

随着销售旺季的临近，我们的顾客急需货物。如延迟交货，将妨碍我们今后的交易。

相信这一订单将是我们之间达成一系列交易的第一步。

---

**PART 2　签约成交函 Letter of Signing**

**Unit 3　合同条款 Contract Clauses**

在外贸函电往来中，往往在正式签订合同之前以邮件正文列出合同条款，以供讨论相关事项。前述邮件中已有部分示例，下面是完整的合同条款示例。

1. 价格条款，包含币种、金额、计量单位、贸易术语等要素。

【邮件示例】
Unit Price: USD 59 PER PC CIF Singapore
单价：新加坡港 CIF 价格每件 59 美元

2. 品名，包含商品编号和名称。

【邮件示例】
Product: No.25003 24K Gold Decoration
品名：编号 25003 款 24K 黄金饰品

3. 规格或质量要求，有两种表示方法：一是文字说明；二是以样品实物表示。

【邮件示例】

Description:24K Pure gold, Scape: 24.5CM, Flowers in diameter: 6.5CM, Leaves: 6CM, Gold Weight: 1g

规格：24K 纯金，花茎：24.5cm，花朵直径：6.5cm，叶：6cm，黄金重量：1g

【邮件示例】

Quality: As per samples No. 2662 submitted by the seller on March 10, 2020

质量：参照卖方于 2020 年 3 月 10 日所交付的第 2662 号样品

4. 数量：欲交易的或是最终合同的交易货物数量。

【邮件示例】

Quantity:100 pcs

数量：100 件

5. 包装：根据货物的特点明确包装方式。

【邮件示例】

Packing:1pc/box, 10boxes/carton

包装：1 件／箱，10 盒／箱

6. 付款方式：根据交易国家和自身的情况选择适合的付款方式。

【邮件示例】

Payment: T/T 100% WITHIN 30 DAYS AFTER SHIPMENT DATE

付款：装运日期后 30 天内电汇 100%

7. 运输方式：选择适合商品的运输方式。

【邮件示例】

Means of transport: BY AIR

运输方式：空运

8. 装运时间：确切告知对方货物装运时间。

【邮件示例】

Shipment: Within 2 weeks of receiving L/C

装运时间：收到信用证后两周内

9. 装运港：出口国所在国家港口。

【邮件示例】

Port of Shipment: Guangzhou

装运港：广州

10. 目的港：进口商所在国港口。

【邮件示例】

Port of Destination: Singapore

目的港：新加坡

11. 运输标志（唛头）：内容繁简不一，由买卖双方根据商品特点和具体要求商定，其作用在于使货物在装卸、运输、保管过程中容易被有关人员识别，以防错发错运。

【邮件示例】

Shipping Mark:

24K Gold Decoration（货品名称）

U.S.A（进口商所在国家）

C/NO. 1–10（装箱顺序号和总件数）

MADE IN JAPAN（货物原产地）

12. 单据，包括所需单据的种类和正本（original）、副本 (copy) 份数。出口商在贸易过程中必须将合同中规定的单据备齐，并在交单 / 寄单时将这些单据提交给银行 / 寄给进口商。

【邮件示例】

Signed commercial invoice in 1 original and 3 copies.

签发的商业发票正本 1 份，复印件 3 份。

13. 保险条款：在 FOB、CFR、FCA 和 CPT 条件下，由买方投保。在 CIF 和 CIP 条件下，由卖方投保，应具体载明投保的险别、保险金额等事项。

【邮件示例】

Insurance: To be covered by the buyer.

保险：由买方投保。

【邮件示例】

Insurance: To be effected by the seller for 110% invoice value against W.P.A. & War Risk.

保险：由卖方按发票金额的 110% 投保水渍险和战争险。

14. 仲裁条款。

【邮件示例】

Any dispute arising from or in connection with this Contract shall be submitted to International Economic and Trade Arbitration Commission for arbitration which shall be conducted in accordance with the PIETAC's arbitration rules in effect at the time of applying for arbitration.The arbitral decision is final and binding upon both parties.

凡因本合同引起的或与本合同有关的任何争议，均应提交国际经济贸易仲裁委员会，在申请仲裁时，仲裁的执行应与 PIETA 的仲裁有效规则一致。仲裁裁决是终局的，对双方均有约束力。

## PART 3 生产前准备 Pre-production preparation

### Unit 1 准备样品 Preparing Samples

根据商业惯例，一个订单的落实，一般需要供应商准备至少两次样品，一个是产前样，另一个是确认样。产前样是生产前给客户确认的样品。确认样是经过客户确认后的样品。产前样应当完全按照确认样来做。

## 常用词汇　*Vocabulary*

### 1. composition　n. 成分；作品；组织

【双语例句】

We examined the rock to find out its composition.

我们检验了这一石块，想弄清它的构成成分。

【用法解析】

相关短语有"in composition with（与…一并）"和"make a composition with（和…妥协）"。

### 2. expedite　vt. 加速；加快；有助于

【双语例句】

We will expedite shipment as much as possible.

我们将尽可能加快装运。

【用法解析】

"expedite"是书面用语，表示加快或加急处理事务。

### 3. dispatch　v. 派遣；发送　n. 急件；派遣；发送

【双语例句】

The firm dispatched the goods to London.

公司将把这批货物送往伦敦。

【用法解析】

在英式英语中，"dispatch"还可写作"despatch"。表示"派遣，发送"时，其后与介词"to"搭配，意为"将某人派往，将某物发送往"，如"dispatch troops to the front（派部队去前线）"；表示"急件"时，相关短语有"carry a dispatch（携带急件）"和"diplomatic dispatches（外交急件）"。

**基本词汇** *Basic Words*

**photo** [ˈfoʊtoʊ]   n. 照片；相片

**freight** [freɪt]   n. 货运

**policy** [ˈpɑːləsi]   n. 政策；方针

**prefer** [prɪˈfɜːr]   v. 较喜欢

**collect** [kəˈlekt]   v. 收集

**initial** [ɪˈnɪʃl]   adj. 最初的；开始的

**情景实例** *Scene Example*

在产前样品制作完成后，供应商发函告知客户将寄送样品，并要求对方支付快递费用。

**英**

It is pleased to get your feedback. Thanks for your appreciation of our items.

Further to the samples, they were just completed and passed our internal inspection. Please check the photos in the attachment. I will send you tomorrow for quality approval.

But as a rule, we have to charge you first. That is a usual way to every customer. I think we could get your support and understanding, too. Which express company do you prefer? Please advise your account for freight collect.

Look forward to your further comments soon.

**中**

很高兴收到您的反馈。感谢你方对我们产品的喜爱。

样品刚刚完成，并通过了我们的内部检查，请查看附件中的照片。明日将寄送你方，以供质量验收。

但一般来说，我们得先收费。这是我们对每一个顾客的惯例。我想也能得到你方的支持和理解。你希望选择哪个快递公司？请告知你的运费到付账号。

期待你方的进一步交流。

在寄送了产前样品之后，供应商发函询问客户是否收到，并询问对方对样品是否满意，有何意见。

**英**

I am writing to check whether you have received our samples. Does everything fine there?

We hope the samples we sent you on May 5 were up to your expectations.

If there are any questions, please don't hesitate to contact me.

**中**

我写信是想确认你方是否收到我们的样品。一切都没问题吗？

希望我们 5 月 5 日寄来的样品符合你们的期望。

如果有任何问题，请随时与我联系。

客户在收到供应商产前样品之后，认为样品未达到己方要求，回函表示希望安排定制，并寄送了试制样品。

**英**

We were in receipt of your sample on May 15.

As the quality of your sample is not in the range of our current import standard, we are prepared to arrange a special production. By our experience, slight changes in its composition are necessary and will only make the goods superior in quality.We shall then show you the trial sample and see if it can be accepted as a quality standard for bulk production.

If you find our proposal acceptable, please let us know and then we can expedite the transaction.

**中**

我们已于 5 月 15 日收到贵公司的样品。

鉴于你方的样品质量未达到我方目前的进口标准，我们准备安排定制。根据我们的经验，产品组成的细微变化是必要的，会使产品的品质更为卓越。我们将给你方展示试制样品，请确认是否可作为大量生产的质量标准。

如果你方能够接受我们的建议，请告诉我们，然后我们可以加快交易进程。

供应商收到客户的试制样品后，由于定制样品需要特别制版，费用不小，于是发函要求客户支付样品费。

**英**

Greetings!

Glad to get your trail samples. Just following up to let you know that we do the new samples strictly according to your request, but please pay for the model charge USD 400 by your side.

After order placed, you could deduct this cost when balancing the payment. Enclosed please find our bank account file.

Please advise your opinion. Thank you!

**中**

向你问候！

很高兴收到你方的试制样品。希望你方知道，我们严格按照你方的要求做新的样品，但我们希望你方能支付 400 美元的制版费。

在下正式订单后，你方可以在付款时扣除此费用。随函附上我方银行账户。

请告知你方意见。谢谢！

收到供应商要求支付样品费的函电后，采购商回函表示样品仅用于测试，拒付样品费。

**英**

We regret to say that we can't pay the sample charge because of the policy of our company. And we can only pay transportation fee by DHL. Our express number is ××××.

If you want us to cooperate with you, you will have to make an effort. Please take note that we do not want to get profits from this sample, only for testing purpose.

**中**

很遗憾，由于我们公司的规定，我们不能支付样品费。我们只能用 DHL 支付运输费。我们的快递账号是 ××××。

如果你方想让我方和你方合作，你方就必须做出努力。请注意，我们要样品不是为了获得利润，只是为了测试目的。

收到客户拒付样品费的回函，供应商方面再次做出解释，说明己方是小公司，无力承担样品费，请求对方理解。

**英**

Thanks for your kind support to me first.

Regarding sample charges, I really hope we can find a way to move forward the project. It is honored for me and our company to work with you and your company. And be sure that we can start the initial order soon.

For the point of charges, I really hope you can do me a favor. We understand Real Inc. of New York is a big company, you have your own rules for samples. But our company is small, and the sample charge for us is quite a lot. Please kindly help us on this point.

We hope you can do your part to pay the charges for samples. Could we get your understanding and support?

Looking forward to hearing from you soon.

**中**

谢谢你对我的友好支持。

关于样品费，我真的希望我们能找到一个推进项目的方法。我和公司都很荣幸能与你和贵公司合作。并相信我们能很快开始做首批订单。

关于费用问题，我真的希望你能帮忙。我们了解纽约真实公司是一家大公司，你有自己的样品规则。但我们是一家小公司，而样品费对我们来说不是小数目。请在这一点上理解我们。

我们希望你方尽你所能支付样品费。我们能得到您的理解和支持吗？

期待尽快收到你的来信。

　　客户在收到供应商产前样品之后，认为样品达到己方要求，回函表示确认，并以样品为生产依据。

**英**

Thank you very much for the samples you sent us on June 4.

Your samples received a favorable reaction from our customers, and you can place the bulk production now. The quality of the order must be the same as your sample.

Please note that NK203 should be as per the sample No. 20 dispatched by you on May 25.

**中**

非常感谢你方 6 月 4 日寄来的样品。

我方客户对你方样品反映良好，现在可以批量生产了。所订货物的质量必须与你方的样品相同。

请注意，NK203 型产品应按照你方在 5 月 25 日寄来的第 20 号样品生产。

## Unit 2 向供应商下单
### Placing Order to Vendor

在确认样品之后，外贸公司就要尽快安排生产，以免因不必要的拖延造成交货延误。如果是贸易公司，就要向自己的供应商下订单，要求对方安排生产。

## 常用词汇 Vocabulary

### 1. purchase　n. 购买；采购

【双语例句】

Take the goods back to your retailer who will refund you the purchase price.

把商品退还给你的零售商，他们会按原价退款的。

【用法解析】

purchase 做动词时，意为购买，词义同 buy，但更为正式，且不可后接双宾语。

### 2. discrepancy　n. 差异；不一致；分歧

【双语例句】

The price tag says $100 and you charged me for $120, how do you explain the discrepancy?

货物标签上标明的是 100 美元，你方向我方索价 120 美元，这个差异该怎么解释？

【用法解析】

相关短语有"discover a discrepancy（发现矛盾）""marked discrepancy（显著的差异）"和"discrepancy in age（年龄方面的差异）"等。

## 基本词汇 *Basic Words*

**payment** [ˈpeɪmənt]　n. 付款

**July** [dʒuˈlaɪ]　n. 七月

**later** [ˈleɪtər]　adj. 后来的

**advance** [ədˈvæns]　n. 预付款

**deliver** [dɪˈlɪvər]　v. 传送；交付

## 情景实例 *Scene Example*

　　某外贸公司只做贸易，没有自己的工厂。在收到欧洲客户的订单后，下单给供应商订货。

## 英

We got a new order from our European customer. The order required 5,000 pcs of shirts. We are enclosing the terms and conditions of the purchase order for your consideration.

We would appreciate if you could start the production at the earliest and deliver the goods to our warehouse no later than the end of July. Also, please find enclosed check of USD $500 as advance payment.

Please feel free to contact me for any clarifications or discrepancy in the order details.

## 中

我们从欧洲客户那里得到了一份新订单。订单要求 5 000 件衬衫。随函附上购货订单的条款和条件，供你方参考。

若能尽早开始生产，并于七月底前将货物运至我方仓库，我们将不胜感激。另外，请查收随函附上的 500 美元预付款支票。

关于订单细节若需任何阐明或有任何异议，请随时与我联系。

**Tips** *如何快速敲定订单？*

1. "二选其一"的问话技巧。例如问"请问您要内销库存鞋还是外贸库存鞋？"只要客户选中一个，就等于下决心购买了。

2. 突出紧迫感。"这种产品只剩最后一批了，你不抓紧买就没有了。"

3. 试销订购。有的产品不方便寄送样品，则可以建议客户先购买一点试用，在试用满意之后，则可能带来大订单。

4. 消除客户疑虑。对于客户说的话，不能仅仅从字面上去理解，而要多思考客户为什么提出这个问题，并从源头上打消疑虑。如上文中关于样品费的交涉，在坦诚表示己方是小公司后，对方也能理解索要样品费的要求。

5. 耐心沉着。如果客户迟迟未回复邮件，可能是对方休假或其他事务耽搁。只要确定己方事务做好了，不必在邮件中催促对方下单，只要礼貌询问是否繁忙，作为提醒即可。

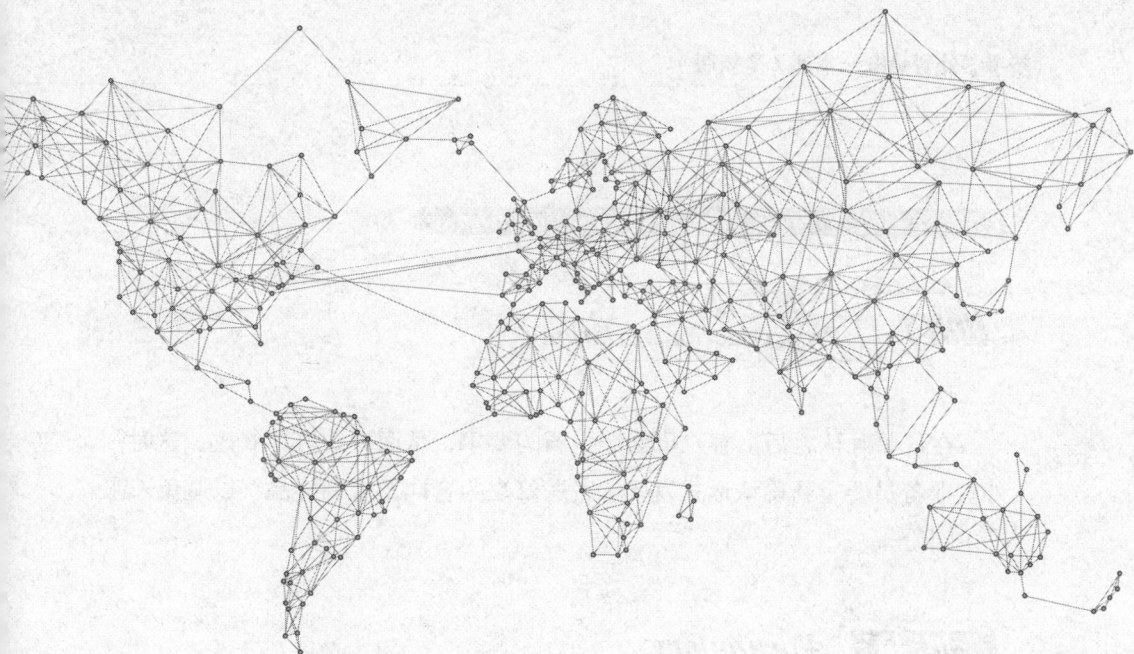

# CHAPTER 06

生产与装运函电

**Production and Shipment Letters**

对于外贸公司来说，价格、质量和交货期是最重要的经营要素。而质量和交货期又与生产和装运息息相关，因此在客户下了订单之后，外贸业务员要密切关注订单的行踪，并及时与客户沟通。

**PART 1 跟踪生产过程 Tracking Production Process**

**PART 2 装运环节 Shipping Links**

**PART 1** *跟踪生产过程 Tracking Production Process*

**Unit 1** 产前变动
*Preproduction Variation*

在订单确认之后，客户可能产生新的要求，从而导致订单修改。这时，外贸业务员要重新确认形式发票、寄送修改的合同及重制样品，以避免未来产生纠纷。

**常用词汇** *Vocabulary*

### 1. variation　n. 变种；变奏曲；变动；变化

【双语例句】

Prices have not shown much variation this year.

今年物价没表现出多大变化。

### 2. modify　v. 修改；更改；缓和；修饰

【双语例句】

The heating system has recently been modified to make it more efficient.

暖气设备最近已进行了改造，使其效率得到提高。

【用法解析】

"modify" 的基本意思是"改变，修改，调整"，强调在一定限度或范围内部分地改变，多用于观点、方法、制度、组织和计划等。

### 3. warehouse　n. 仓库　vt. 存入仓库

【双语例句】

If necessary, please warehouse the goods.

若有必要，请将该货存入仓库。

【用法解析】

表示存储场所的单词还有"storehouse（仓库）""depository（存储处）""stockroom
（仓库）"和"storeroom（储藏室）"等。

## 4. revised　adj. 经过修订的；改进的

【双语例句】

I send you my revised catalog and pricelist in the attachment, in the hope that you
may find something to suit you.

随信寄去新修改的目录和价目表，希望这些商品能适合贵公司业务。

【用法解析】

"revise"指校订原稿或修订较早的版本，相关短语中，"revised edition"指"第
二版"，"revised from"指"根据…修订而成"。

## 基本词汇 Basic Words

**survey** [sərˈveɪ] n. 民意调查

**risk** [rɪsk] n. 危险；风险

**quality** [ˈkwɑːləti] n. 质量

**change** [tʃeɪndʒ] n. 改变；变化

**package** [ˈpækɪdʒ] n. 包；盒

**infiltration** [ˌɪnfɪlˈtreɪʃən] n. 渗入

**urgent** [ˈɜːrdʒənt] adj. 紧急的

**hurry** [ˈhɜːri] v. 赶快；匆忙

## 情景实例 Scene Example

### 1. 修改包装

　　某采购商收到报告，指出公司一直采用的包装容易导致货物受损，于是
紧急发函告知供应商需要修改包装。

## 英

According to a recent survey, the package we usually use leads to a high risk of water infiltration.

We must modify our packing requirement to avoid future losses. Please see attached files and let us know whether these specifications can be met by you and whether they will lead to an increase in your prices.

It's an urgent change. so we must receive the final samples within next week. Please hurry up!

**中**

根据最近的一项调查可知，我们通常使用的包装会导致水渗入的高风险。

为了避免将来的损失，我们必须修改包装要求。请参阅所附文件，确认你方是否能满足相应要求，并告知新方法是否会引致价格上涨。

这是一个紧急修改。所以我方必须在下周之内收到最终样品。请快点！

## 2. 重制形式发票

　　收到采购商要求重新修改包装的要求，供应商修改了形式发票以便确认，并说明下周将寄送样品。

**英**

In response to your request, dated May 13, please check our attached proforma invoice for confirmation.

The requested samples will be sent out from our warehouse within the next week. Please take note, no shipping on Public holiday.

We look forward to hearing from you.

**中**

根据你方 5 月 13 日的要求，请查收我方形式发票以供确认。

所要求的样品将在下周内从我们仓库寄出。请注意，在公共假日不发货。

我们静候您的消息。

## 3. 修改合同

在采购商确认了已方发送的形式发票之后，供应商发送修改后的销售合同副本要求对方确认，并说明确认后即寄送正本。

**英**

As per our discussion, please see attached copy of our revised Sales Contract. Please check and confirm it ASAP.

We will send you the original by air as soon as you confirmed the items and conditions of the revised S/C.

**中**

根据我们的讨论，请参阅所附的修改后的销售合同副本。请尽快查看和确认。

一旦你方确认了修改后的销售合同的条款和条件，我们将立即把正本空运给你。

## 4. 重新寄送样品

应采购商要求，供应商重新制作了样品，在制作完毕后，发函通知对方样品已寄送。

**英**

We've done the production of samples, and we have airmailed you a box containing 50 pieces of them so that you can try them out. This will allow you to experience the quality and the value for sample charge. If you find the quality of samples acceptable, please contact us as soon as possible.

**中**

我们已完成了样品的制作，并空运寄去一盒，共 50 件，以便你方试用。这会让你方体验到样品费的物有所值。若你方觉得样品质量不错，请尽快联系我们。

# Unit 2 告知客户生产情况
## Claiming the Production Status

在产品生产过程中，外贸业务员要保持与客户的联系，及时沟通，让对方了解产品的生产情况。除了有助于维护客户关系外，如果产品出现问题，不至于措手不及。

## 常用词汇 *Vocabulary*

### 1. workload   n. 工作量

【双语例句】

He's always grousing about the workload.

他总是抱怨工作量大。

【用法解析】

相关短语有"a heavy workload（工作压力很大）""expanding workload（日益增多的工作量）"和"projected workload（预定工作量）"等。询问工作量，可以说"How's your workload?"，回复则说"I have a lot"。

### 2. queue   n. 长队；行列；辫子 v. 排队等候；使成队列

【双语例句】

People are queuing to buy tickets.

人们正排队买票。

【用法解析】

相关短语有"form/make a queue（排队）""join a queue（排入队伍）"和"be in a queue（排在队伍中）"等。

## 3. batch  n. 一批；一炉；一次所制之量  v. 分批处理

**【双语例句】**

We're still waiting for the first batch to arrive.

我们还在等着第一批货的到来。

**【用法解析】**

"batch"的基本意思是指面包、糕饼等的"一炉"，引申可指人或物的"一批，一组，一群"。相关短语有"batch processing（成批处理）""fresh batch（新到的一批）""in batches（分批地）"和"a batch of ten（十人一组）"等。

### 基本词汇 *Basic Words*

**update** [ˈʌpdeɪt]  v. 更新          **line** [laɪn]  n. 线；线条

**weekly** [ˈwiːklɪ]  adv. 每周        **mass** [mæs]  adj. 大批的

**upon** [əˈpɑːn]  prep. 当…时候

### 情景实例 *Scene Example*

某外贸业务员在产品准备生产、即将生产、开始生产、即将生产完毕和已经生产完毕的这5个阶段，都给客户发送了通知邮件。

## 英

Sample 1

In regard to your order No. 145 which you placed with our company on February 4. Now the factory is too busy due to peak season, the production is under full workload, so we are still waiting in the queue.

I will give you more information once I get more updates.

Sample 2

With reference to your order No. 145, we wish to inform you that the goods will be in production after 5 days and supposed to be finished in 10 days.

Sample 3

Your order No. 145 has been in line yesterday night. I will keep following the production, checking to make sure the products are of good quality and will keep you informed of the production status weekly.

Sample 4

In regard to your order No. 145, the factory is trying their best to speed up the production to meet the closing time. Now the goods are near to be finished, and the finished ones of the whole batch are packing now. We can deliver the goods a few days later no later than a week.

Sample 5

Regarding your order No. 145, the mass production is completed. Please check the attached photos for your reference. Goods will be shipped upon your balance cleared. And please advise us the shipping instructions.

## 中

示例 1

关于你方 2 月 4 日向我方下的 145 号订单。现在工厂处在生产旺季，太过忙碌，生产满负荷，所以我们仍然在排队等待。

一旦我方得到更多信息，会立即通知你方。

示例 2

关于你方 145 号订单，我们想通知你，货物将在 5 天后生产，应该会在 10 天内生产完毕。

示例 3

你方 145 号订单昨天晚上已开始生产。我方会继续跟进生产，在产品质量上严格把关，并将生产情况和进度每周详细报告给你方。

示例 4

关于你方 145 号订单，工厂正在努力加快生产以赶上截单时间。现在货物即将完工，其中已生产完毕的货物正在打包装。我们几天后就可以交货，最迟不超过一个星期。

示例 5

关于你方 145 号订单，已经大批量生产完成。请查看所附的照片以供参考。收到余款后，我们将开始发货。并请告知装运通知。

PART 1 跟踪生产过程 Tracking Production Process

## Unit 3 第三方验厂 Factory Audit

越来越多的跨国客户希望供应商在质量、社会责任（人权）、反恐等方面的管理体系达到一定的要求，因此在下订单之前会自己或者委托第三方公证行检查工厂状况，在确认工厂没有大的、严重的问题存在后，才将工厂纳入合格供应商名单，才会下订单并长期合作。

常用词汇 Vocabulary

## 1. audit　n. 审计；查账　vt. 旁听；验厂

【双语例句】

The bank first learned of the problem when it carried out an internal audit.

银行在一次内部审计时首次得知这个问题。

【用法解析】

相关短语有 "audit program（审查程序）""financial audit（财政审计）" 和 "limited audit（局部审计）" 等。

## 2. recapitulate　vt. 摘要；总结，扼要重述

【双语例句】

Let's just recapitulate the essential points.

我们再来回顾一下要点。

I will now briefly recapitulate the foregoing cases.

我现在将上述各项事实，扼要地重述一遍。

**【用法解析】**

在平时应用时，可简写为"recap"。

## 3. Corrective Action Plan　整改行动计划

**【双语例句】**

In regards to QC department, we should keep our wastage level to the minimum and implement our internal corrective action plan to avoid any more quality issues.

在质量控制部门，我们将把废品率控制在最低水平上，并且实施内部整改行动计划避免产生更多质量问题。

**【用法解析】**

在外贸中，一般缩写为 CAP，验厂常用，表示对验厂中出现的问题提出的改正措施。

## 4. deficiency　n. 缺乏；不足；缺陷；缺点

**【双语例句】**

It was the deficiency we were struggling with to correct.

此缺点我们正在努力改进中。

**【用法解析】**

"deficiency"可表示"缺陷"，也可表示"不足"。相关短语有"cover up the deficiency（掩饰缺点）"和"fill up a deficiency（弥补不足）"等。

## 基本词汇　*Basic Words*

convention [kənˈvenʃn]  n. 惯例

cooperation [kəʊˌɒpəˈreɪʃn]  n. 合作

deadline [ˈdedlaɪn]  n. 最后期限

share [ʃer]  v. 共有；合用

recap [riˈkæp]  vt. 重述要点

validate [ˈvælɪdeɪt]  v. 证实

**情景实例** *Scene Example*

## 1. 要求验厂

采购商向供应商发函以了解对方是否通过验厂审核，若没有审核经验，他们希望对方进行 SGS 审核。

**英**

Please advise whether your factory has passed any Factory Audit. If yes, please send me a copy of the audit report.

If not, can you start to look into audit by SGS? We require both technical audit and SMETA audit.

As a convention, we share the costs of the audit with our supplier.

**中**

请告知贵厂是否已通过任何工厂审核。如果是的话，请寄给我一份验厂报告的复印件。

如果没有，你方能进行 SGS 的验厂吗？我们要求进行技术和 SMETA 审核。

作为惯例，我们会分担供应商审核的费用。

## 2. 验厂报告

第三方审核机构在验厂过后，给采购商发去了验厂报告，并在邮件中大致说明报告内容和评定情况。

**英**

We would like to thank you for your cooperation during the most recent Responsible Sourcing audit. A full audit report has been enclosed for your reference. The point to recap is:

A description of the compliance violations.

Notes or comments from the auditor.

High-level information about how the factory can address the issue.

The deadline or "correct by" date for addressing each issue.

Once you have submitted your CAP, it will be reviewed for acceptance. If all safety violations are validated as being correct, the audit report will be assessed as a rating B.

During the time that your CAP is being reviewed, orders can be shipped and placed.

Please see attached report from the audit of points raised and agreed actions. If you have any questions please do not hesitate to contact me.

**中**

我们感谢你方对于最近的验厂工作的合作。随函附上完整的验厂报告供参考。摘要包括：

违反法规的描述。

验厂员的意见或评论。

关于工厂如何处理问题的高层次信息。

每个问题的截止日期或"修正"日期。

你方提交整改行动计划后，它将被审查验收。如果所有安全隐患被证实已改正，验厂报告将评定为等级 B。

在你方整改行动计划被审查期间，可以照常运货和订货。

请参阅验厂报告所提出的要点和商定的行动。如果你方有任何问题，请随时与我们联系。

## 3.CAP 报告

在收到验厂报告之后，由于整体通过验厂，仅有一处小问题不符合，供应商直接以邮件作为对客户的 CAP 报告。

# 英

We already passed the factory audit, a full audit report has been enclosed for your reference. Below is our completed corrective action plan.

Description of deficiency: There is video surveillance system, but video recordings are not maintained for a minimum of 30 days.

Desired Outcome: buy big hard drives to store all the files and maintain the video recordings for 60 days.

Due Date: In a week.

We sincerely hope you find our action satisfying.

# 中

我们已经通过了验厂，随函附上一份完整的验厂报告供你方参考。以下是我们的整改行动计划。

缺陷描述：有视频监控系统，但录像未保存至少 30 天以上。

理想结果：购买大容量硬盘以存储所有文件，并保存 60 天内的录像。

截止日期：一周内。

我们真诚地希望你方会满意我们的行动。

## PART 1 跟踪生产过程 Tracking Production Process

## Unit 4 请第三方验货
### Applying 3rd Party for Inspection

相对于验厂，验货的标准更为个性化。在验货之前，外贸业务员一定要和客户确认好检验标准，审核项目应完全按照客户的标准来进行，避免不必要的麻烦。

## 常用词汇 Vocabulary

### 1. undergo vt. 经历；遭受；承受

【双语例句】

He underwent an agonising 48-hour wait for the results of tests.

他苦苦等待了 48 个小时，化验结果才出来。

【用法解析】

"undergo"指经历某事本身的过程，或指经受不愉快的、痛苦的或危险的事物；也可以表示"遭受，蒙受"的意思。

### 2. accredited adj. 可信任的；质量合格的 v. 相信；委托

【双语例句】

Only accredited journalists were allowed to entry.

只有正式认可的记者才获准入内。

【用法解析】

在私募中，需要小规模数量合格投资者，即"Accredited Investor"。

### 3. submit vt. 提交；递交 vi. 屈从

【双语例句】

We should submit our plans to the council for approval.

我们应该向理事会提交计划以求批准。

【用法解析】

"submit"的基本意思是"服从"，指顺从某人的意愿或权威，使自身无法反抗或失去反抗的念头，强调在抵抗另一人的意志后确认反抗不会奏效而绝对服从。

## 基本词汇 Basic Words

legal [ˈliːgl] adj. 合法的

custom [ˈkʌstəm] n. 海关

fail [feɪl] v. 失败

Kenya [ˈkɛnjə] n. 肯尼亚

laboratory [ˈlæbrətɔːri] n. 实验室

fabric [ˈfæbrɪk] n. 织物；布料

## 情景实例 Scene Example

### 1. 要求验货

某采购商由于所在国政策，进口货物必须经过 SGS 检验，于是发函告知供应商相关流程。

**英**

Please note it is a legal requirement that all shipments coming into Kenya have to undergo PVOC pre–shipment inspection by SGS.

You will require an Import Declaration Form which we shall apply from customs office at this end and we shall send you a copy. You will be required to apply for inspection from your end from the SGS office which is close to your factory. They will require your factory to show the quality certificates such as ISO, and CE from any certification authority.

Upon carrying out inspection you will be issued with a Certificate of Conformity which we shall collect from SGS at this end.

**中**

请注意，所有进入肯尼亚的货物必须由 SGS 进行 PVOC 装运前检验，这是法律要求。

你方需要一个进口申报表，我们将在这边的海关申请，并给你方一份副本。你方需要向你方工厂附近的 SGS 机构申请检验。他们将要求你方工厂出示来自认证机构的 ISO 和 CE 等质量证书。

在检查完毕后，你方将收到合格证书，我们能通过这边的 SGS 查看。

## 2. 验货报告

某供应商应客户要求，通过对方指定的检验机构进行了验货，收到了如下验货报告。

**英**

Please find the final inspection report for T602 as follows.

Final results fail due to reasons below.

1.Surface

Bulk average point count is 22.6, fail.

2.GSM

REQ:160

ACTUAL :146.6 (−8.3%)

Please don't ship this fabric without correcting the GSM.

3.Color

Bulk looks lighter. If our customer rejected this color you should make a new batch.

Please confirm.

**中**

请看以下关于 T602 的最终验货报告

由于下列原因，最终结果是不通过。

1. 外观

整批货物平均分 22.6 分，不通过。

2. 克重

要求：160gsm

实际：146gsm（−8.3%）

克重不改善的话，这批货不能出货。

3. 颜色

整批货物看起来颜色浅了点。若客人拒绝这个颜色的话，你们需要重做一批新的。

请确认。

**PART 1** 跟踪生产过程 *Tracking Production Process*

## Unit 5 未通过验货 Failure in Inspection

　　在货物未通过检验的情况下，首先要再三确认，是否完全按照客户的标准进行检验，若多检验了一些项目或检验要求高于客户的标准，要及时与客户沟通。若的确需要改进，则应说明情况，供对方裁决。

## 常用词汇 *Vocabulary*

### 1. inspection　n. 视察；检查

【双语例句】

I gave the radio a thorough inspection before buying it.
我把收音机彻底检查了一遍才买下来。

【用法解析】

相关短语有"routine inspection（常规检查）""acceptance inspection（承兑验收）""field inspection（现场检验）""random inspection（随机抽查）"和"visual inspection（外观检验）"等。

### 2. upgrade　vt. 升级；提高；改善　adv. 向上地　n. 升级；上坡

**【双语例句】**

We must try to upgrade our cattle to the required standard of meat.

我们必须努力提高牛的品级，使之达到所要求的食用肉标准。

**【用法解析】**

相关短语有"upgrade the pay（提高工资）""upgrade the status（提高地位）"和"upgrade to（提高到…标准）"等。

## 基本词汇 *Basic Words*

**add** [æd]　v. 增加

**engineer** [ˌendʒɪˈnɪr]　n. 工程师

**simply** [ˈsɪmpli]　adv. 简单地

**cost** [kɔːst]　n. 费用；花费

**clarify** [ˈklærəfai]　v. 阐明

**point** [pɔɪnt]　n. 要点

## 情景实例 *Scene Example*

在收到验货机构的检验不合格报告后，供应商在充分了解情况之后，向采购商发函提供了具体解决方案，并请求考虑到时间因素，尽快确认。

**英**

You may already receive the inspection report from SGS. From our view, the solution is not the best, as it adds more cost, and is complicated.

Regarding the STANDARD TECHNICAL FEATURES, the relative engineers clarified that these points are simply and easily to upgrade, no need to modify anything. Please see the solution reports attached.

Now I think we'd better focus on the main points. You know we must make shipment on March 28. But the rework and re-inspection required several days. Our time is limited. Therefore, please kindly take all these into considerations. We, at our side, are always preparing to do our best to fulfill the shipment.

Awaiting your further comments soon.

**中**

你方可能已经收到 SGS 的检验报告。我们认为，该解决方案不是最好的，因为它增加了更多的成本，而且复杂。

关于标准技术特性，相关工程师申明说，这些方面的升级是很简单容易的，不需要修改任何东西。请参阅附件的解决方案报告。

现在，我们最好把重点放在要点上。你知道我们必须在 3 月 28 日装货上船，但返工和复检需要几天时间，我们的时间有限。因此，请将所有这些因素纳入考虑。就我方而言，我们会尽最大努力完成装运。

等候你方的进一步反馈。

**PART 1 跟踪生产过程 Tracking Production Process**

**Unit 6  申请重验**
**Requesting a Re-inspection**

　　一般验货未通过，除了得到客户的特别许可外，都是需要重验的，这样才能保证产品的质量在整改后能达到客户的要求。

**常用词汇  Vocabulary**

**1. in light of  adj. 考虑到（从…观点；由于…结果）**

【双语例句】

You can sell more this year in light of the market conditions at your end.
根据你们地区的市场情况来看，今年可以销售更多。

【用法解析】

"light" 本义是 "亮光"，可以引申为 "观察或考虑事情的方式"，因此 "in light of" 表达根据一定的事实而做出来的判断，并不是唯一导致这个结果的原因。与之近似的短语是 "on the basis of/upon"。

## 2. unannounced　adj. 未经宣布的；未通知的

**【双语例句】**

He had just arrived unannouncedly from South America.

他刚刚从南美来到这里，事先没有打招呼。

**【用法解析】**

飞行检查（Unannounced Inspection），简称飞检，就是在不提前通知的情况下，进行检查。

### 基本词汇 | *Basic Words*

**afford** [əˈfɔːrd]　vt. 给予；提供

**charge** [tʃɑːrdʒ]　n. 要价；收费

**specific** [spəˈsɪfɪk]　adj. 特定的

**whole** [hoʊl]　n. 整个；整体

**hygiene** [ˈhaɪdʒiːn]　n. 卫生

**brought** [brɔːt]　v. 带来

### 情景实例 | *Scene Example*

## 1. 申请重验

　　由于验货未通过，在产品经过整改之后，供应商发函向客户申请重验，在信中表达了歉意并说明将承担重验费用。

**英**

I am writing to inform you that we failed in the final inspection. You can find the report in the attachment. With deep regret, we want to apply the re-inspection, and we will afford the whole charge.

Please kindly let us know if you think the re-inspection is needed, we sincerely apologize for the inconvenience we brought to you.

**中**

我写信是想告诉贵方，我们没有通过最终验货。你可以在附件中看到报告。怀着深深的歉意，我们想申请重验，我们会承担重验的费用。

如果您认为重验是有必要的，敬请告知，我们对给您带来的不便深表歉意。

## 2. 重验通知

在收到重验申请之后，第三方检验机构向供货商发函表示接受重验，并提醒对方重验并不限于上次检验中出现问题的项目。

**英**

I acknowledge receipt of your request for your food hygiene rating to be reassessed. This was received on Aug. 10.

In light of the information that you have provided about the actions you have taken to address the issues raised at your inspection on Aug. 4, we agree with your request.

The re-inspection will take place sometime between three and six weeks following the date of your inspection. As you know, the visit will be unannounced, in other words, we will not tell you the specific date and time in advance.

I should remind you that we are focusing on standards, not just at the specific areas you have been working on and try to improve, so your rating could go up, down or remain the same.

**中**

我方确认你方 8 月 10 日提出的重新评估食品卫生等级的要求。

鉴于收到贵公司所提供的信息，对 8 月 4 日的检察所发现的问题，你方采取了整改措施，我们同意贵方的要求。

此次重验将在上次检查后的三至六周内进行。如你所知，这次访问将是不通知的，换句话说，我们不会提前告诉你具体的日期和时间。

我要提醒你的是，我们关注整体标准，而不仅仅是你一直在努力改进的特定领域，所以你的评级可能会上升、下降或保持不变。

## PART 2 装运环节 Shipping Links

### Unit 1 讨论装运细节
### Shipping Details Discussion

在货物备齐准备装运之前，按照国际贸易的一般做法，供应商应该在约定装船前向采购商发出货物备妥通知，并询问装运指示。采购商在接到供应商发出的通知后，应该在约定的时间内，将包装要求和装船要求等通知卖方。

## 常用词汇 Vocabulary

### 1. facilitate  vt. 促进；帮助；使…容易

【双语例句】

The new underground railway will facilitate the journey to all parts of the city.
新的地下铁路将为去城市各处提供方便。

【用法解析】

"facilitate"更多地指给予便利，使事情更容易做，而不是直接提供帮助，类似汉语的"方便"。

### 2. emphasize  vt. 强调；着重；使突出

【双语例句】

We cannot emphasize the importance of learning English more.
我们再怎样强调学英文的重要性也不为过。

【用法解析】

"emphasize"在英式英语中写作"emphasise"。相关短语有"emphasize the

importance of sth. （强调某事的重要性）" "emphasize repeatedly（反复强调）"
和 "emphasize sth to sb.（向某人强调某事）" 等。

## 3. withstand    vt. 对抗；经得起；承受

【双语例句】

This dress material will withstand repeated washing.

这种衣料经得住反复洗涤。

【用法解析】

相关短语有 "withstand an attack（顶住进攻）" "withstand hardship（能吃苦）"
和 "withstand severe tests（经得住严峻的考验）" 等。

## 基本词汇 / *Basic Words*

available [əˈveɪləbl]   adj. 可找到的

draw [drɔ:]   v. 吸引

venture [ˈventʃər]   v. 冒险

otherwise [ˈʌðərwaɪz]   adv. 否则

steamer [ˈstiːmər]   n. 汽船

fact [fækt]   n. 实际情况

choice [tʃɔɪs]   n. 选择；挑选

damage [ˈdæmɪdʒ]   n. 损失；损害

## 情景实例 / *Scene Example*

## 1. 请求装运指示

　　某供应商已基本生产完毕客户订购的产品，于是发函告知客户，并请求
对方给予装运指示。

**英**

We are now pleased to inform you that we have almost completed the bulk
production and the goods are scheduled to be shipped by the first available
steamer in July.

After finishing shipment, we'd like to draw your attention to the fact that is up to the present moment, we haven't received your shipping instructions. Please let us have your shipment advice immediately.

We look forward to hearing from you.

## 中

我们高兴地通知贵方，我方已基本完成批量货物生产，货物将在 7 月由第一艘可供装运的轮船装运。

在装运完毕后，我们希望贵方注意到目前为止，我们还没有收到你们的装船指示。请立即让我方知悉。

我们期待你方的来信。

## 2. 发出装运指示

某采购商收到供应商询问装运指示的来信，于是发函告知对方，详细说明了装船时间和包装要求。

## 英

We appreciate your email asking about the shipping instructions. We are now writing to facilitate your arrangement for the shipment of the goods.

Since the selling season is approaching, we venture to ask you to advance shipment to the end of this month. We know that our request to advance shipment will greatly inconvenience you, but we have no choice.

As our products are easily fragile, it is quite necessary to pay special attention to packaging. Frankly speaking, our packaging requirements are quite strict. The details are written in our packing instruction, which is attached. However, I'd like to emphasize the following three points.

1.The packaging must be of good quality, strong enough to withstand the shocks and loadings normally encountered during transport.

2.The products are to be wrapped in leak-proof boxes before being packed in wooden cases.

3.The package markings must be attached on the outside of the overpack.

We believe you will give special care to the packaging to avoid any possible damage.

Please mark the bales with our initials, with the destination and contract number as follows: KT LONDON 250

This will apply to all shipments unless otherwise instructed. Please advise us by email as soon as shipment is effected.

**中**

感谢你方询问装运指示的电子邮件。为了便于你们安排货物装运，我们现在写信给你们。

由于销售季节临近，所以我们冒昧地要求你们提前到本月底装运。我们知道要求提前装运会给你们带来极大的不便，但是我们没有办法。

由于我们的产品容易损坏，所以特别要注意包装。坦率地说，我们的包装要求很严格。详细资料在附件中的包装说明上。但是，我想强调以下 3 点。

1. 包装材料必须质量优良，能承受运输过程中通常会遇到的较强的冲击载荷。

2. 产品须装在防漏的盒内，然后再用木箱包装。

3. 包装标志必须在外包装外再贴一层。

我们相信你方会特别注意包装，以避免任何可能的损坏。

请在唛头上注明我们的首字母，目的地和合同编号如下：KT 伦敦 250。

除非另有指示，这将适用于所有装运。一旦装运，请电邮通知我们。

*PART 2* 装运环节 *Shipping Links*

*Unit 2* **告知客户装运情况**
*Keeping Customer Informed of Shipment Status*

在安排好装船后，供应商应该及时将装运情况告知客户，以便客户办理保险并做好卸货的准备。

## 常用词汇 *Vocabulary*

### 1. steamship　n. 汽船；轮船

**【双语例句】**

We saw that there was an oncoming steamship on the river.

我们看到河面上有一艘汽轮正在向这边驶来。

**【用法解析】**

ship、steamer、vessel、steamship 都有船只的意思，其区别如下："ship"是最普通的用词，泛指大大小小的各种船只；"steamer"在国际贸易中常常用来统指一切远洋船，在商业书信中用得最多；"vessel"包括一切大小船只，一般指载运货物的大型船只，在商业书信中也常用；在船名前面，则常用"steamship"的缩写 S.S.、S/S、s.s. 或 s/s，以及"motor vessel"的缩写 M.V.、M/V、m.v. 或 m/v。

### 2. Estimated Time of Departure　估计出发时间

**【双语例句】**

If the container has exported, I need the Vessel Name, ETD and ETA to Los Angeles.

如果这个集装箱已经出口了，我需要了解这个集装箱的名字，还有预计出发到洛杉矶的起止时间。

**【用法解析】**

"Estimated Time of Departure"在外贸术语中常缩写为 ETD，还有"Estimated Time of Arrival（估计到达时间）"缩写为 ETA。

### 3. stipulation　n. 规定；契约；条款

**【双语例句】**

Your remarks break the stipulation of the contract.

你们的意见是违反合同规定的。

## 【用法解析】

相关短语有"on the stipulation that（以…为条件）""non-essential stipulation（非主要条款）"和"optional stipulation（选择性规定）"等。

## 4. Bill of Lading　提单

### 【双语例句】

The Date of Bill of Lading shall be taken as the actual date of the delivery of the TECHNICAL DOCUMENTATION.

提单的日期应根据技术文件的实际交付日期而定。

### 【用法解析】

根据货物是否装船，可分为"已装船提单（Shipped B/L）"和"备运提单（Received for shipment B/L）"。"备运提单"上加注"已装船注记"后，即成为"已装船提单"。

## 基本词汇 *Basic Words*

**detail** [ˈdiːteɪl]　n. 全部细节

**August** [ˈɔːgəst]　n. 八月

**port** [pɔːrt]　n. 港口

**expect** [ɪkˈspekt]　v. 预料；预期

**favour** [ˈfeɪvər]　n. 支持

**patience** [ˈpeɪʃns]　n. 耐心

## 情景实例 *Scene Example*

## 1. 订舱通知

　　某供应商在安排好装船事项后，发函告知客户订舱编号、船名、预计开船和到达时间。

**英**

We are glad to have been able to execute your order as contracted, and we wish to inform you that the goods will be dispatched on Sep. 19.

The shipping details are expected to be.

COSCO booking NO.: 15432380

M/V: MSC AURORA 3FAT3

ETD Xiamen: 5 July 2020

ETA Savannah: 8 August 2020

We hope the goods will turn out to be satisfactory. If you have any questions, please let me know.

**中**

我们很高兴能按合同执行你方订单，并告知你方货物将于 9 月 19 日发运。

预计装船细目如下。

中国远洋运输集团订舱编号：15432380

船名：MSC AURORA 3FAT3

预计开船时间（从厦门）：2020 年 7 月 5 日

预计抵达萨瓦那的时间：2020 年 8 月 8 日

我们希望货物能使你方满意。如果你有任何问题，请告知我。

## 2. 开船通知

某供应商在船只顺利出航之后，发函通知客户船只名称、起运港和起航时间，并附上已装船提单附件。

**英**

We are pleased to inform you that we have completed the shipment of your order No. 239 in accordance with the stipulations set forth in  L/C. The MSC

AURORA 3FAT3 has sailed from Xiamen on 5 July 2020.

Our bank has informed us that you have opened a letter of credit in our favour and we have handed the following documents to be transmitted to your bank in London: commercial invoice, certification of origin, insurance certificate and bill of lading.

We trust the consignment will arrive in good order and give you complete satisfaction. If you find any problem, please let us know as soon as possible.

## 中

我们很高兴地通知你方，我们已按照信用证规定，完成了你方第239号订单的装运。船只 MSC AURORA 3FAT3 已于 2020 年 7 月 5 日从厦门起航。

我方银行已告知我方，贵公司已开具以我方为受益人的信用证，我方已将下列单据交给伦敦银行：商业发票、原产地证明、保险证书和提单。

我们相信这批货一定会正常运到，并使你方完全满意。如果你方发现任何问题，请尽快通知我们。

## 3. 交货通知

　　某供应商在货物顺利抵达目的地港之后，发函通知客户前去卸货，并表示了对延迟交货的歉意。

## 英

We are glad to notify you that the goods you ordered are now in loading port and available for pick up, and we wish that the goods will be in good condition.

Please accept our sincerest apologize for the delay in delivery and we thank you for your patience in this matter. If further assistance is needed, please call us at any time.

**中**

我们很高兴地通知你方所订购的货物现已运至卸货港，可供接收，希望货物的情况良好。

请接受我们对延迟交货的真诚歉意，我们感谢你方在这个问题上的耐心。如果需要我们提供进一步的帮助，请随时打电话给我们。

---

**Tips** *如何快速完成出货？*

1. 最重要的事项是要保持与客户的沟通。不论好坏，任何进度都要让客户了解与参与。特别是不寄送样品而仅通过照片展示产品的，要尽可能地把包装和产品的各个角度呈现给客户。

2. 特别注意客户在邮件往来中关心的问题。确认产品生产和物流运输中有没有特别的要求，出口报关和客户清关会不会有问题。

3. 跟踪订单进度。经常关注车间现有订单的生产进度，能够很好地避免生产货期拖延和产品质量问题。及时跟踪，及时发现问题，能够有更多的时间来处理，可及时向客户汇报，也能让客户产生信任感，方便后续的合作。

4. 产品质量的稳定性。产品合格率把控得好，合格率高，自然就能准时出货，顺利完成订单。需要注意的是，若因质量问题导致未能如期交货，万万不能以次充好，要根据实际问题妥善处理，才更有利于与客户的长期合作。

---

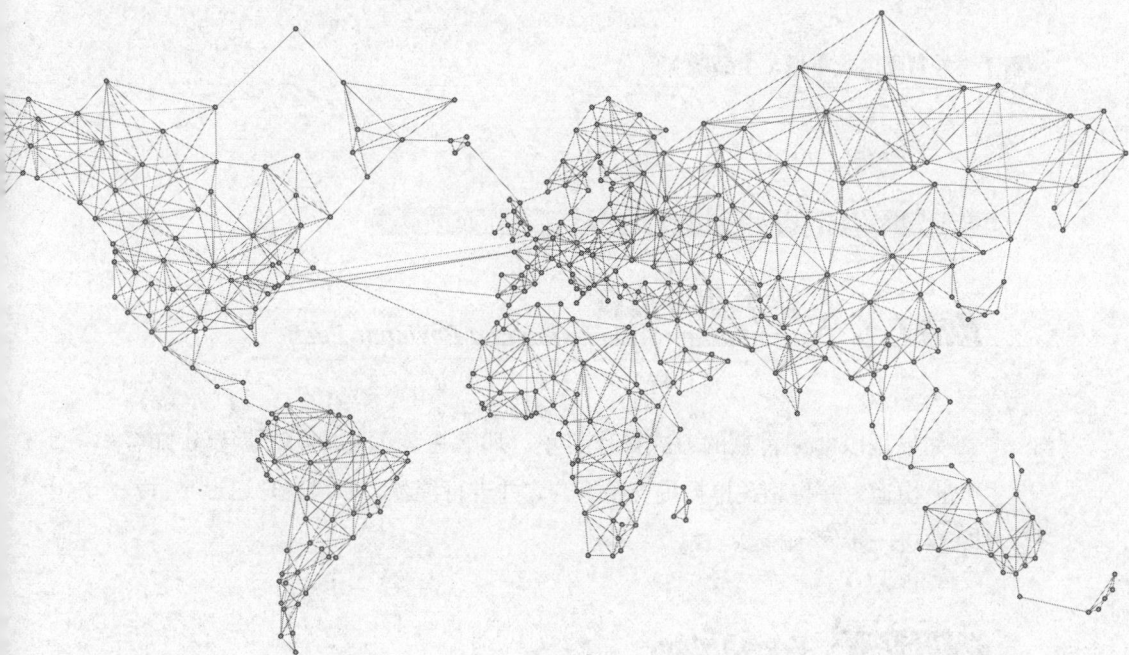

# CHAPTER 07

支付结算和信用证

*Payment, Settlement and Letter of Credit*

在国际贸易中，买卖双方签订销售合同后，最重要的就是货款的结算，对于货款支付时间和支付方式等都需要企业倍加小心。而信用证是国际贸易中使用最广泛的结算方式，需要重点把握。

## Unit 1 提供单据并催款
### Documentary Submission and Payment Push

如果是以即期付款的方式操作订单，那么在装运完成后，需要告知客户货物已出运，并将相关单据提交给客户，并进行催款。如果客户迟迟不付款，则需要进一步发函催款。

## 常用词汇 Vocabulary

### 1. norm　n. 规范；标准

【双语例句】

Everyone should abide by our social norms.

我们每个人都应该遵守社会行为准则。

There's a production norm below which each worker must not fall.

每个工人的产量都不得低于生产指标。

【用法解析】

相关短语有"abide by the norms（遵守准则）""reach the norm（达到标准）""violate the norms（违反准则）""diplomatic norms（外交准则）"和"above/below the norm（超过／低于标准）"等。

### 2. overdue　adj. 过期的；未兑的；迟到的

【双语例句】

Your payment is 6 months overdue in total.

贵公司的应付款项总计已过期 6 个月。

【用法解析】

相关短语有"debt overdue（过期债务）""overdue ship（误期船只）"和"overdue

check（过期支票）"等。

## 3. resort   n. (度假) 胜地；手段；凭借 vi. 诉诸；常去

**【双语例句】**

If other means fail, we shall resort to the law.

如果其他手段均失败，我们就将诉诸法律。

**【用法解析】**

"resort" 一般用作不及物动词，基本意思是"求助于"，常与介词"to"连用构成及物动词短语。

## 基本词汇 *Basic Words*

demand [dɪˈmænd]   n. 要求

contact [ˈkɑ:ntækt]   v. 联系

past [pæst]   adj. 过去的

steel [sti:l]   n. 钢

buyer [ˈbaɪər]   n. 买方

business [ˈbɪznəs]   n. 商业；买卖

pipe [paɪp]   n. 管子；管道

force [fɔ:rs]   v. 强迫；迫使

## 情景实例 *Scene Example*

### 1. 正常催款

某供应商已经将客户订购的毛毯出货，于是发函告知客户，并附上发票、装箱单和提单副本，催促客户尽快付款。

**英**

As we have completed my order of delivering 500 blankets to your place. In the attached you can find the invoice, packing list and copy of B/L. Would you please kindly make our payment as soon as possible, according to our contract norms? The blankets are manufactured in concern with all the demands which you have mentioned in the contract according to the needs of buyers.

Request you to expedite the process and make our payment at your earliest convenience. We hope to receive your reply at an early date.

Please accept our thanks in advance for your usual kind attention, and feel free to contact our company and discuss the details of next year's orders at any time.

**中**

我们已经完成了向你们运送 500 条毛毯的订单。在附件中你能找到发票、装箱单和提单副本。请按照我们的合同规范尽快付款。毛毯是根据您在合同中提到的基于买方需要的所有要求制造的。

请您尽快办理手续并尽快付款。我们希望早日收到你方回复。

请允许我提前感谢您平日的关照，并请随时与我们沟通联系，讨论下一年的订单细节。

## 2. 久不付款

某供应商几经提醒，客户仍旧没有为采购钢管的订单付款，且已经逾期 20 天，于是发函催促付款，并警告对方继续拖延将走法律途径。

**英**

I am writing to inform you that while we sincerely appreciate doing business with you in the past, but accordingly to our records, your payment of order No. 741 of steel pipes is long overdue by more than 20 days now.

We had sent you a reminder before to ensure that you make the payment on time, but there was no response to that from your end. You are a valuable customer for our firm and we want to continue to serve you diligently. To maintain healthy relations, we request you to please clear the overdue within the next 10 days by March 30 at the latest. If we do not receive the amount by March 30 then we would be forced to resort to a legal proceeding against you.

If for any reason you cannot make the entire payment at one go, then please contact us within 3 days so that we can decide upon partial payment terms which are mutually acceptable for both of the parties.

Please feel free to contact our office if you have any other queries regarding this matter. Your prompt attention to this issue will be highly appreciated by us. We look forward to assisting you in the future.

**中**

我在此写信是想提醒你方，尽管我方真诚地感谢你方和我们做生意，但是，根据我们的记录，你方第 741 号钢管订单的款项已经逾期 20 天了。

我们曾给你方发过提醒，以确保按时付款，但没有收到你方的任何答复。你方是我们公司的宝贵客户，我们希望继续竭诚为你方服务。为了保持良好的关系，我们要求你方在 3 月 30 日前，最迟 10 天内将逾期款项结清。如果我们在 3 月 30 日还没有收到这笔账款，对此我们将不得不诉诸法律程序。

如果由于任何原因不能一次性支付全部货款，请在 3 天内与我们联系，以便我们决定双方都可以接受的部分付款方式。

如果你方对此事有任何其他疑问，请随时与我们办公室联系。你方对此事的迅速关注将得到我们衷心感谢。我们期待着在以后的日子里为您提供帮助。

---

**PART 1** 支付结算事宜 *Payment and Settlement Matters*

**Unit 2** | **请客户提供银行流水单**
**Asking for Bank Statement**

对于已经提交单据多日却未见付款，但客户信誉良好或者回函说明已付款的情况，外贸业务员就应当考虑是否是汇款的某一个环节出错了，导致未收到款项。这时可以要求客户检查和提供银行流水单。

## 常用词汇 / *Vocabulary*

### 1. procedure n. 程序；手续；步骤

【双语例句】

These procedures are highly irregular.

这些程序是很不合乎规则的。

【用法解析】

相关短语有"adhere to procedure（遵守规程）""proper procedure（常规步骤）""procedure for（…的程序）"和"procedure in production（生产过程）"等。

### 2. reject vt. 拒绝；排斥；驳回；丢弃 n. 不合格产品；被拒之人

【双语例句】

His request was rejected.

他的请求遭到拒绝。

【用法解析】

"reject"的基本意思是"拒绝，抵制"，表示主观上不肯承认、接受或服从，语气强烈，用于外交和商业条款之类的正式场合。"reject"还可作"抛弃，丢掉，剔除"解，表示把无用的、不能令人满意的或无价值的东西扔掉。

## 基本词汇 / *Basic Words*

careful ['kerfl] adj. 小心；注意

compare [kəm'per] v. 比较；对比

yet [jet] adv. 还没

error ['erər] n. 错误；差错

record [rɪ'kɔːrd] v. 记录；记载

## 情景实例 / *Scene Example*

某供应商在催促客户付款后，客户回函已付款，但检查账户后发现依旧未收到货款，于是发函要求对方检查和提供银行流水单。

### 英

With a careful check of this order, we regret to tell you that there must be an error in your payment procedure. We haven't received your remittance yet, maybe your payment was rejected by the bank.

Please kindly check our account information in attachment and compare it with the bank receipt. By the way, could you please also send us the bank receipt for record? We hope to hear your earliest reply as it is so urgent.

### 中

仔细检查此订单后，我们遗憾地告诉你方，你们的付款程序中一定有错误。我们还没有收到你方汇款，也许是付款被银行拒绝了。

请检查附件中的账户信息，并与银行流水单进行比较。顺便说一下，你方可以把银行流水单也发给我方，以便存档记录吗？鉴于此事紧急，我们希望尽快收到你方的答复。

### PART 1 支付结算事宜 *Payment and Settlement Matters*

**Unit 3** 收到客户回应
Receiving the Response from Customers

在外贸业务员发出请求付款信函后，通常会收到客户付款通知的邮件，有时也会收到要求延期付款的邮件。

### 常用词汇 *Vocabulary*

**1. remittance  n. 汇款**

【双语例句】

Sorry, your remittance has not reached us yet.

对不起，您的汇款还没有到我们这里。

**【用法解析】**

表示汇款的单词有"remit（汇出）""transfer（转账）""send（发出）""wire（电汇）"等。

## 2. instance　n. 例子；场合；情况；要求；诉讼程序　vt. 举例说明

**【双语例句】**

This is only one instance out of many.

这不过是许多例子中的一个。

**【用法解析】**

"instance"作为动词解释为"举例说明"，前面一般加单词"as"，不过也可以省略"as"，但是加"as"使用比较普遍。

## 3. jeopardize　vt. 危及；使处于危险境地；影响

**【双语例句】**

If you are rude to the boss, it may jeopardize your chance of success.

如果你对老板没有礼貌，那也许会危及你事业的成功。

**【用法解析】**

相关短语有"jeopardize one's chances（危及可能性）""jeopardize one's life（冒生命危险）"和"jeopardize the whole operation（破坏整个行动）"等。

## 基本词汇　*Basic Words*

slip [slɪp]　n. 纸条；便条

owe [oʊ]　v. 欠（债）

occur [əˈkɜːr]　v. 发生

incident [ˈɪnsɪdənt]　n. 严重事件

successful [səkˈsesfl]　adj. 有成就的

intend [ɪnˈtend]　v. 打算；计划

plane [pleɪn]　n. 飞机

## 情景实例 *Scene Example*

### 1. 付款通知

某采购商收到供应商要求支付货款的邮件，于是回函表示 10 万美元的货款已付，并附上汇款凭单的复印件。

**英**

On March 25, 2020, the amount of USD $100,000 as payment for your invoice No. 3890 was transferred into your account. Please check and send us your confirmation.

Attached is the copy of the remittance slip for your reference.

We are pleased that this first transaction with your company has come to a successful conclusion. We look forward to a continuing and mutually beneficial trade between our companies.

**中**

2020 年 3 月 25 日，我方已经将发票号码为 3890 的货款 100 000 美元汇入你方账户。请你方查收并确认。

附件是汇款凭单的复印件，供参考。

我们很高兴与贵公司的首次交易取得圆满成功。期待我们之间会有一个持续的、互利的贸易关系。

### 2. 请求延期付款

由于生意不好，为了减少损失，某采购商迟迟未支付供应商货款，在收到对方的催款邮件后，回函请求允许延期一个月再付款。

**英**

Through this letter, I apologize to you for the inconvenience caused to you, owing to the delay in payment of order No. 387 from my side. This was not intended, and considerable loss in business due to office relocation issues has made it impossible for me to pay the balance on the discussed date.

This is the first instance that our organization has not cleared the payment on time, and we would really appreciate it if you give us an extension of one month to pay the due. I assure you that I will pay back all my due on April 20. I sincerely regret this delay in the payment and promise you that we would make sure such a delay doesn't occur in the future.

We add that we are pleased with the way by which you executed our order. The goods arrived exactly on time by a United Airlines plane. I have been happy with our business relationship and trust this incident will not jeopardize our future dealings.

**中**

由于我方第 387 号订单延期付款，给你方带来的不便，我深表歉意。这不是存心的，由于办公室搬迁问题，我们生意不好，为了减少损失，所以我无法在讨论的日期付清余款。

这是第一次我们公司没有按时付款，如果你方允许我们延期一个月再付款，我们将非常感激。我方向你们保证，我方会在 4 月 20 日付清所有款项。我对延迟付款感到由衷的歉意，并向你方保证以后不会再发生这样的延误。

另外，我们很高兴你方执行订单的方式。通过美国航空公司的飞机，货物送达完全准时。我为我们的业务关系感到高兴，相信这一事件不会影响我们今后的交易。

*PART 1* 支付结算事宜 *Payment and Settlement Matters*

**Unit 4** 告知客户收到款项
*Informing Clients of Receiving Funds*

在客户告知已汇款后，外贸业务员就要及时查询己方账户，若发现收到款项，就要及时告知客户并表示感激，这除了是商务礼节，也节省了客户核查的时间。

## 常用词汇 *Vocabulary*

### 1. due   adj. 应有的；到期的；预定的；应付的 n. 应得物；会费

【双语例句】

He received a large reward, which was no more than his due.

他得到了一大笔奖金，这是他应得的。

【用法解析】

"due" 的意思与义务、责任和债务有关，表示"应得的"时常置于名词前作定语；"due" 作"应付的"解时，常置于名词之后作定语。

### 2. dedication   n. 奉献；献词；献堂礼

【双语例句】

Her dedication to her work was admirable.

她对工作的奉献精神可钦可佩。

The book's dedication reads "To Mother".

本书献词写道：献给母亲。

【用法解析】

"commitment, devotion, dedication" 都有"贡献，投入"的含义，其区别在于"commitment"指义务上的奉献；"dedication"多用来表示为重要工作付出的长期的奉献；"devotion"多指"对某人或事的热爱和献身"。

## 基本词汇 *Basic Words*

sincerely [sɪnˈsɪrli]  adv. 真诚地

side [saɪd]  n. 一边；一侧

promise [ˈprɑːmɪs]  v. 许诺；承诺

admire [ədˈmaɪər]  v. 钦佩

customer [ˈkʌstəmər]  n. 顾客

maintain [meɪnˈteɪn]  v. 维持；保持

## 情景实例 | *Scene Example*

在收到客户对订单的支付汇款后，供应商发函告知对方已确认收到款项，并表达了感谢。

### 英

We are writing to inform you that we have received your payment that was due last month. Thank you for remitting this payment to us.

We sincerely appreciate your promptness regarding all payments from your side. You have always fulfilled the promises made by you regarding deadlines and payments. We admire your sincerity and dedication that you have always maintained as a customer.

We would like to take this opportunity to thank you for being a valued customer with us for so long. We are looking forward to serving you again in the future.

If you have any other concerns that you would like to address us, please feel free to contact us. We are more than willing to address your needs.

### 中

我们写信告知你方，我们已收到你方上个月的付款。谢谢你方的汇款支付。

我们衷心感谢你方所有的及时付款。你们坚持履行对期限和付款的承诺。我们钦佩你方作为客户一直保持的真诚和奉献精神。

借此机会，我们感谢你方与我方长期合作。我们期待未来再次为你方服务。

如果你方有任何其他想解决的问题，请随时与我们联系。我们非常愿意满足你们的需求。

**Unit 1** 请客户接受信用证差异点
Proposing Acceptance Discrepancy of L/C

信用证的开立一般在生产前，在最终交单时，由于各种原因就可能产生不符点。如果不是特别严重，银行只要得到客户的确认和接收指示，就可以继续偿付。

## 常用词汇 *Vocabulary*

### 1. amend vt. 修正；改进

【双语例句】

Please amend your copy of the contract accordingly.
请将你的合同副本作相应的修正。

【用法解析】

"amend" 的基本意思是"修改，修订"，指对文件、建议和法律等进行略微改进或稍微改动，也可指为使某人或某事物变得更好而"改过，改善，改良"。

### 2. oblige vt. 迫使；责成；使感激；施恩于 vi. 帮忙

【双语例句】

I am obliged to you for your gracious hospitality.
我很感谢你的热情好客。

【用法解析】

"oblige" 的基本意思是"在武力或法律的制约下不得不做某事"。引申可表示"答应请求，施惠于"，在表示此意时，"oblige" 只指小事情，不指大事情，施惠的具体内容用"by doing sth." 或"with sth." 来表示。

## 基本词汇 *Basic Words*

**clerk** [klɜːrk]  n. 职员

**commercial** [kəˈmɜːrʃl]  adj. 商业的

**term** [tɜːrm]  n. 期限

**exactly** [ɪɡˈzæktli]  adv. 确切地

**guarantee** [ˌɡærənˈtiː]  v. 保证

**matter** [ˈmætər]  n. 事情；问题

## 情景实例 *Scene Example*

供应商接到议付行通知，由于信用证存在不符点，被美洲银行拒付。检查后发现是工作人员输入数据时出错，于是发函向客户解释，并附上更正后的装箱单和发票，希望其尽快付款。

**英**

We are very concerned when yesterday we received the notification from the Bank of America complaining about the discrepancies under L/C No. YT–LC–20040526.

After investigation of the matter, we found they are made as a result of our clerk's carelessness. We feel really sorry for all the trouble we have bought you and assure you that such a matter will never occur again. Enclosed please find our amended packing list and commercial invoice in 4 copies, respectively.

However, we can guarantee that the quantity of the goods is exactly in line with the stipulations of the relative contract.

Since our goods have been shipped on time, would you be kind to give the Bank of America your acceptance? Then we could get the payment soon.

We would be greatly appreciated that you could help us in consideration of the long–term trade relations between us and thank you for your kind cooperation.

We are looking forward to your favorable reply.

**中**

昨天我们收到通知，因为存在不符点，美洲银行拒付 YT-LC-20040526 号信用证，这让我们非常担心。

在调查此事后，我们发现这个问题是由于我们职员的疏忽。对我们给你方造成的麻烦，我们深表歉意，并向你方保证，这种事不会再发生了。随函分别附上我们修改后的装箱单和商业发票一式 4 份。

但是，我们可以保证货物的数量与有关的合同规定完全一致。

由于我们的货物准时装运，你能向美洲银行确认付款吗？这样我们可以快速得到支付。

如果能考虑我们之间长期的贸易关系，我们将不胜感激，谢谢你们的友好合作。

我们期待您的答复。

---

*PART 2 关于信用证 About L/C*

## *Unit 2* 请客户更改信用证
### *Proposing Amendment to L/C*

在前期开立信用证时，外贸业务员收到客户开出的信用证要及时检查。如果需要修改，就要回信告知客户具体需要修改的地方。一般来说，会请客户提供草稿件，双方核对无误后再向银行申请开立，就免去了申请修改的时间和金钱。

### 常用词汇 *Vocabulary*

**1. clause   n. 条款；[语] 从句**

【双语例句】

There is a contentious clause in the treaty.

这份协议中有一条有争议的条款。

【用法解析】

一般指法律文件等的条款。

## 2. partial　adj. 不完全的；部分的；偏袒的；偏爱的

【双语例句】

His partial attitude called forth a lot of criticism.

他的偏袒态度招致了不少批评。

【用法解析】

相关短语有 "partial to( 偏爱的 )" "partial eclipse of the moon( 月偏食 )" 和 "partial in one's judgement（判断不公平的）" 等。

## 基本词汇　*Basic Words*

**several** [ˈsevrəl]　pron. 几个；数个

**mistake** [mɪˈsteɪk]　n. 错误

**prepaid** [ˌpriːˈpeɪd]　adj. 预付款的

**negotiation** [nɪˌɡəʊʃiˈeɪʃn]　n. 谈判

**amendment** [əˈmendmənt]　n.（法律、文件的）改动

## 情景实例　*Scene Example*

某供应商收到客户开出的信用证草稿件，在经过检查后，发现了四处错误，于是回函告知对方需要修改的内容，并请开立信用证正本。

**英**

We have received your L/C draft for order No.435 with many thanks. However, on checking its clauses we found with regret that your Letter of Credit has several mistakes. You are kindly requested to make the below amendments:

1.Extend shipping date to September 30.

2.Permit partial shipments.

3. "Freight Prepaid" should be "Freight Collect".

4.The credit is to be valid for negotiation in China instead of in Italy.

All other terms and conditions remain unchanged. Please make the above amendments and open the original L/C so that we may make arrangements for shipment.

A prompt reply will greatly oblige us.

## 中

我们已收到你方为 435 号订单开出的信用证草稿件，万分感谢。然而，经过条款核对，我们遗憾地发现你方信用证有几处错误。请做以下修改：

1. 延长装运日期为 9 月 30 日。

2. 允许分批装运。

3. "运费预付"应该改为"运费到付"。

4. 信用证应在中国议付有效，而不是在意大利。

所有其他条款及条件保持不变。请确认以上的修改，并开出信用证正本，以便我们能够安排装运。

敬请迅速答复，不胜感激。

### PART 2 关于信用证 About L/C

**Unit 3** 收到客户回应
Receiving the Response from Customer

　　在要求客户进行信用证修改后，对于客户发来的已修改邮件，外贸业务员要进行仔细检查，核对无误后表示确认。

## 常用词汇 *Vocabulary*

### 1. expiry　n. 满期；逾期

【双语例句】

The licence can be renewed on expiry.

执照期满时可延期。

【用法解析】

信用证上的"expiry date"即有效期，过期信用证即作废。有效交单的条件是任何时候不能超过信用证的有效期，且必须在提示期以内。

### 2. usual terms　惯常条款

【双语例句】

We must insist on our usual terms of payment.

我们必须坚持通常的支付条件。

【用法解析】

可以用"terms as usual"代替"usual terms"。

## 基本词汇 *Basic Words*

**May** [meɪ]　n. 五月　　　　**condition** [kənˈdɪʃn]　n. 状态；状况

**instead** [ɪnˈsted]　adv. 代替　　　**Italy** [ɪtəlɪ]　adj. 意大利

**utmost** [ˈʌtmoʊst]　n. 极限　　　**once** [wʌns]　conj. 一旦

## 情景实例 *Scene Example*

　　收到供应商对己方开出的信用证的修改意见后，采购商进行了修改，并回函告知对方已修改的内容，并催促对方尽快安排装运。

## 英

Thanks for the email asking us to make an amendment to our L/C. As requested, the amendment to our L/C No. 657 has been made as follows.

1.Date of Expiry: 4 June 2020

2.Last Date of Shipment: 15 May 2020

3.Any Other Conditions: The credit is to be valid for negotiation in China instead of in Italy

We regret the mistake we've made and have now instructed the Bank of America to make the amendment. The amendment advice will reach you soon. Please try your utmost to complete the shipment once you confirm our amendment.

We expect to receive the first shipment at the date stated in the contract.

## 中

感谢你方要求我方修改信用证的电子邮件，对我方第 657 号信用证的修改如下。

1. 截止日期：2020 年 6 月 4 日

2. 最后装运日期：2020 年 5 月 15 日

3. 其他条件：信用证应在中国议付有效，而不是在意大利

我们对所犯的错误感到遗憾，并已指示美洲银行做出修正。修改意见很快就会到达。一旦你方确认我们对信用证的修正，请尽全力完成装运。

我们希望在合同中规定的日期内收到第一批货。

## PART 3 新支付结算方式 New Payment Settlement

## Unit 1 申请新的付款方式
### Requesting New Payment Methods

贸易双方初次合作时，一般采用信用证或者高额定金的方式操作，以避

免风险。在合作较熟悉之后，供应商就会要求采用一些便捷且利于资金流动的付款方式。

## 常用词汇 *Vocabulary*

### 1. prevailing　adj. 盛行很广的；盛行的，广泛流传的；主流的

【双语例句】

Your price is out of line with the prevailing international market.

你方价格与现行世界市场行情不一致。

【用法解析】

相关短语有"prevailing rate（现行汇率）""prevailing wage（现行工资）"和"prevailing price（普遍价格）"等。

### 2. propose　v. 打算；计划；向……提议；求婚；提名

【双语例句】

The committee proposed that new legislation should be drafted.

委员会建议着手起草新法规。

【用法解析】

"propose"的基本意思是"提议，建议"，多指在讨论或争辩中提出明确的意见或建议，强调要求对方予以考虑或同意，引申可表示"打算，计划（做某事）"。

## 基本词汇 *Basic Words*

**moment** [ˈmoʊmənt]　n. 时刻

**economic** [ˌiːkəˈnɑːmɪk]　adj. 经济的

**rate** [reɪt]　n. 速度

**irrevocable** [ɪˈrevəkəbl]　adj. 不可更改的

**tie** [taɪ]　v. 系；拴

**climate** [ˈklaɪmət]　n. 气候

**document** [ˈdɑːkjument]　n. 文件

## 情景实例 | *Scene Example*

### 1. 笼统请求

　　某供应商和采购商已经合作得较为熟悉，由于信用证的支付方式占用资金较大，因此发函请求对方提供更加合理的付款条件。

**英**

In the past, our purchases of steel pipes from you have normally been paid by confirmed, irrevocable letter of credit.

This arrangement has cost us a great deal of money. From the moment we open the credit until our buyers who pay us normally tie up funds for about four months. This is currently a particularly serious problem for us in view of the difficult economic climate and the prevailing high–interest rates.

If you could offer us more reasonable payment terms, it would probably lead to an increase in business between our companies. We propose either cash against documents on arrival of goods, or drawing on us at three months' sight.

We hope our request will meet with your agreement and look forward to your early reply.

**中**

过去，我们从你们那里购买钢管通常是用保兑的、不可撤销的信用证支付的。

这样的安排已经花了我们一大笔钱。从我们开具信用证到我们的买家付款，这期间通常会积压 4 个月的资金。鉴于目前的经济环境困难和普遍存在的高利率，对我们来说，这是一个特别严重的问题。

如果你们能给我们提供更合理的付款条件，它可能会使双方公司之间业务量增加。我们建议以货到付款交单方式付款，或以三个月的即期付款交单方式向我方付款。

希望就我们的要求能得到你方同意，并期待你方早日答复。

## 2. 具体请求

　　某供应商和采购商已经合作得较为熟悉，由于信用证的支付方式不太便捷，因此请求对方采用见单据付款的支付方式。

**英**

In the past, we have traded with you on a sight credit basis. Now we would like to propose a different arrangement. When the goods are ready for shipment and the freight space is booked, you telex us and then we remit the full amount by telegraphic transfer (T/T).

We are asking for this concession so that we can give our customers a specific delivery date and also save the expense of opening a letter of credit. As we believe that this arrangement should make little difference to you, but could help our sales, we trust that you will agree to our request.

We look forward to receiving confirmation to the new arrangements for payment.

**中**

过去，我们以即期信用证的方式与你们进行交易。我们现在想提出一个不同的安排。当货物准备好装运，并且舱位已订好时，你方电传给我们，然后我们用电汇全额支付。

我们要求这种让步，这样我们就可以给我们的客户一个具体的交货日期，也节省了开立信用证的费用。我们认为这种安排对你方没有多大影响，但对我们的销售有帮助，我们相信你方会同意我们的要求。

我们期待收到你方对新付款安排的协议的确认。

**PART 3** 新支付结算方式 *New Payment Settlement*

## Unit 2 回复新付款方式
### *Responding by New Payment Methods*

当客户提出想要更改付款方式时，外贸业务员可根据自身情况，回函进行答复。

## 常用词汇 *Vocabulary*

### 1. adhere  vi. 遵守；坚持；黏附

【双语例句】

They failed to adhere to our original agreement.
他们未能遵守我们原定的协议。

【用法解析】

"adhere"的基本意思是"黏附，附着"，引申于人时则指有意或自愿接受教义或信仰等，即坚持决定、习惯、意见和计划等。

### 2. exceed  vt. 超过；超出  vi. 领先

【双语例句】

Demand began to exceed supply.
开始供不应求。

【用法解析】

"exceed, excel, outdo, outstrip, surpass, transcend"的共同意思是"超过"，其区别在于："exceed"指超出权利、权力的限度或管辖的范围，也指超出规定的时空范围，还指在大小、数量和程度上超过；"excel"指在成就或学识上胜过他人；"outdo"指有意打破先前的纪录或胜过前人；"outstrip"指在竞赛、竞争中超过对手；"surpass"指在质量上、气力上、速度上和技术上等超过对方；"transcend"原指超越世俗和物质世界等，暗示高高凌驾于一切事物之上。

## 基本词汇 | *Basic Words*

**current** [ˈkɜːrənt]  adj. 当前的

**association** [əˌsoʊsiˈeɪʃn]  n. 协会

**ready** [ˈredi]  adj. 准备好

**practice** [ˈpræktɪs]  v. 练习

**figure** [ˈfɪɡjər]  n. 数字

**spend** [spend]  v. 用；花

## 情景实例 | *Scene Example*

### 1. 拒绝更改

在收到客户要求更改付款方式的邮件后，由于己方公司一直坚持信用证的付款方式，因此外贸业务员回函表示拒绝。

## 英

Thank you for your letter of 19 January asking for a change in payment terms.

There is nothing unusual in our current arrangement. From the time you open credit until the shipment reaching your port spends normally about three months. In addition, your L/C is only opened when the goods are ready for shipment.

I regret to say that we must adhere to our usual practice and sincerely hope that this will not affect our future business relations.

## 中

感谢您 1 月 19 日要求更改付款条件的来信。

我们目前的安排是合适的。从你开立信用证直到装船到达你方港口，通常需 3 个月。此外，只有在货物准备装运时，你方才需要开立信用证。

很遗憾，我们必须坚持一贯的做法，并衷心希望这不会影响我们今后的业务关系。

## 2. 同意更改

在收到客户要求更改付款方式为承兑交单后，由于风险太大，外贸业务员回函表示拒绝，但可以破例接受其他的付款方式。

**英**

Thank you for your letter of 15 April regarding payment terms, and noted your proposal for payment under D/A terms.

We regret that we are unable to consider your request for payment under D/A terms, the reason is that we generally ask for payment by Letter of Credit. But, as an exceptional case, considering we have established close long-term partner relationship, we are prepared to accept payment on 30% T/T in advance and 70% D/P basis.

However, we wish to make it clear that in future transactions, direct payment will be accepted only if the amount involved for each transaction is less than USD $5,000. Should the amount exceed that figure, payment by letter of credit will be required.

We would like to say that this exception is allowed only in the light of our long and mutually beneficial association. We sincerely hope that the above payment terms will be acceptable to you and look forward to hearing from you soon.

May the future discussions between our companies will lead to further mutually beneficial business.

**中**

感谢你方 4 月 15 日关于付款方式的来函，并注意到你方提出的以承兑交单方式付款的建议。

很遗憾，我方无法接受你方承兑交单的要求，理由是我们一般要求用信用证付款。但是，考虑到我们建立了密切的长期合作关系，我们准备破例接受以电汇预付 30% 货款和付款交单 70% 货款的方式付款。

然而，我们希望明确表明，在今后的交易中，只有每笔交易金额少于 5 000 美元，才可接受直接付款。如果金额超过这个数字，那么付款方式为信用证付款。

需要说明，这是因为双方长期的互惠互利关系，才存在这种例外。我们真诚地希望上述付款条件能为贵方所接受，并期待尽快得到贵方的答复。

我们希望通过公司之间的交流促进我们之间互利互惠的贸易。

---

**Tips** *如何快速完成收付款?*

1. 信用证和电汇。对卖家来说是最安全的，但如果客户仅需向卖家支付几十美元至几百美元，就会显得非常麻烦。此种收款方式适合于大金额的外贸交易。

2. PayPal 收款方式。有两种用法，一种是直接把账号给买家，另外一种是开账单给买家付款。PayPal 对于买卖双方来说都比较安全，而且最易被购买商品的新商户接受。适合零售型外贸商户或批发兼零售的小金额交易。

3. 速汇金、西联汇款。只需把自己的名字告诉给买家，然后带着对方提供的汇款信息，就可以在指定银行填表接受汇款。由于资金是瞬间到账，容易被一些国际欺诈所利用，假设卖家有欺诈行为，买家将拿卖家毫无办法。比较适合金额较大的对外贸易。

4. 国际支付宝。一般用于"速卖通"，是速卖通上的首选收款方式。具体使用方法参照国内支付宝。

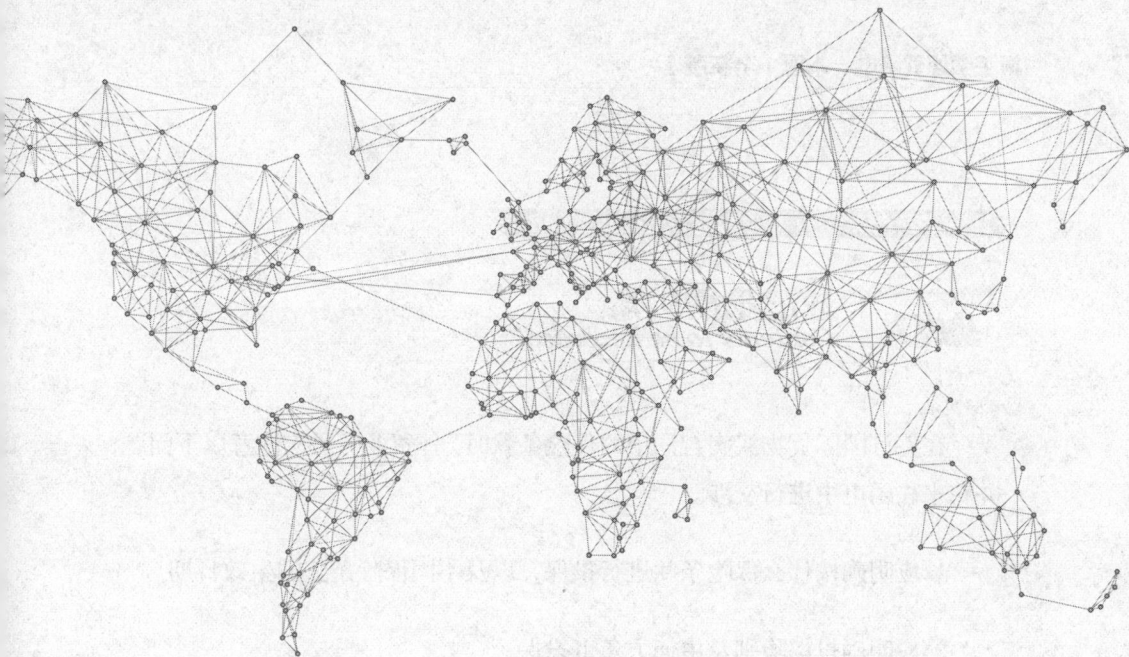

# CHAPTER 08

保险与售后函电

*Insurance and After-sale Letters*

在订单操作过程中，外贸业务员需要处理好保险问题，
以免在发生意外后，双方因保险索赔问题产生纠纷。
在售出产品后，应及时跟进，询问产品和市场情况，
改进产品和推荐相关产品，以维系客户关系。

PART 1  与保险有关的函电 *Insurance Letter*

PART 2  往来商议保险条款 *Insurance Terms Negotiation*

PART 3  售后跟进函电 *After-sale and Follow-up Letter*

## Unit 1 应记载的内容
### Contents to be Recorded

在签订国际货物买卖合同中的保险条款时，外贸业务员应注意以下问题，并在来往函电中进行交涉。

1. 应明确按什么保险条款进行投保，以及不同保险条款的生效日期。

2. 应明确投保险别及由何方负责投保。

3. 应明确投保加成率。如加保战争险，应明确"若有关保险费率发生调整，所增加的保费由买方负担"。

在具体交涉保险条款时，双方来往信函的写作步骤如下。

1. 提示合同、货物等。

【邮件示例】
We refer you to Contract No. ...
关于第…号合同。

2. 说明具体保险要求或意见。

【邮件示例】
Owing to ... we would appreciate it if you ...
由于…如果…我们将不胜感激。

【邮件示例】
With regard to…we regret being unable to accept ...
关于…很遗憾不能接受…

3. 希望对方同意。

【邮件示例】

We wish you can accommodate us in this respect.

希望你方在此方面给予照顾。

PART 1 与保险有关的函电 Insurance Letter

## Unit 2 常用术语和句型
## Common Terms and Sentences

在与保险有关的函电中，常用术语如下。

| 术语 | 含义 | 术语 | 含义 |
| --- | --- | --- | --- |
| Natural Calamity | 自然灾害 | Fortuitous accidents | 意外事故 |
| General Extraneous Risks | 一般外来风险 | Special Extraneous Risks | 特殊外来风险 |
| Actual Total Loss | 实际全损 | Constructive Total Loss | 推定全损 |
| General Average | 共同海损 | Particular Average | 单独海损 |
| Sue and Labor Expenses | 施救费用 | Salvage Expenses | 救助费用 |
| Special Expenses | 特别费用 | Basic Coverage | 基本险别 |
| General Additional Coverage | 一般附加险 | Special Additional Coverage | 特别附加险 |

除了常用术语，在交涉保险条款时，还会用到以下常用句型。

Insurance is to be covered by the seller for a sum equal to the amount of the invoice.

卖方按发票金额进行投保。

We shall provide such insurance at your cost.

我们将投保这种险别，费用由你方负担。

As to the goods priced on CIF basis，our company will insure against All

Risks for 110% of invoice value.

按到岸价格成交的货物，由我公司按发票金额的 110% 投保综合险。

After loading the goods on board the ship, you must go to the insurance company to have them insured.

货物装船后，你必须去保险公司为货物投保。

We have covered insurance on the 100 metric tons of wool for 110% of the invoice value against all risks.

我们为 100 公吨羊毛货物按发票金额的 110% 投保综合险。

The insurance covers only W.P.A. and War Risk. If additional insurance coverage is required, the buyer is to bear the extra premium.

该项保险仅保水渍险和战争险。若投保一般附加险，则由买方负担额外保险费。

Our quotation is On CIF basis. If you prefer to have the insurance to be covered at your end, please 1et us knows so that we may quote you CFR prices.

我方报价是 CIF 价，若你方想自己投保，则请告知，以便我方给你方报 CFR 价。

Should the damage be incurred, you may, within 60 days after the arrival of the consignment, file a claim with the insurance company.

如果发生损失，你方可以在收到货物后 60 天内向保险公司提出索赔。

We are enclosing details of the shipment to be insured under our usual conditions.

随函附上我方通常条件下要投保的货物详细情况。

## PART 1 与保险有关的函电 Insurance Letter

## *Unit 3* 样函
### Sample Letter

在对外贸易中，保险纠纷的发生往往与保险当事人保险业务知识匮乏和外贸合同条款签订欠妥有关。因此，在具体交涉保险事宜时，双方一定要确认清楚相关条款，达成一致的认识。

## 常用词汇 *Vocabulary*

### 1. premium   n. 额外费用；奖金；保险费

【双语例句】

He's had to lay his car up for he can't afford the insurance premiums.
因付不起保险费，他只得把汽车搁置起来。

【用法解析】

相关短语有"at a premium（以超过一般的价格）""insurance premium（保险费）""basic premium（基本保险费）"和"additional premium（附加保险费）"等。

### 2. coverage   n. 新闻报道；覆盖范围；承保范围

【双语例句】

This is an insurance policy with extensive coverage.
这是一项承保范围广泛的保险。

【用法解析】

相关短语有"coverage test（覆盖测试）""coverage note（投保单）"和coverage ratio（保付比率）"等。

### 3. incur   vt. 招致；遭受；惹起

【双语例句】

If you don't do the job properly, you will incur blame.
如果你不把工作做好，你将会招人责难。

The city incurred great losses in the earthquake.
该市在这次地震中蒙受重大损失。

**【用法解析】**

相关短语有"incur debts( 负债 )""incur great expense( 须付巨额费用 )"和"incur sb's anger（惹某人生气）"等。

## 基本词汇 *Basic Words*

**extra** [ˈekstrə]  adj. 额外的

**arrival** [əˈraɪvl]  n. 到达；抵达

**insurance** [ɪnˈʃʊrəns]  n. 保险；保险业

**loss** [lɔːs]  n. 损失；亏损

**average** [ˈævərɪdʒ]  adj. 平均的

## 情景实例 *Scene Example*

某供应商收到客户咨询保险事宜的邮件，于是回函告知客户保险条款、险种和索赔事宜。

**英**

Thank you for your letter of June 28, in which you inquired about the insurance of your Order No. 235.

Generally speaking, if goods are sold on CIF basis, as it is in your case, we insure goods against ALL Risks for 110% of the invoice value. Should the buyer require broader coverage, the extra premium is for buyer's account.

We would like to inform you that there are three kinds of basic insurance coverage under the Ocean Marine Cargo Clauses of the People's Insurance Company of China: F.P.A.(Free from Particular Average), W.P.A.(With Particular Average), and A/R(All Risks). A/R is the broadest form of coverage.

Should the damage be incurred, you may, within 60 days after the arrival of the consignment, file a claim with the insurance company. In case of the claim, the insured is required to submit the following documents.

1.Original Policy or Certificate of Insurance

2.Original or copy of B/L

3.Packing List and Invoice

4.Certificate of Loss/Damage, or Short-landed Memo, and Survey Report

5.Statement of Claims

Please feel free to contact us again if you have any further questions.

### 中

感谢你方 6 月 28 日的来信，询问关于 235 号订单的保险事宜。

一般来说，货物按 CIF 价格出售，如你方的情况，我们按发票金额的 110% 投保一切险。如买方需要更广泛的覆盖范围，额外的保费由买方负担。

我们希望告知你方，中国人民保险公司制定的海洋运输货物保险条款，包括 3 个基本险别：F.P.A.（平安险）、W.P.A.（水渍险）和 A/R（一切险）。A/R 是覆盖最广泛的险别。

如果发生损失，你方可以在收到货物 60 天内向保险公司提出索赔。进行索赔时，被保险人应提交下列文件。

1. 保险单或保险凭证正本

2. 提单正本或副本

3. 装箱单和发票

4. 丢失 / 损坏证书或货差证明，调查报告

5. 索赔声明

如果你方有任何问题，请再与我们联系。

---

*PART 2* 往来商议保险条款 *Insurance Terms Negotiation*

### *Unit 1*  安排投保事宜
### *Arranging Insurance Cover*

　　在对外贸易中，如果采用 CIF 价格进行交易，则卖方需要安排投保事宜。

除此之外，如果买方希望卖方代办保险，也可进行安排，保险费需要买方另行汇款进行支付。

## 常用词汇 *Vocabulary*

### 1. debit　n. 借方；借项；借；缺点　vt. 记入借方

【双语例句】

Loss incur through this mishap amount 20,000 dollars which debit your a/c.

此次灾祸造成 20 000 美元的损失，须由你方负担。

Per our conversation just now, we will send Debit Note to you for this request.

鉴于刚刚我们的谈话，我们会按要求发送收款单给你方。

【用法解析】

"debit" 的词根 "debt" 与 "owe" 意义相同，表示 "债务，义务"。

### 2. stipulate　v. 规定；保证　adj. 有明文规定的

【双语例句】

The company fails to pay on the date stipulated in the contract.

该公司没有按合同中规定的日期付款。

【用法解析】

"stipulate" 一般是一些明确规定和要求，尤指在协议或建议中规定、约定和讲明条件等。通常在正式场合使用，比如合同、法律和法规等。

### 3. proceed　vi. 继续进行；开始；着手

【双语例句】

We received approvement to proceed with our plans.

我们获准继续进行我们的计划。

【用法解析】

"proceed" 的基本意思是沿特定路线行进或朝某特定方向前进，引申可表示

"进行，继续下去"。相关短语有"proceed to（去往，转入）""proceed along（沿着…前进）"和"proceed with（继续做）"等。

## 基本词汇 | *Basic Words*

**toy** [tɔɪ]  n. 玩具

**print** [prɪnt]  v. 打印

**inconsistency** [ˌɪnkənˈsɪstənsi]  n.（行为的）反复无常

**desire** [dɪˈzaɪər]  v. 渴望；期望

**sight** [saɪt]  n. 看见；视野

## 情景实例 | *Scene Example*

### 1. 要求保险

某采购商与供应商以 CFR 条件成交了订单，这种方式是不含保险的。由于采购商希望对方代办保险，于是发函告知要求。

**英**

We would like to refer you to our Order No.1289 for 500 cases of toys, from which you see that this order is placed on CFR basis.

As we desire to have the shipment insured at your end. Please insure the same on our behalf against All Risks at invoice value plus 10%. We shall, of course, refund the premium to you upon receipt of your debit note, or if you like, you may draw on us at sight for the amount required.

We sincerely hope that our request will meet with your approval.

**中**

请你方注意，我方 1289 号订单下的 500 箱玩具是以 CFR 条件交易的。

因我方希望你方来进行投保，请代表我方，按照发票票面金额的 110% 投保一切险。一收到你方的索款通知，我方就将保费支付给你方。或者如果你方愿意，也可以开具相应金额的即期汇票给我们。

真诚地希望你方能同意我方的要求。

## 2. 安排保险

　　由于疏忽，合同上规定的 CFR 条款与信用证规定的 CIF 条款不一致，供应商在检查到这个问题后，发函告知客户，说明为避免延误装运，将代办保险事宜。

**英**

We refer to contract No. 645 for 500 pieces of printed cotton.

The contract was made on a CFR basis, whereas your letter of credit stipulates CIF. This inconsistency must be resolved.

To avoid any further delay in shipping, we suggest that we arrange the necessary insurance cover.

The premium will cost USD $140 and we could deduct it from the 2% commission payable to you. The balance of the commission will be remitted to you as soon as the proceeds from the letter of credit have been collected.

We trust that this arrangement will be acceptable. Please send us your confirmation as soon as possible.

**中**

此函是关于第 645 号采购 500 件印花棉的合同。

合约是建立在 CFR 价格条款的基础上的，而你方信用证规定的是 CIF 价格。很显然，必须要解决该矛盾。

为避免进一步延误装运，我们建议投保必要的保险。

保费将耗资 140 美元，我们暂时从应付给你方的 2% 佣金里扣除。一旦收到信用证的收益，佣金余额将立即汇给你方。

我们相信，这样的安排是可以接受的。请尽快确认。

## Unit 2 收到客户回应
### Receiving the Response from Customers

在 CIF 条件下，保险事宜是由供应商安排的，外贸业务员需要与客户积极沟通，取得客户的确认，否则可能产生误解，损失投保金额。

## 常用词汇 Vocabulary

### 1. quotation　n. 语录；引用；行情；引语；报价

【双语例句】

With regard to our quotation, we will discuss it later.

关于我们的报价，以后再讨论。

【用法解析】

相关短语有"black market quotations（黑市行情）" "the quotations for（…的行情）" "a quotation of prices（报价）"和"quotations on a foreign market（国外市场报价）"等。

### 2. particular　adj. 专指的；特殊的；挑剔的　n. 详情；细节

【双语例句】

He gave full particulars of the stolen property.

他详细列出全部被盗的财物。

【用法解析】

"particular"用作名词的意思是"细节，详情"，指一个事件的具体事实。常与介词"of"连用。

### 3. rebate　n. 回扣　vt. 减少；变钝　vi. 减少

【双语例句】

Could you grant me a premium rebate?

你能给我保险费折扣吗？

【用法解析】

相关短语有"rent rebate（租金回扣）""freight rebate（运费回扣）""export rebate（出口退税制度）"和"tax rebate（退税）"等。

## 基本词汇　*Basic Words*

**wheat** [wi:t]　n. 小麦（植物）

**underwriter** [ˈʌndəraɪtər]　n. 承保人

**consequently** [ˈkɑːnsɪkwentli]　n. 因此

**position** [pəˈzɪʃn]　n. 位置；地方

**interval** [ˈɪntərvl]　n. 间隔；间隙

**harmonic** [hɑːrˈmɑːnɪk]　adj. 和声的

## 情景实例　*Scene Example*

### 1. 接受保险

　　某采购商收到供应商的来信，说明商品应该额外办理破碎险，超出的保费应由卖方承担，于是回函表示同意对方的提议。

**英**

We are pleased to receive your letter of May 25.

We are in agreement with you to cover Risk of Breakage and we agree on your insurance terms. We accept that the extra premium is to be paid by ourselves. We know that according to your usual practice, you insure the goods only for 10% above invoice value, therefore the extra premium will be for our account.

We look forward to a long and harmonic relationship with you.

# 中

我们很高兴收到你方 5 月 25 日的来信。

我们同意你方投保破碎险的建议，且我们同意你方的保险条款。我们接受额外的保费由我们自己来缴纳。我们知道按你方惯例，你方货物的投保金额仅为发票金额的 10%，因此额外保险费由我方负担。

我们期待着与贵公司建立长期而和谐的伙伴关系。

## 2. 拒绝保险

某采购商收到供应商按 CIF 条件下的报盘，由于己方有固定的合作保险商，于是回函表示拒绝保险，请对方提供 C&F 条件下的报盘。

# 英

Thank you for your letter of 1 November, quoting us for 500 metric tons of wheat.

Your quotation is for CIF terms. We regret to say that we prefer to have your quotation and offers on C&F terms.

Our position is that we have taken out an open policy with Lloyds of London. Under the policy, when a shipment is made, all we have to do is to advise them of the particulars. We are on good terms with our underwriters and consequently receive premium rebates at regular intervals.

However, we would also like to know the scope of cover as per your customary practice for our reference.

We look forward to hearing from you.

# 中

感谢你方 11 月 1 日就 500 吨小麦报盘的来信。

你方所报价格是成本加保险费和运费，但是，我方希望你方能给予成本加运费的报价。

我方的情况是，我们的保险单通常由伦敦莱德商船协会办理。合作时，只需在装运时告知详情即可。此外，我们合作非常愉快，并且会定期收到保险回扣。

然而，我方也希望了解和参考你方惯用的投保范围。

希望收到你方回复。

## Unit 1　跟进产品销售情况
### Following up Product Sales

在一笔交易完成后，供应商应及时跟进客户，除了感谢客户的支持和告知售后服务信息外，更重要的是询问产品的销售情况，如果产品销售较好，可以起到加深印象、维系关系的作用，即使产品销售不好，也可以汲取经验，从而改进自身的产品。

## 常用词汇　Vocabulary

### 1. boost up　托起；支援；增强力量

【双语例句】

Doing this will definitely boost up your productivity.

这样做肯定会提高你的生产率。

【用法解析】

口语中"boost up"指"振奋起来"。

### 2. coupon　n. 息票；参赛表；票券；礼券；（购物）优惠券

【双语例句】

To take advantage of our special offer, simply fill in the coupon and send it to us.

要得到我们的优惠，只需填写这份优惠表格并把它寄回给我们。

【用法解析】

"coupon"的基本意思是"礼券，优惠券"，指证明持有人有做某事或获得某物的权利的票据，一般可以撕下。也可作"参赛表"解，通常指剪自报纸等的参赛表。

## 3. revert　　vi. 恢复；回复；归还

【双语例句】

We'll revert to your enquiry as soon as fresh supplies are available.

一旦有货，我们就回复你方询价。

【用法解析】

相关短语有"revert to（回到）"和"revert statement（回复语句）"等。

### 基本词汇　Basic Words

**client** [ˈklaɪənt]　n. 委托人

**grateful** [ˈɡreɪtfl]　adj. 感激的

**hotline** [ˈhɑːtlaɪn]　n. 热线

**growth** [ɡroʊθ]　n. 增加；增长

**award** [əˈwɔːrd]　v. 授予；奖励

**role** [roʊl]　n. 地位；角色

### 情景实例　Scene Example

在产品售出后，供应商发函感谢客户的支持，提供优惠券，并告知售后服务信息，然后询问对方市场上己方产品的销售情况，请求给予反馈。

**英**

I am writing to you to specifically thank you for your recent order. Our clients play an important role in the growth of our company, and we're so grateful that you chose to do business with us.

We hope that you are satisfied with our products. Your purchase really boosted up our profits of this month. With that, I would like to appreciate your purchase and also award you with a discount coupon which is attached to the letter. Next time you place an order, you will be able to buy goods at a lower price.

In case of any problem and queries, please feel free to contact our After-sale Service Hotline at 419-888-8800. Our qualified team will be available to serve you anytime. We are glad to assure you full after sales support service.

One more thing, how's the current selling situation at your end? If you could revert your feedback to us, we would be grateful. Any comments from you will contribute a lot to our future service to you and other clients.

We look forward to hearing from you.

**中**

我写信给你，是为了感谢你方最近的订单。客户对我们公司的发展起着重要作用，我们非常感谢你方选择与我们合作。

我们希望你方对我们的产品感到满意。你方的购买行为使我们本月得到了利润增长。因此，我方非常感谢你方购买我们的产品，同时赠送一张优惠券，在附件中可见。下次你方订货，就能够以一个较低的价格购买商品。

如果有任何问题和疑虑，请随时拨打我们的售后服务热线 419-888-8800，我们的专业团队将随时为您服务。我们很高兴为你方提供全面售后支持服务。

最后一件事，目前你方销售情况怎么样？如果能将你方意见反馈给我们，我们将不胜感激。任何来自你方的意见，对我们将来为你方和其他客户提供服务都是很有帮助的。

等待你方的回信。

---

**PART 3 售后跟进函电 After-sale and Follow-up Letter**

**Unit 2** 掌握最新市场动向
**Mastering the Latest Market Trends**

在后续跟进中，外贸业务员要时刻关注市场信息，根据海外市场的最新动向来进行产品的推荐。此外，还可以向客户询问市场信息，互相交换情报，这不仅可以加深双方联系，也便于己方加深对客户的了解。

## 常用词汇 *Vocabulary*

### 1. capture  vt. 捕获；占领；夺取；吸引 n. 捕获；战利品

【双语例句】

The company looks forward to capturing the Canadian market.

该公司期待占据加拿大市场。

【用法解析】

"capture" 的基本意思是"捕获"，指凭武力、谋略或计划在经过较量取得胜利或克服较大的障碍、困难或反抗之后的获得。用于比喻，"capture" 可表示"迷住，使感兴趣"，指到了爱不释手、近于发狂的程度。

### 2. requisite  adj. 必要的；需要的 n. 必需品

【双语例句】

The state provided the requisite capital for this farm.

国家为这个农场提供了必要的资金。

【用法解析】

相关短语有"requisite variety（必要多样性）"和"requisite condition（必要条件）"等。

### 3. retailer  n. 零售商（店）

【双语例句】

The retailer accepted the shipment on consignment.

零售商收到了运来的寄售物品。

【用法解析】

相关短语有"big retailer（大零售商）""online retailer（网上零售商）"和

"independent retailer（独立经营的零售商）"等。

## 基本词汇 *Basic Words*

**notice** [ˈnoʊtɪs]　n. 注意；理会

**launch** [lɔːntʃ]　v. 上市；发行

**engine** [ˈendʒɪn]　n. 发动机

**pace** [peɪs]　n. 速度；步速

**applause** [əˈplɔːz]　n. 鼓掌；喝彩

**vehicle** [ˈviːəkl]　n. 车辆

## 情景实例 *Scene Example*

　　某供应商新推出的发动机产品在海外市场引起热烈反响，在注意到这一点后，该供应商发函给老客户推荐这款产品，并向其询问汽车市场的动向。

**英**

I would like to bring to your kind notice that our recently launched engine motor is capturing the market at a very fast pace. The product really got a lot of applause in the market. So, for your information, I'm sending you a file of our new product specification in the attachment.

In the meanwhile, we would be really grateful to you if you could provide us the literature and requisite details of your market. As far as I know, lots of US retailers begin to sell vehicles with rechargeable lithium batteries, but we need detailed information.

We would be grateful if you could take prompt action on our request. And you can be sure of our immediate attention to your order, which we are looking forward to receiving.

**中**

我想通知你方，我们最近推出的发动机正以很快的速度占领市场。该产品在市场中得到了广泛的赞誉。因此，我在附件中附上了我们新产品的规格文件，以供你方参考。

同时，如果你方能提供你方市场资料和必要的细节，我们会很感激你。据我所知，美国的很多零售商开始出售车辆的充电锂电池，但我们需要详细的信息。

如果你方能对我们的要求迅速采取行动，我们将不胜感激。此外，请相信我们会立即处理您的订单，我们期待着收到你方的订单。

PART 3 售后跟进函电 After-sale and Follow-up Letter

## Unit 3　提供改进方案
### Solutions to Defect

不同客户有着不同的需求，如果客户指出产品某方面的不足，外贸业务员应该虚心接受，多次反复地与客户进行沟通，并按照客户的要求进行产品质量改进，最后向客户提供改进产品的方案和样品。

## 常用词汇　Vocabulary

### 1. defect　n. 缺点；缺陷　vi. 背叛

【双语例句】

With all its defects the little play has a real charm.

尽管有许多不足之处，这出小戏仍颇具魅力。

We know that it is a defect in his character.

我们知道这是他性格上的缺点。

【用法解析】

"defect" 和 "fault" 都有 "缺点，缺陷" 的意思，其区别在于："defect" 强调不影响全局，美中不足，而 "fault" 强调不十分严重，无伤大雅。用于人时，"defect" 多指人体器官上存在的缺陷，而 "fault" 多指道德行为上的缺点；用于物时，"defect" 指易于察觉的缺陷，而 "fault" 则指功能方面的缺陷。

## 2. corresponding  adj. 相当的；相应的；一致的

【双语例句】

Sales are up 10% on the corresponding period last year.

销售额和去年同时期相比增长了10%。

【用法解析】

"corresponding"的意思是"相当的，对应的"，指一方适应另一方而使双方相称或相等，也可作"符合的，一致的"解，在句中多用作定语，偶尔可用作表语。

## 3. half and half  平分

【双语例句】

I think the loss ought to be shared by both parties — let us say half and half.

我认为损失应由双方承担，我们就各负担一半吧。

【用法解析】

表示平分的短语还有"go fifty-fifty（平分，分摊）""on a fifty-fifty basis（对等地）"和"meet each other half way（对半分）"等。

### 基本词汇 *Basic Words*

**test** [test]  v. 测验；考查

**thickness** [ˈθɪknəs]  n. 厚；厚度

**align** [əˈlaɪn]  v. 排整齐；校准

**gas** [gæs]  n. 气体

**section** [ˈsekʃn]  n. 部分；部门

**degassing** [ˈdeɪgəsɪŋ]  n. 去气；排气

### 情景实例 *Scene Example*

某供应商生产的塑料制品被采购商指出不足后，努力改进技术，在出成果之后发函告知对方，询问是否愿意尝试样品。

# 英

Regarding your request, we have tested the particular item and find there
is some room to improve the quality of it. Please see the defects and our
corresponding solutions below.

Sink Marks: Reducing the thickness of the thickest wall sections.

Vacuum Voids: Ensure that mold parts are perfectly aligned.

Warping: Select plastic materials that are less likely to shrink and deform.

Burn Marks: Optimize gas venting and degassing.

How do you think? Would you like to try the evolved samples for us?
We'd like to receive your valuable comments. Please note that due to the
evolution, the price of this item has to be added USD $1 per unit. We
suggest that we share the cost by half and half.

Awaiting your earliest reply.

# 中

根据您的要求，我们已经测试了特定的产品，发现有改进产品质量的空间。产品
的缺陷和我们相应的解决方案如下。

凹痕：降低厚壁部分的厚度。

真空空隙：确保模具部件完全对齐。

变形：选择不易收缩变形的塑性材料。

烧痕：优化气体排出和脱气的技术。

能否告知你方的想法？是否愿意尝试升级后的样本？我们希望能收到你方的宝贵
意见。请注意，由于产品升级，本产品的价格每单位必须增加1美元。我们建议，
双方对半分担费用。

等待你方的尽早答复。

# Unit 4 推荐相关产品 Recommending Related Products

除了客户询盘涉及的产品外，外贸业务员也要适当推荐公司生产的其他相关产品，以便创造其他的合作机会。

## 常用词汇 Vocabulary

### 1. sourcing  v. 采购

【双语例句】

Many large companies are now sourcing overseas.

现在很多大公司都向海外采购。

I contacted some Chinese suppliers and began sourcing wool products in China.

我联系了一些中国供应商，然后开始在中国采购羊毛产品。

【用法解析】

在工厂采购中，"sourcing"的方式一般具有策略性和一次性，一旦选定合适的供应商并进入正轨，任务就基本完成。

### 2. apparel  n. 衣服；装具 vt. 装饰；使…穿衣

【双语例句】

The store sells women's and children's apparel.

这家商店出售女装和童装。

Have textile and apparel industries in U.S.A declined?

美国纺织业和服装业衰败了吗？

【用法解析】

在表示"服装"的词汇中，"apparel"比较中性客观，现在常用。

## 基本词汇 *Basic Words*

**produce** [prəˈduːs]　v. 生产；制造

**dealing** [ˈdiːlɪŋ]　n.（商业）活动

**manufactory** [ˌmænjəˈfæktərɪ]　n. 工厂

**silk** [sɪlk]　n.（蚕）丝

**continue** [kənˈtɪnjuː]　v. 持续

## 情景实例 *Scene Example*

　　某供应商原本只生产布料，最近拓展了公司的经营范围，新增了成衣的销售业务，于是决定向一些合作企业主动推荐自己的丝绸服装，以期获取与合作企业更多的交易机会。

## 英

It's been six months since we executed your last order. At that time, you informed us that you were sourcing for finished apparel while we regret to say our factory produces only cloth.

However, I'd like to inform you that recently, we step in the apparel manufactory field and got in large quantities of silk apparel. We produce high-quality silk apparel and would be able to manufacture clothing of your own designs to the highest European standards.

Attached please find the catalog of our new products. If you find yourself interested, please contact us ASAP.

We look forward to our continued mutually-profitable business relationship and wish you every success in your business dealings.

**中**

距离我们上次合作已经半年了。在那时，你告诉我们，你在采购成衣，而我们遗憾地告诉你我们工厂只生产布料。

但是，我们想告知你方，最近我们踏入了服装生产领域，并生产大量的丝绸服装。我们生产高质量的丝绸服装，并能够按照你方设计要求，生产满足欧洲最高标准的服装。

随函附上我们最新的产品目录。如果你方感兴趣，请尽快与我们联系。

我们期待与你方继续保持互惠互利的商业关系，并祝您生意兴隆。

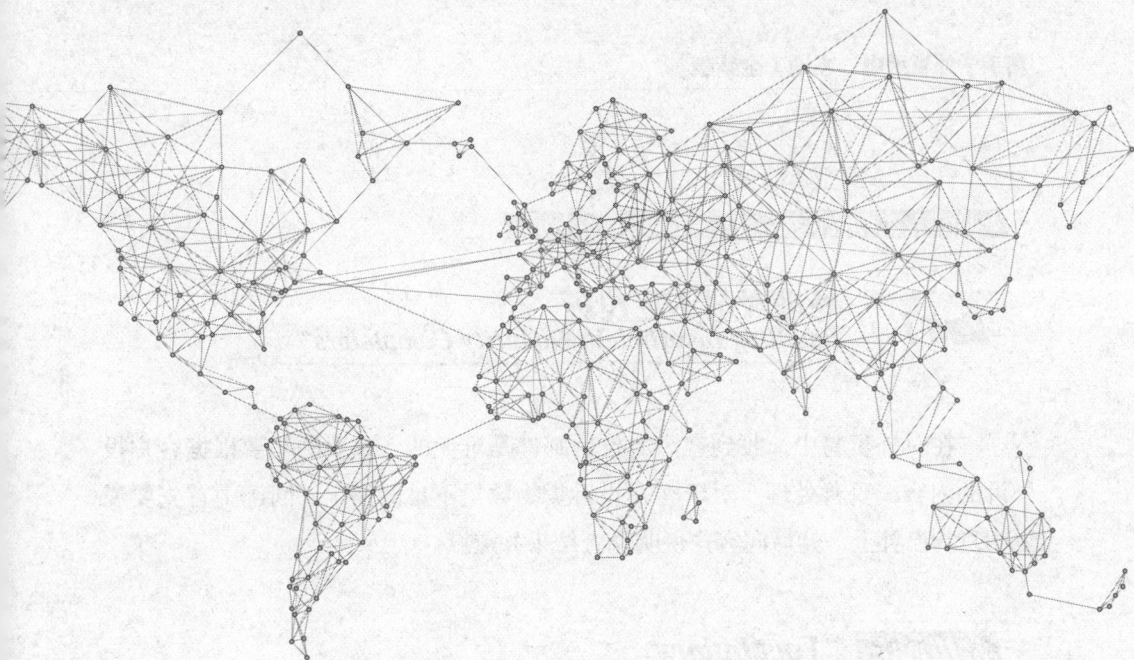

# CHAPTER 09

投诉与索赔函电

*Complaints and Claims Letters*

客户投诉或客户索赔是很多外贸业务员常常遇到的问题，不管是货物迟交、少交、损坏还是其他品质问题，都可能造成外贸双方合作关系出现裂痕。对此，外贸业务员要积极沟通，第一时间处理并给出答复。

*PART 1 处理投诉问题 Handling Complaints*

*PART 2 索赔函电 Claim Letter*

## Unit 1 处理数量不足投诉
### Handling Insufficient Quantity Complaints

在对外贸易中，收到客户的投诉邮件是难免的，重要的是要根据客户投诉的内容，妥善处理。对于客户投诉货物数量不足的情况，回函中首先要说明货物已补上，然后向客户说明调查结果并道歉。

## 常用词汇 *Vocabulary*

### 1. shortage  n. 不足；缺少，短缺

【双语例句】

The shortage can be put down to bad planning.

短缺是由计划不周造成的。

【用法解析】

"shortage"指按规定应具备或需要的数量而没有达到。相关短语有"weight shortage（重量短少）""labor shortage（劳力短缺）"和"severe shortage（严重缺乏）"等。

### 2. tamper  v. 干预；玩弄；贿赂；篡改；损害

【双语例句】

The seal on the ballot box is tampered with.

投票箱上的封条已被损坏。

Why would he tamper the document?

他为什么要篡改这份文件？

【用法解析】

"tamper"指用不正当手段去影响事物。

## 基本词汇 Basic Words

**discover** [dɪˈskʌvər]  v. 发现

**evidence** [ˈevɪdəns]  n. 根据；证明

**failure** [ˈfeɪljər]  n. 失败

**receive** [rɪˈsiːv]  v. 拿到；接到

**number** [ˈnʌmbər]  n. 数量；编号

**department** [dɪˈpɑːtmənt]  n. 部；局

**fault** [fɔːlt]  n. 过错；过失

**worker** [ˈwɜːrkər]  n. 工作者

## 情景实例 Scene Example

### 1. 投诉信

某采购商在收到货物后，检查发现缺少了 10 件订购的货物，于是发函向供应商投诉，要求对方尽快调查和处理。

**英**

We have just received the cartons of goods ordered on May 10.

On checking the goods we discovered that there is a shortage in the number of articles you sent us. We received only 10 pieces of item No. 389 and there should be 20 pieces instead of 10.

We inspected the packing cases, which were in good order and showed no evidence of tampering so that it appears that the shortage is due to a failure in your packing department.

Please investigate the matter and send us the missing goods ASAP.

We are looking forward to your reply. We trust that this kind of mistake will not occur again.

**中**

我们刚刚收到了 5 月 10 日订购的货物。

在检查货物时，我们发现你方寄来的货物数量短缺。我们只收到了 10 件 389 号货物，但应有 20 件，而不是 10 件。

我们检查了包装箱，情况良好，没有任何损坏的迹象，所以看来货物短缺是你方装运部门的错误所致。

请调查此事，并尽快寄给我们不足的货物。

我们期待着你方的回复。相信这样的错误不会再次发生。

## 2. 处理投诉

某供应商收到客户邮件投诉，收到的货物少了 10 件，在调查并补发货物后，回函向客户坦白承认了错误。

**英**

With reference to your letter dated June 2, which complained about the shortage of the goods, we assure that the remaining items as per your order of May 10 last, precisely, 10 pieces of item No. 389, are already on their way to you.

In fact, we have dispatched them by DHL courier, the tracking number is 20650004 and you should receive the missing goods within five days at the latest.

As you pointed out, the fault was due to a failure of one of our packing workers, and we have arranged new checking procedures to avoid such mistakes happening again.

We hope that you will continue to place orders with us and that we can serve you better in the future. Please accept our apologies for any inconvenience caused.

**中**

关于贵公司 6 月 2 日来函投诉货物短缺的情况，我方保证，贵方 5 月 10 日最后一批订货所缺货物，确切地说，10 件 389 号货物，已发往你方。

实际上，我们是通过 DHL 快递寄出的，快递查询号码是 20650004，你方最迟会在 5 日内收到缺失的货物。

正如你方所指出的，该失误是我方的一位包装工人的错误导致的，我们已经安排了新的检查程序，以避免此类错误再次发生。

我们希望你方继续向我方订货，今后我们能更好地为你方服务。对造成的不便，请接受我们的歉意。

**PART 1** *处理投诉问题 Handling Complaints*

## Unit 2 处理错发货物投诉
### Handling Wrongly Delivery Complaints

对于客户投诉错发货物的情况，首先要做的是及时安排缺少货物的装运，然后向客户说明调查结果并道歉。对于错发的货物，可以请求客户暂存以待后续处理，也可以请客户收下作为赔礼。

**常用词汇** *Vocabulary*

## 1. presume   vt. 假定；推测；姑且认定  vi. 越权行事；利用

【双语例句】

We presume that the factory has been fully engaged.
我们推测工厂的生产已经满负荷了。

【用法解析】

"presume" 的基本意思是 "以为，假定"，可用于有经验证明或从已知事实经逻辑推理而得出的事情。用于第一人称时多表示 "冒昧地做…"，为客套用语。

## 2. disposal   n. 处理；处置；布置

【双语例句】

We placed everything at his disposal.
我们把一切事情都交给他处理。

**【用法解析】**

相关短语有"at one's disposal（由某人支配）""leave sth at sb's disposal（把某物交给某人处理）""entire disposal（完全的处置权）"和"disposal of（…的处置权）"等。

## 3. content　n. 内容；目录；含量

**【双语例句】**

A bag with its precious contents was missing.

一个装有贵重物品的包不见了。

**【用法解析】**

"content"可表示"所含之物"，指某一物体中所含的具体东西；表示一本书或文章中所包含的具体或抽象的"内容"；表示某一容器的"容量"或某一物质在另一物质中的"含量"。

**基本词汇** *Basic Words*

except [ɪkˈsept]　prep. 除…之外

assemble [əˈsembl]　v. 收集

situation [ˌsɪtʃuˈeɪʃn]　n. 情况

porcelain [ˈpɔːrsəlɪn]　n. 瓷；瓷器

cutlery [ˈkʌtləri]　n. 餐具；刀具

meantime [ˈmiːntaɪm]　adv. 在…期间

**情景实例** *Scene Example*

## 1. 投诉信

某采购商在收到货物后，检查发现 46 号箱中装的不是己方订购的货物，于是发函向供应商投诉，要求对方更换错误的货物，并提供了采取行动需要的相关文件。

## 英

We refer to our order No. 252.

We have taken delivery of the goods which arrived at Marseilles on July 22. Thank you for the prompt delivery of the order. The goods are correct and in good condition except for one case, number 46.

When we opened case No. 46, we found that it contained porcelain which we had not ordered. We presume that a mistake has been made in the order of shipment. In case No. 46 there should be cutlery.

As we need the articles we ordered to complete our range of cutlery, please make arrangements to dispatch the missing items at once. We attach a list of what should have been in case No. 46. Please check this with our order and your copy of the invoice.

In the meantime, we are holding case No. 46 at your disposal. Please let us know what to do with it.

## 中

来信是关于 252 号订单。

我们已于 7 月 22 日收到了抵达马赛港的货物。感谢你方对订单的及时交货。除了 46 号箱以外，其余货物正确无误，状况良好。

当我们打开 46 号箱时，我们发现它含有我们没有订购的瓷器。我们猜测装运顺序有错误，46 号箱中应该是餐具。

鉴于我方需要将我们订购的特定餐具组成我们的餐具系列，所以请立即安排寄送出错的货物。我们附上一份列表，以说明 46 号箱中应该是什么餐具。请对这份列表和我方订单以及发票副本进行检查。

在此期间，我们暂时保存 46 号箱。请通知我们应该如何处理。

## 2. 处理投诉

某供应商收到客户邮件投诉，收到了错误的货物，在调查并补发货物后，回函向客户坦白承认了错误并道歉。

## 英

Thank you for your letter of July 23 referring to your order No. 252. We are glad to hear that the consignment was delivered promptly.

We regret, however, that case No. 46 did not contain the goods you ordered. We have arranged for the correct goods to be dispatched to you at once. The relevant documents will be mailed to you as soon as they are ready.

We have investigated this issue and find that we did make a mistake in putting the order together. Please keep case No. 46 and its contents until they're called for by our agents who have been informed of the situation.

We apologize for the inconvenience caused by our error.

## 中

感谢你方 7 月 23 日关于 252 号订单的来信。我们很高兴听到货物迅速交付。

不过，我们很抱歉，46 号箱中没有包含你方订购的商品。我们已立即安排正确货物的装运。相关文件准备好后就会邮寄给您。

我们调查了这件事情，发现我们把两个订单的货放在一起，造成了错误。请保存 46 号箱及其中货物，我方代理人会在了解情况后致电你方。

对于我们的错误造成的不便，我们深表歉意。

*PART 1 处理投诉问题 Handling Complaints*

**Unit 3** 处理品质投诉
*Handling Quality Complaints*

对于客户投诉品质不佳的情况，要及时调查，并向客户道歉。一般来说，货物要作退款或退货处理，如果货物较为贵重，则可向客户提供免费维修和技术服务。

## 常用词汇 *Vocabulary*

### 1. refund  n. 偿还；退款  vt. 偿还；退还

【双语例句】

We will refund you if the purchase has any quality defect.

如果所购物品存在质量问题，我们将退款给您。

【用法解析】

相关短语有"claim for refund（要求退款）""tax refund（退税）""refund offset（退税补偿）"和"refund policy（退款政策）"等。

### 2. function  n. 职务；功能；函数；取决于  vi. 运行；起作用

【双语例句】

The machine will not function properly if it is not kept well-oiled.

机器若不能保持良好的润滑性，就不会顺利地运转。

【用法解析】

相关短语有"discharge one's function（尽职）""leading function（主要职责）""function as（担任）"和"primary function（首要任务）"等。

## 基本词汇 *Basic Words*

autumn [ˈɔːtəm]  n. 秋天；秋季              fade [feɪd]  n. 变淡；变暗

pending [ˈpendɪŋ]  prep. 直到…为止          complaint [kəmˈpleɪnt]  n. 抱怨

motor [ˈmoʊtər]  n. 发动机                 oversight [ˈoʊvərsaɪt]  n. 疏忽；忽略

## 情景实例 *Scene Example*

### 1. 投诉信

某采购商在销售衣物后，顾客投诉衣物质量差，容易褪色。采购商经过检查，发现库存商品也存在这个问题，于是发函向衣物的供应商投诉并要求处理。

**英**

We refer to our order No. 150 of Aug. 12 for clothes, your Autumn Catalog.

Some of our customers' report that the colors were fade away after first washing in the washing machine and have asked for a complete refund of their purchase. We checked the remaining clothes we have in stock and we found that many of them had the same problem, due to a defect in manufacturing.

As stated, you must provide us with goods of superior quality. Although this is the first time that we have had to complain about your products and this is the only consignment appears to have such problems. You will understand that we cannot continue to sell your clothes.

Therefore, we are keeping the goods for the time being until you make a solution.

**中**

我们来信是关于 8 月 12 日的 150 号订单，根据你方秋季目录采购的衣物。

一些顾客说，衣服第一次在洗衣机里洗完后就褪色了，并要求全额退款。我们检查了库存中剩下的衣服，发现由于质量问题，许多衣物也有同样的问题。

按规定，你方必须向我们提供品质优良的商品。虽然这是我们第一次抱怨你们的产品，且这是唯一一批看起来有问题的货物，但相信你方能理解，我们不能再售卖你方衣物。

因此，我们暂时保留你方衣物，直到你方做出处理。

## 2. 处理投诉

某供应商收到客户投诉，所购电机质量差，受到顾客抱怨。于是回函表示全权负责，请客户安排退货，己方支付退款。

## 英

Following your complaint of the poor quality of our Universal Motor, we have checked the matter with our manufacturing control. We found that a whole batch of motors, sent out from our factory after June 1 had been poorly constructed because of an oversight of the assembly line controller.

We realize that any accident to our customers, however slight, would have extremely negative effects on our marketing as well as possible legal complications. We would, therefore, ask you, as our long-standing retailers, to contact directly all customers who have purchased the faulty motors and offer to replace it free of charge immediately. We will be more than happy to refund you fully of this.

We rely on your help to overcome the unfortunate circumstances and we assure you that an inconvenience of this kind will not be repeated.

That you very much for your cooperation.

## 中

在你方投诉我们的通用电机质量不好之后，我们检查了生产控制流程，发现在 6 月 1 日之后生产的电机，都因为装配线控制的疏忽导致电机质量差。

我们意识到，对于客户而言，意外无论多小，都会对我们的营销产生极其负面的影响，甚至可能会产生法律纠纷。因此，作为我们长期的零售商，我们希望你方直接联系所有购买错误电机的顾客，并立即提供免费更换。我们将很乐意地为此支付全部退款。

我们需要依靠你方的帮助渡过难关，我们向你方保证，这种事情不会再发生。

感谢你方的合作。

　　某印刷机厂收到了客户的投诉，称机器不能正常工作。由于这些机器价格非常昂贵，于是工厂回函表示愿意派技师免费维修，并提供印刷机的日常维护培训。

**英**

Thank you for your letter of January 26.

We are very sorry to hear about the difficulties you are having with your new 4CP60 printing press.

When our engineers installed the machine last month, they satisfied themselves that it was functioning perfectly. They did, however, have some reservations about the ability of your operatives to carry out routine preventive maintenance.

We believe it is essential that one of our engineers come to your factory for a period of two weeks for the purpose of.

1.putting the press into perfect working order.

2.training at least two of your operatives in routine preventive maintenance.

We hope you will agree to our proposal. There will be no charge since the press is still under guarantee.

We apologize for any inconvenience you have experienced.

**中**

感谢你方 1 月 26 日的来信。

我们非常抱歉得知您使用新的 4CP60 型印刷机遇到了困难。

当我们的技师上个月安装机器时，他们认为机器已经成功运行了。但是，他们对你方操作人员的日常预防性维护技能没有教学到位。

我们相信以下行动是必要的，我们将派一位技师在您的工厂进行为期两周的培训，目的是。

1. 修理印刷机，使其正常工作。

2. 为你方培训至少两名能够进行日常预防性维护的人员。

希望您能同意我们的建议。由于印刷机尚在保修期内，将不收取任何费用。

对你方造成的不便，我们深表歉意。

## Unit 4 处理误期投诉
### *Handling Delivery Delay Complaints*

对于客户投诉未及时交货的情况，要向客户说明原因，并明确告知货物的发货和预计抵达日期，诚恳地向客户道歉。

## 常用词汇 *Vocabulary*

### 1. punctual adj. 准时的；严守时刻的；正点的

【双语例句】

Not being punctual is his greatest shortcoming.

不守时是他的最大缺点。

【用法解析】

相关短语有"punctual for（对…准时的）""punctual in（在…方面不误期的）"和"punctual to the minute（准时，一分不差）"等。

### 2. backlog n. 积压待办事项；存货；垫底大木头 v. 积压

【双语例句】

Orders are starting to backlog faster than we can process them.

订单开始形成积压，我们来不及处理。

【用法解析】

相关短语有"backlog of orders（现有定货量）""significant backlog（有效储备）""backlog document（积压文件）"和"backlog of unfilled orders（未完成订单）"等。

## 基本词汇 / *Basic Words*

**mug** [mʌg]　n. 大杯；缸子

**novelty** [ˈnɑːvlti]　n. 小玩意儿

**compel** [kəmˈpel]　v. 强迫；迫使

**limit** [ˈlɪmɪt]　n. 限度；限制

**season** [ˈsiːzn]　n. 季；季节

**advertise** [ˈædvərtaɪz]　v. 做广告

**cancel** [ˈkænsl]　adv. 取消；撤销

**realize** [ˈriːəlaɪz]　v. 意识到

## 情景实例 / *Scene Example*

　　某采购商订购了 5 000 个马克杯，准备为圣诞节销售季做准备，但供应商迟迟未发货，于是发函投诉对方，并表示如不及时采取行动，接下来将取消订单并寻找替代供应商。

**英**

We refer to our order of November 5 for 5,000 pieces of mugs.

These goods were ordered on the clear understanding that they should reach us by mid–October. They are in fact a fashionable novelty, which we intended to advertise particularly for the Xmas season.

The Xmas sales are now approaching and we received neither the goods nor an explanation. We may run out of stock and be unable to meet our clients' requirements. You will understand that this delay could cause us a loss of business.

As we all know, punctual delivery of the goods is the basis for our good business relationships. Under the circumstances, we cannot wait any longer. So if we do not hear from you by the end of this week, we shall be compelled to cancel the order and seek alternative suppliers.

Please look into this matter immediately and reply us as soon as possible.

**中**

来信是关于 11 月 5 日 5 000 个马克杯的订单。

在订购这些货物时，我们达成了清晰共识，它们将在 10 月中旬抵达我方。由于货物新潮时尚，我们打算在圣诞季做推销。

圣诞节销售季即将来临，而我们既没有收到货物也没有收到任何解释说明，我们也许会用光库存，无法满足顾客的需求。希望你方能明白，这种延误可能会使我们失去生意。

我们都知道，准时交货是我们良好业务关系的基础。在这种情况下，我们不能再等了，所以如果我们在本周末之前没有接到你们的消息，我们将被迫取消订单并寻找替代供应商。

请即刻检查相关情况，并尽快回复我们。

因延误了订单的交货，某供应商收到了客户的投诉，于是回函告知对方延误是由于工厂员工罢工，已安排对方订单的装运，并表示歉意。

**英**

Yesterday, we received your letter complaining about the delivery of 5,000 pieces of mugs you ordered on November 5 and we are very sorry for the trouble caused by the delay.

Unfortunately, a strike in our factory stopped the production for a period of two weeks. The strike has now been settled but we are now faced with a backlog of orders. We are however doing our best to keep the delay of the scheduled deliveries within reasonable limits, and we've arranged dispatch of your order so that you will be able to receive the consignment by the end of next week.

We are extremely sorry for the delay, which you will realize is due to circumstances beyond our control. Please accept our apologies for the inconvenience caused.

We look forward to receiving an early reply.

## 中

我们昨天收到你方的来信，投诉 11 月 5 日订购的 5 000 个马克杯的交货问题，我们对延误造成的损失深表歉意。

遗憾的是，罢工使工厂生产停止了两周。罢工问题已经解决，但我们现在面对着大量订单的积压。不过，我方已尽最大努力将交货期延迟到合理的限度内，并已安排发运你方的货物，以便你方能在下周末前收到货物。

我们为延误感到非常抱歉，希望你方理解这是出于我们无法控制的情况。请接受我们对为你方带来的不便表达的歉意。

期待你方早日答复。

PART 1 *处理投诉问题 Handling Complaints*

## *Unit 5* 处理服务投诉
### *Handling Service Complaints*

对于客户投诉服务态度的情况，要向客户说明原因，并明确告知货物的发货和预计抵达日期，诚恳地向客户道歉。

## 常用词汇 *Vocabulary*

### 1. manner   n. 举止；礼貌；方式；习俗

【双语例句】

The work should have been done in a more satisfactory manner.

这项工作本来可以用更令人满意的方法进行。

【用法解析】

"good manners" 指"有礼貌"，"bad manners" 指"没礼貌"。"manner" 作单数使用时，可以解释为"大方的态度"。

## 2. supervision　n. 监督；管理

【双语例句】

New workers often need close supervision.

新工人通常需要严密的管理。

【用法解析】

相关短语有"under the supervision of someone（在某人监督之下）""technical supervision（技术监督）"和"close supervision（严密监督）"等。

### 基本词汇 *Basic Words*

**appal** [ə'pɔːl]　v. 使惊骇

**employee** [ɪm'plɔɪiː]　n. 受雇者

**distress** [dɪ'stres]　v. 使忧虑

**witness** ['wɪtnəs]　v. 当场看到

**behave** [bɪ'heɪv]　v. 表现

**argue** ['ɑːrgjuː]　v. 争论；争吵

### 情景实例 *Scene Example*

　　某采购商在请求水晶公司检查自己订单时遭到了对方员工的粗鲁拒绝，于是发函向该公司客户经理投诉。

**英**

I am writing to you today to explain about a bad experience I had yesterday. While I was worried about my order and asked one of your sales representatives, Danny, to check the consignment according to my order.

It is appalling to witness an employee of such a respected company behave in such a manner. He brutally refused my request and told me I annoyed him. I was both shocked and disappointed to have been treated in this way. I believe you should be made aware of your employee's actions.

I trust that this is not the way that Crystal Inc. does business and that you will mention my concern with Danny about the incident. I am open to discussing the matter further and should hope that you will respond with a solution to prevent this incident happening again.

I look forward to hearing from you.

# 中

今天我写信给您是为了说明我方昨天的一段糟糕的经历。由于我方很担心订单，就要求你方一位销售代表丹尼，根据我们的订单检查货物。

令我震惊的是，这样一个受人尊敬的公司，员工的行为却是如此。他粗鲁地拒绝了我的请求，并认为我打扰了他。被这样对待，我既震惊又失望，并认为你方应该了解你们员工的行为。

我相信这不是水晶公司做生意的方式，并且希望你会告诉丹尼我的担忧。我愿意进一步讨论这件事，希望你们能采取对策来防止这类事件再次发生。

我期待着你方的来信。

收到客户对员工服务态度不好的投诉，水晶公司的客户经理立即回复表示抱歉，并告知问题已解决，以安抚客户情绪。

# 英

We were distressed to receive your letter of May 4 about the rudeness of our sales representative.

We apologize for the way he acted. His refusal to check the consignment against your order was quite unforgivable. We have checked with our export department and a mistake was made in your order No. 454. The matter is now in hand, and you will receive the missing goods within the next ten days.

We looked into the matter and found out that the representative in this issue was in the process of leaving our company. You happened to telephone him on his final day. It was his lack of responsibility that allowed him to argue with you. We apologize for what has happened.

Due to your complaint, we have intensified the training and supervision of our sales staff.We can assure you that you will receive more courteous and helpful service in future.

## 中

我们很抱歉收到你方 5 月 4 日关于我公司销售代表的无礼的来信。

我们为他的行为道歉，他拒绝根据你的订单检查货物的行为是不可原谅的。我们已与我方的出口部门联系，你的 454 号订单的确出现了错误。这件事已解决，你方将在 10 天内收到丢失的货物。

我们调查了这件事，发现那个代表正要离职，你碰巧在他离职的最后一天给他打电话，是他缺乏责任心促使了他和你争论，我们为所发生的事道歉。

鉴于你的投诉，我们加强了对销售人员的培训和监督，我们向你保证，今后你将得到更礼貌且更友善的服务。

## PART 2 索赔函电 Claim Letter

## Unit 1 客户提出索赔 Compensation Claim

如果客户提出索赔，一般都会明确提供索赔的理由和赔偿金额。对此，外贸业务员既要诚挚表达歉意，又不能鲁莽行事，要做进一步调查后才能对索赔要求进行处理。

## 常用词汇 Vocabulary

### 1. expense   n. 费用；花费；代价

【双语例句】

I can't afford the expense of redecorating my house.

我负担不起重新装修房子的费用。

【用法解析】

"expense"泛指"费，费用"。相关短语有"at sb's expense（由某人付费）""free of expense（免费）" "regardless of expense（不惜费用）" 和"with great expense（花费大）"等。

## 2. amount　n. 数量；总额 vi. 总计；等于

【双语例句】

The total cost of repairs amounted to 100 dollars.

修理费用总计 100 美元。

【用法解析】

"amount"用于表示"量，额"，如重量和金额等。相关短语有"in amount（总计）" "to the amount of（总计达）"和"reach a certain amount（达到一定数量）"等。

## 基本词汇　*Basic Words*

**dozen** [ˈdʌzn]　n. （一）打

**burst** [bɜːrst]　v. （使）爆裂

**compensate** [ˈkɒmpenseɪt]　v. 补偿

**blouse** [blaʊs]　n. 衬衫

**poor** [pʊr]　adj. 劣质的

**tight** [taɪt]　adj. 拮据的

## 情景实例　*Scene Example*

### 1. 提出索赔

　　某采购商收到的货物包装受损，为此不得不更换新包装，于是发函向供应商提出索赔，要求支付新包装的费用。

**英**

We refer to our order No. 848 for 500 dozen silk blouses.

The goods were unloaded yesterday. On examination, the cartons were found be in a damaged condition. Consequently, we feel that we must make a claim against you.

Of the 100 cartons, 40 had burst open due to poor packing. The rest were in a damaged condition.

We have now repacked the whole consignment in new cartons for delivery to our customers. The expense involved amounted to USD $115.

In view of the tight profit margin on this consignment, we must insist that you compensate us for the repacking.

You will be aware that customers are likely to get a false impression of the quality of goods that are poorly packed. We suggest that, in future, you make sure that the goods are properly packed.

We look forward to hearing from you.

**中**

来信是关于 500 打丝绸衬衫的 848 号订单。

昨天货物已卸货。在检查中，我们发现纸箱已损坏。因此，我方认为，我们必须向你方提出索赔。

在总计 100 箱中，40 箱由于包装不良而爆裂。其余的都已损坏。

我们现在已经将全部货物重新包装，放入了新的货箱，以交付给我们的客户。涉及的费用为 115 美元。

鉴于这批货物的利润不大，我们要求你方赔偿我们重新包装的费用。

你方应该知道，客户很可能会对包装不良的商品的质量产生消极印象。我们建议你方今后确保货物妥善包装。

期待你方的回复。

## 2. 道歉并调查

某供应商收到客户发来的邮件，告知收到了受损的货物，为此发函向客户表示歉意，并请求对方提供调查报告和照片，以便展开调查。

## 英

We regret to hear that you received damaged goods and we apologize for any inconvenience.

We will thoroughly investigate the matter and try to resolve it as quickly as possible.

To avoid any delays in processing your claim, please email the survey report and photos to damage@crystal.com. We will contact you within 48 hours upon receipt of the survey report and photos. Thank you for your cooperation and we appreciate your business.

Should you have any questions, please do not hesitate to contact me.

## 中

我们很遗憾得知你方收到了损坏的货物，我们为造成的任何不便表示歉意。

我们将彻底调查此事，并尽快解决。

为了避免处理你方索赔时的任何延误，请将调查报告和照片发到这个邮箱 damage@crystal.com。我们将在收到调查报告和照片的 48 小时内与你方联系。谢谢你方的合作，我们感谢你方与我们进行的交易。

如果你方有任何问题，请随时与我们联系。

---

**PART 2** 索赔函电 *Claim Letter*

## Unit 2 确定赔款金额
### Determining the Amount of Compensation

对于客户的索赔要求，外贸业务员不能一味向客户让步或全盘拒绝，而要根据实际情况，与客户协商确定合理的金额，这样才不会影响未来的合作。

## 常用词汇 *Vocabulary*

### 1. claim　n. 要求；断言；声称　vt. 请求；主张；声称；断言

【双语例句】

The government would not even consider his claim for money.

政府甚至不考虑他的赔款要求。

【用法解析】

相关短语有"claim against（有权利要求得到）""put in a claim for（提出有权得到）""claim back（要求付还）"和"set up a claim to（提出…的要求）"等。

### 2. rest with　归于；在于；取决于

【双语例句】

It rests with the committee to decide.

这事要由委员会来决定。

【用法解析】

"rest upon"指"依赖于，取决于"，而"rest with"除了"取决于"的含义，还有"在…手中，存在于，归属于"的含义。

## 基本词汇 *Basic Words*

admit [əd'mɪt]　v. 承认　　　　　　unfair [ˌʌn'fer]　adj. 不公正的

rest [rest]　v.（使）倚靠　　　　　fee [fiː]　n. 报酬

value ['væljuː]　n.（商品）价值

## 情景实例 *Scene Example*

　　某供应商收到了客户对受损货物的索赔函，在经过调查后，发现货物受损是由于己方包装拙劣，于是回函表示将发去替换品，并愿意赔偿对方受损货物的价值和商检费。

**英**

We've looked into your claim as to the damaged goods, and with much regret we have to admit the unsatisfactory packing resulting in your receiving the damaged goods. We'll complete your order and send replacements for the damaged ones.

However, we couldn't agree to accept all your claim. It is unfair to make a claim against us for all the losses, including your retail margin. We've completed your order in time and the goods are of high quality as always.

Since the responsibility rests with us, we are ready to pay the value of the damaged goods and your inspection fee. Meanwhile please return the damaged goods back to us, we will pay the freight fee.

Sorry again for the inconvenience we caused. We should be obliged by your early reply.

**中**

我们已调查了你方对受损货物的索赔，带着深深的歉意，我们不得不承认，包装拙劣是导致你方收到受损货物的原因。我们会完成你方的订单，为你方发去受损货物的替换品。

然而，我们不能接受你方的所有索赔要求。向我们索赔所有的损失，包括零售利润在内，这是不公平的。我们及时完成了订单，货物也一如既往的高质量。

因为责任在我们，我们愿意支付受损货物的价值和你方所支付的商检费。同时请将破损的货物送回给我们，我们将支付运费。

再次抱歉给你方带来了不便。若能尽快回信，将不胜感激。

---

**PART 2  索赔函电 Claim Letter**

**Unit 3  请求分期赔款**
**Asking for Installment**

在支付客户赔偿金时，请求对方允许分期赔款是一个很好的方式。既能缓解公司流动资金压力，也能在每一次支付赔款时，用通知邮件打动客户的心，重新挽回客户。

## 常用词汇 *Vocabulary*

### 1. compensation  n. 补偿；赔偿；赔偿金

【双语例句】

They disallowed our claim for compensation.

他们否决了我们的索赔要求。

【用法解析】

"compensation" 一般常用作不可数名词，意思是"补偿，赔偿"，后面常接介词"for"，表示"损失或损伤的赔偿"。

### 2. indemnity  n. 保证；赔偿；保险

【双语例句】

You will get the sum of the indemnity if the freight were procrastinated.

如果货运耽搁，你会收到全额退款。

【用法解析】

"indemnity" 含有担保及赔偿的双重意义，即一方担保不使他方受有损害，他方若受有损害则由该方负责赔偿或补偿。

## 基本词汇 *Basic Words*

| | |
|---|---|
| **improper** [ɪmˈprɑːpər]  adj. 不合适的 | **prepare** [prɪˈper]  v. 有准备 |
| **offer** [ˈɔːfər]  v. 主动提出 | **isolate** [ˈaɪsəleɪt]  v.（使）隔离 |
| **appropriate** [əˈproʊprieɪt]  adj. 合适的 | **affect** [əˈfekt]  v. 影响 |

情景实例 *Scene Example*

某供应商收到了客户对受损货物的索赔函，要求 3 万美元的赔偿。由于无力支付，于是回函请求降低索赔金额为 1 万美元，并请求允许分期付款。

**英**

The letter is with the reference to the claim letter, which we have received on October 7, regarding the goods received in a damaged condition.

Under investigation, it was found that the goods damaged due to the improper packaging. Please accept our apology for the damaged goods and inconvenience caused. We are pleased to inform you that we'll complete your order and send replacements for the damaged ones. Also, appropriate action has been taken by the delivery department to avoid further damages.

Again, we sincerely apologize for the damage and loss you came across over the incident. However, it is impossible for us to accept the compensation charge which is up to USD $30,000. We are prepared to offer $10,000 in full and final compensation. As our factory is small, it is the best compensation we can offer. Please note that we must pay in installments of 3 months, with the first payment to be two weeks later, then once a month after that, for we are not able to make you a settlement at the moment.

We truly hope that due to this isolated incident, our business relations will not be affected. We look forward to serving your company better in future.

**中**

来信是关于 10 月 7 日我们收到的货物运到时处于受损状态的索赔信。

经调查，发现货物受损是包装不当造成的。为损坏的货物和给你方造成的不便我们深表歉意。我们希望你方了解，我们会完成你们的订单，给你们发去受损货物的替换品。同时，装运部门也采取了一定措施，以避免再造成类似的损坏。

为此事中你方遭受的破坏和损失，我们再次真诚地道歉。然而，我们不能接受高达 30 000 美元的赔偿金。我们准备 10 000 美元作为全部最终补偿。因为我们的工厂很小，这是我们能提供的最高的赔偿金。请注意，由于我们目前实在无力结清该账目，必须分期 3 个月付款，两个星期后付首期款，以后每个月付一次。

我们真的希望这一个别事件不会影响我们的业务关系。我们期待着未来更好地为贵公司服务。

## PART 2 索赔函电 Claim Letter

### Unit 4　请求延期赔付
### Asking for Deferred Compensation

协商赔偿金，是要在不得罪客户的情况下，尽量为公司争取最大的利益。因此，如果客户拒绝减免赔偿金，那么外贸业务员可以先请求延期赔付，这往往能在争取时间的同时，取得客户的退让。

## 常用词汇　Vocabulary

### 1. negligence　n. 疏忽；不修边幅；渎职

【双语例句】

He was sharply reprimanded for his negligence.
他因玩忽职守而受到严厉的申斥。

【用法解析】

"negligence, neglect" 都可表示 "疏忽"，其区别在于："neglect" 指该做而没做，针对疏忽或弃置工作，表示有意识地明知故犯；"negligence" 特指人或团体对工作的态度不认真、责任心不强或疏忽大意等，往往有经常不注意的意思。

### 2. mishandle　vt. 粗暴对待；马虎对待

【双语例句】

We wish to assure you that such mishandling will not occur again.

我方保证今后此类失误不再发生。

**【用法解析】**

相关短语有 "mishandle babies（虐婴）" "abuse mishandle（侵害）" 和 "mishandle a ball（没掌握好球，接球失误）" 等。

## 3. allowance　n. 零用钱；津贴；限额，定量；允许；折扣；考虑

**【双语例句】**

We may offer you allowance on a sliding scale in order to open up the new market.
为了开拓市场，我们可以给你提供浮动折扣。

**【用法解析】**

"allowance" 的基本意思是 "津贴，补助，零用钱"，这种津贴或补助一般是按一定规律或为某种特殊目的定时供应之物（多为钱）。"make allowance" 后接事物时，表示 "考虑到，估计到"；后接人时，表示 "体谅，谅解"。

### 基本词汇　*Basic Words*

**railway** [ˈreɪlweɪ]　n. 铁路　　　　**entire** [ɪnˈtaɪər]　adj. 全部的

**apology** [əˈpɑːlədʒi]　n. 道歉　　　**settle** [ˈsetl]　v. 解决

**assure** [əˈʃʊr]　v. 使确信

### 情景实例　*Scene Example*

　　某供应商收到客户对货物受损的抱怨邮件后，为了挽回客户，回信解释原因，表示免费更换，给予折扣承诺，并告知对方将给予 2 万美元的利润补偿。

**英**

Your letter dated February 25 complaining about damaged goods has been duly received. We are sorry to learn that by some negligence on the part of our packing department and partly due to the mishandling of goods by the railway, you have received the consignment in a damaged condition.

As a token of apology, the company has decided to give you a 20% allowance for your further purchase from our company and also to replace the entire damaged products without charging any additional cost. Also, our company would offer your margin loss on these items. We shall remit to you an amount of $20,000 in compensation for the loss, which will be settled after 6 months.

We regret once again the inconvenience caused to you and would like to assure you that such things will not happen in future.

**中**

你方 2 月 25 日投诉货物损坏的来信已收到。我们很遗憾地得知你方收到了破损货物，由于我们包装部门的疏忽及铁路运输的装卸失误。

为了表示歉意，公司决定下一单给你方 20% 的折扣，并在不收取额外费用的情况下更换全部损坏的产品。另外，我公司将为你方损失的利润进行赔偿。我们准备汇给贵方 20 000 美元，以赔偿由此引起的损失，款项将在 6 个月后汇出。

我们再次对给您造成的不便表示遗憾，并向您保证，以后不会发生这样的事情。

*PART 2 索赔函电 Claim Letter*

**Unit 5** 商议代替赔款的方式
*Negotiation for Alternatives*

索赔不一定要用钱来解决，外贸业务员可以和客户协商如给予下一次订单优惠，用货物残余价值冲抵部分赔偿，补上损失货物甚至发运更好的货物等方式，尽量避免赔款。

## 常用词汇 *Vocabulary*

### 1. dispose  v. 清除；处理掉；解决；杀死；打败

【双语例句】

Most complaints can be disposed of pretty quickly.

大多数投诉可以很快地解决。

【用法解析】

"dispose"的基本意思是"处置，处理"，表示性情、情绪、脾气和态度等影响某人采取某种态度或已受影响而采取了这种态度。引申可作"布置，准备做"解。

### 2. inferior  adj. 次等的；不如的；下级的  n. 下级；属下

【双语例句】

They never sell inferior goods.

他们从不销售次货。

【用法解析】

相关短语有"inferior by comparison（相形见绌）""inferior in（在…方面低下的）""inferior to（低于，劣于）""inferior court（初级法庭）"和"inferior limit（下限）"等。

## 基本词汇 *Basic Words*

**financial** [faɪˈnænʃl]  adj. 财政的

**obtainable** [əbˈteɪnəbl]  adj. 可获得

**secondly** [ˈsekəndli]  adv. 第二

**carry** [ˈkæri]  v. 拿；提

**perfect** [pərˈfekt]  adj. 完美的

## 情景实例 *Scene Example*

某供应商不愿向客户支付赔款，向客户发函商议代替赔款的方式，提出用破损货物冲抵赔偿金、发运优质货物替换及给予下一单优惠等方式。

**英**

Since we face a difficult financial situation, I am writing for your permission of alternatives.

Firstly, we are not going to carry these damaged goods back. If you care to dispose of the inferior goods at the best price obtainable, we'd like to use the payment as our compensation fee.

Secondly, we will send perfect goods with a qualified certificate to you. Should you prefer, of course, we will pay the freight charges.

Lastly, we are willing to give you an 18% allowance of the next shipment to compensate you for the loss.

We are completely responsible for this accident. We warrant that we won't make this kind of mistake again.

**中**

鉴于现在我们面临着困难的财务状况，我方请求你方接受替代方案。

首先，破损货物我们不打算运回了。如果你方能以最优惠的价格处理劣质货物，我们希望以这部分款项作为赔偿金。

其次，我们将寄送最优质的货物给你方，并附有产品合格证书。如果你方愿意，当然，我们会支付运费。

最后，下一次的货物订单，我方准备给予 18% 的折扣，以补偿你方的损失。

这次事故完全是由我方失误造成的，我方保证今后不再发生这类错误。

---

*PART 2 索赔函电 Claim Letter*

## Unit 6 拒绝向客户赔款
### Declining a Request For a Claim

客户的索赔并非都是有理有据的，如果调查表明问题的责任方不是供应商，就应该说明真相，让对方向真正的责任方索赔。如果客户纯粹出于主观的对货物不满进行索赔，则应解释清楚，得到客户理解。

## 常用词汇 Vocabulary

### 1. lodge　n. 小屋；门房　v. 存放；安顿；提出（报告、抗议等）

【双语例句】

The buyer has the right to lodge a claim on the defective goods.

对于不合格的货物，买方有权提出索赔。

【用法解析】

相关短语有"lodge a protest（提出抗议）""lodge an appeal（提出恳求）""lodge firmly（强烈地抗议）"和"lodge against（提出…控诉）"等。

### 2. inventory　n. 详细目录；存货（清单）vt. 编制（详细目录）

【双语例句】

All of the inventory has been tagged and referenced.

所有存货清单都被贴上了标签，以备参考。

【用法解析】

相关短语有"average inventory（平均存货）""inventory turnover（存货周转率）"和"optimal inventory（最优库存）"等。

## 基本词汇 Basic Words

**rough** [rʌf]　adj. 粗暴的

**render** [ˈrendər]　v. 使成为

**complex** [ˈkɑ:mpleks]　adj. 复杂的

**transit** [ˈtrænzɪt]　n. 运输；运送

**carpet** [ˈkɑ:rpɪt]　n. 地毯

**perhaps** [pərˈhæps]　adv. 可能；大概

## 情景实例 Scene Example

### 1. 非己方责任

收到货物受损的投诉后，供应商经过调查认为己方装运时没有差错，责任应在船运公司方面，于是发函向客户解释。

**英**

We are regret to receive your complaint about damage to the porcelain we sent you on March 23.

However, we would like to assure you that the goods were packed with great care strictly in accordance with your instructions and were in perfect condition when they were on board the ship, and the damage must have occurred by rough handling during transit. Thus, we could not find any error on our part, and we are not responsible for the damage.

We suggest that you lodge a claim with the shipping company. We shall be ready to render any assistance to you.

We are deeply sorry to learn from you about this unfortunate incident and we hope you will be able to find a satisfactory settlement soon.

**中**

我们很遗憾收到你方对 3 月 23 日抵达的瓷器受损的投诉。

然而，我们向你方保证，货物包装是严格按照你方指示进行的，在装船时处于完好状态，破损一定是运输途中的粗鲁搬运造成的。因此，我方认为我们不是过错方，此次货物损坏不是我方的责任。

我们建议你方向船运公司提出索赔，我们随时准备向你方提供帮助。

我们很遗憾听说这一不幸的事，希望你方能尽快找到令人满意的解决办法。

### 2. 无理索赔

某采购商向供应商订购了一批地毯，规格和设计均按照己方要求特别定制，但收货后认为不满意想要退货。供应商发函表示拒绝。

**英**

Thank you for your letter of 10 March regarding your order No. 354 for 50 carpets manufactured according to your client's design and specifications.

We are appreciate for your questions. At the same time, we are sure that you can understand the difficulties we had in satisfying your client's complex specifications.

Since the consignment is a special design, made to order for your client, we are unable to return it to our inventory. Consequently, we cannot fulfill your request.

Perhaps your client can find another use for these specially designed carpets.

Thank you for giving us this opportunity to explain the situation.

**中**

感谢你方 3 月 10 日关于订单 354 号的来信，该订单是根据你方客户的设计和规范要求而生产的 50 条地毯。

我们感谢你方提出的问题。同时，我们相信你方能明白，要满足你方客户复杂的规格要求，我们面临很大的困难。

既然此货物是为你方客户的订单而特别设计的，我们无法收回作为库存。因此，我们不能答应你们的请求。

也许你们的客户能为这些特别设计的地毯找到别的用处。

谢谢你方给我们这个机会来解释情况。

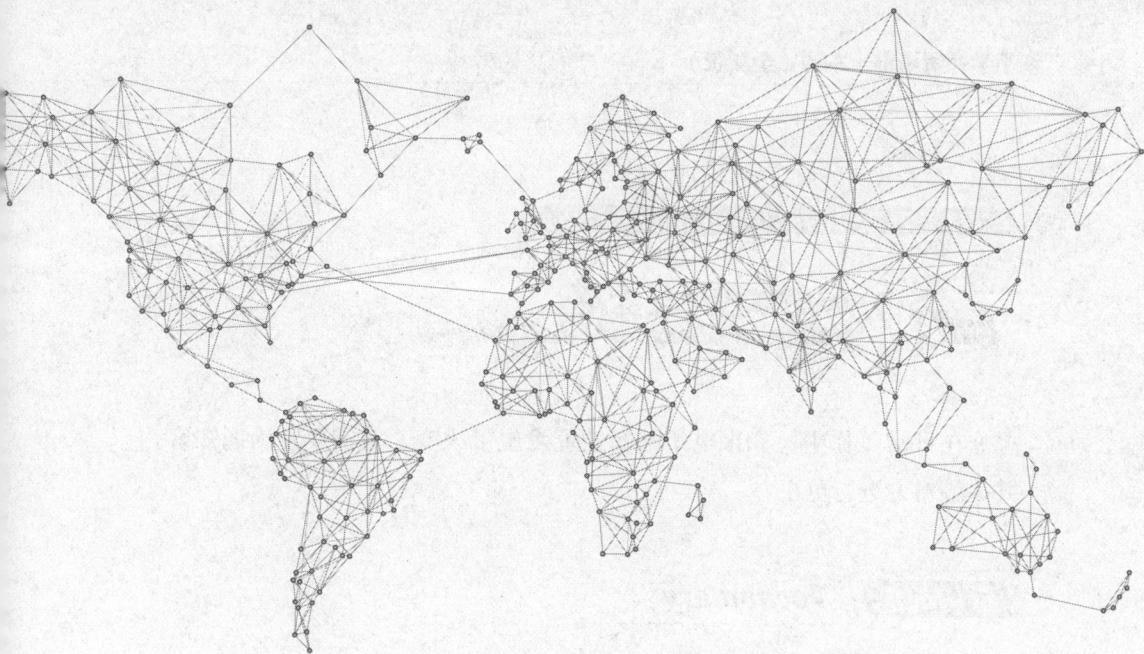

# CHAPTER10 | 其他外贸函电

## *Other Foreign Trade Letters*

外贸业务员平时还需要处理一些不一定直接与工作相关的函电，如日常通知、节日问候、生病慰问和升职祝贺等。这些函电尽管不与生意直接挂钩，但对于维护新老客户关系具有十分重要的作用。

**PART 1** 日常通知函电 *Daily Inform Letter*

**PART 2** 问候函电 *Greetings Letter*

**PART 3** 其他函电 *Other Letter*

## Unit 1 通知邮箱地址变更
### Notice on Change of Email Address

在日常工作中，如果电子邮箱地址发生了改变，就需要发函通知客户，并提醒对方进行更正。

### 常用词汇 Vocabulary

#### 1. terminate   v. 结束；终止；满期；达到终点

【双语例句】

Your contract has been terminated.

你的合同已经被终止。

【用法解析】

相关短语有"terminate in（以…为结尾）"和"terminate contract（解约）"等。

#### 2. accordingly   adv. 因此；相应地；于是

【双语例句】

I have told you the circumstances, so you must act accordingly.

我已将情况告诉你，所以你必须酌情处理。

【用法解析】

"accordingly"作"照着，相应地"解时，常用于句末。

### 基本词汇 Basic Words

email ['iːmeɪl]  n. 电子邮件

direct [dəˈrekt]  adj. 直接的

cause [kɔːz]  v. 导致

previous [ˈpriːviəs]  adj. 先前的

keep [kiːp]  v. 保持

**情景实例** *Scene Example*

某公司将从 5 月 23 日起使用新的电子邮件地址，于是统一发函给客户说明这一事项，并提醒对方及时更新通讯录。

# 英

Our email address has been changed, please update your records.

We shall start using a new email address"gt@abc.com" from May 23, and the previous address of "gtc@abc.com" will be terminated accordingly.

Please update our contact information in your address book and direct your messages to our new email address.

Your messages are important to us, thanks for keeping our information up to date. We are sorry for any inconvenience that may be caused for you.

# 中

我们的电子邮件地址已更改，请更新你的记录。

从 5 月 23 日起，我们将开始使用新的邮件地址"gt@abc.com"，以前的邮箱地址"gtc@abc.com"也将因此被终止。

请更新你通讯录中的联系信息，并发送信息到我们的新电子邮件地址。

你的消息对我们很重要，谢谢你更新我们的联系方式。对于给你造成的不便，我们感到抱歉。

**PART 1 日常通知函电** *Daily Inform Letter*

**Unit 2** **通知公司地址变更**
*Notice on Change of Company Address*

公司也会遇到搬迁的情况，外贸业务员在发函通知客户时，需要简要说明原因，如搬迁到更宽阔的场地可以更好地发展等，然后提醒对方进行信息更正。

## 常用词汇 *Vocabulary*

### 1. reflect  v. 反映；反射；反省；归咎；显示

【双语例句】

Take time to reflect before doing important things.

在做重大事情之前要从容考虑。

【用法解析】

"reflect" 的基本意思是"反射，照出，映出"，指反射光、热或声音等，也指镜子或水面照的映像。引申可作"反映，表明"解，也可作"考虑"解。

### 2. correspondence  n. 通信；信件；相符，相似；一致，相当

【双语例句】

We have carried on a correspondence for years.

多年来，我们一直互相通信。

【用法解析】

相关短语有"address correspondence（写信）""begin a correspondence（开始通信）""hold correspondence with（和…保持通信）"和"commercial correspondence（商业信函）"等。

## 基本词汇 *Basic Words*

**east** [iːst]  adv. 在东面

**telephone** [ˈtelɪfoʊn]  n. 电话

**service** [ˈsɜːrvɪs]  n. 公共服务系统

**province** [ˈprɑːvɪns]  n. 省份

**above** [əˈbʌv]  adv. 在（或向）上面

**allow** [əˈlaʊ]  v. 允许

## 情景实例 *Scene Example*

广州贸易有限公司在搬迁到新地址后，发函提醒客户更新信息，并表示除地址变更外，公司一切照常运行，并将提供更好的服务。

**英**

Please be advised that we have moved and that we now have a new mailing address. Please update your records. Our NEW ADDRESS is:

No.12, Xingang East Road

Guangzhou City, Guangdong Province

Our telephone number will remain the same: (000)000–0000.

Please change your records to reflect our new contact information and direct all future correspondence to the new address found above. We will continue to offer the same friendly service at our new address, which will allow us to offer an even larger selection of products and services.

You are of great value to our company. Please do not hesitate to contact us if you have any questions.

**中**

请注意，我们公司已经搬迁，现在有了新的邮寄地址，请更新你的记录。我们的新地址是：

新港东路 12 号

广东省广州市

我们的电话号码将保持不变：（000）000-0000

请更新你的记录，以显示我们新的联系信息，并将以后所有的信函发送至上述新地址。在新的办公地点我们将继续提供同样优质的服务，并且在新的办公地点我们能够提供更多的产品和服务选择。

你方对我们公司有很大的价值。如果你有任何问题，请随时与我们联系。

## Unit 3　通知公司新规定
### Notice on Change of Policy

公司有时会出台一些新规定，外贸业务员要及时将这些信息通知客户，并解释原因，以免不必要的误解来影响双方的正常交易。

## 常用词汇　Vocabulary

### 1. incentive　adj. 刺激的；鼓励的　n. 刺激；鼓励；动机

【双语例句】

The company offers a bonus as an incentive to higher speed and efficiency in production.

公司提供红利，作为提高生产速度和效率的激励。

【用法解析】

相关短语有"give incentive（激发）""chief incentive（主要动机）""powerful incentive（强有力的刺激）"和"incentive to（对…的动机）"等。

### 2. be of　具有…性质；内容

【双语例句】

My advice may be of use for you.

我的意见也许对你有用。

【用法解析】

相关短语有"be of help（有帮助）""be of benefit（有益）""be of age（成年）"和"be of effect（有效）"等。

## 基本词汇 *Basic Words*

**indeed** [ɪnˈdiːd]　adv. 真正地

**interest** [ˈɪntrəst]　n. 兴趣

**enable** [ɪˈneɪbl]　v. 使能够

**pleasure** [ˈpleʒər]　n. 高兴

**forward** [ˈfɔːrwərd]　adv. 向前；进展

## 情景实例 *Scene Example*

　　某供应商修改了销售条款，规定对装运途中损坏的货物不负任何责任。其外贸业务员发函将这一改变告知客户。

### 英

It has been a pleasure to serve you in the past, and we look forward to doing business with you in the future.

I am writing to you regarding a change in our policy. To continue to offer you reasonable and competitive prices, we have amended our terms of sale to stipulate that we are not responsible for goods damaged while in shipment. Fortunately, this will enable you to select any freight company who will best serve your interests.

Indeed, we will continue to serve you to the best of our abilities. Please call me at (000)000−0000 if I may be of any service to you.

### 中

一直以来为你服务是我们的荣幸，我们期待以后继续与贵公司做生意。

我们写信给你方是想告知关于我们公司政策改变的情况。为了继续向你方提供合理而有竞争力的价格，我们修改了我们的销售条款，规定我们对在装运途中损坏的货物不负任何责任。因此，你可以任意选择最符合你方利益的货运公司。

事实上，我们将一如既往地竭诚为您服务。如果需要我的效劳，请致电（000）000−0000。

**Unit 4** | *通知离职*
*Notice on Resignation*

外贸业务员不应贸然辞职，而要发函通知自己负责的客户，告知对方接任人员及其联系方式。否则将对原公司造成极大损失，这是不负责任的行为。

*常用词汇* | ***Vocabulary***

## 1. absence  n.缺席；缺乏

【双语例句】

His long absence raised fears about his safety.

他长期不在引起了大家对他的安全的担心。

【用法解析】

"absence"的基本意思是某人"缺席，离开，不在场"，通常指"该在而不在"。指"不在"或"缺席"这一事实时是不可数名词，指"不在场的次数或时间"时是可数名词，有复数形式。引申可表示某人、某物或某事"缺乏"或者"不存在"，即不具有应具备或想要的东西。

## 2. roaring business  生意兴隆

【双语例句】

I wish a roaring business for you all and a continued development in our business dealings!

祝大家生意兴隆，买卖越做越好！

【用法解析】

除"roaring（咆哮的）"外，祝对方生意兴隆，还可以使用"booming（兴旺的）""prospering（繁荣的）""thriving（欣欣向荣的）"和"brisk（活跃的）"

等词汇。

## 基本词汇 *Basic Words*

**pursue** [pərˈsuː]  v. 致力于

**career** [kəˈrɪr]  n. 职业

**estate** [ɪˈsteɪt]  n. 房地产；地产

**together** [təˈgeðər]  adv. 在一起

**real** [ˈriːəl]  n. 真正的

## 情景实例 *Scene Example*

ABC 公司的外贸业务员即将离职，在离职前，他发函向客户表达感谢，并向其说明继任者的名字及联系方式。

**英**

It has been my pleasure to serve you for the past two years. Indeed, I hope that you have been pleased with my service as well.

I am writing to inform you that I will be leaving ABC Co. to pursue a new career in real estate. In my absence, I wish to introduce Lisa(lisa@abc.com), who will serve you in the same capacity as I have.

Allow me again to thank you for the opportunity to work together. If, for any reason, you need to contact me, please do not hesitate to call me at my new number (000)000–0000.

May you a good health and roaring business.

**中**

在过去的两年里为你服务是我的荣幸。我希望你也对我的服务感到满意。

我写信是想告知你，我将离开 ABC 公司，去从事一项新的房地产事业。由于我的离去，我想向你介绍丽莎（lisa@abc.com），她会像我一样为你服务。

请允许我再次感谢有机会与你一起工作。如果因为任何原因，你需要联系我，请随时打我的新电话（000）000-0000。

祝你身体健康，生意兴隆。

## Unit 5 通知休假
### Notice on Holiday Closing

在迎接国庆节或春节等放假较长的假期前，公司应该发函统一通知客户，避免因为误解导致客户流失。

## 常用词汇 Vocabulary

### 1. process  n. 工序；过程 v. 加工；处理；起诉；列队前进

【双语例句】

The plans are now being processed.

计划现在正在审定中。

【用法解析】

"process"作为名词时，意思是"工艺流程，过程"，转化为动词，意思是"加工，列队行进"，即指对某种材料或数据等进行加工处理，有秩序地列队进入某处。

### 2. switchboard  n. 配电盘；电话总机

【双语例句】

The switchboard is manned twenty-four hours a day.

电话总机是一天 24 小时由人操纵的。

【用法解析】

相关短语有"dispatch switchboard（调度交换台）"和"relay switchboard（继

电器盘）" 等。

## 基本词汇 *Basic Words*

**lunar** [ˈluːnər]  adj. 阴历的

**dial** [ˈdaɪəl]  v. 拨（电话号码）

**Chinese** [ˌtʃaɪˈniːz]  adj. 中国的

**public** [ˈpʌblɪk]  adj. 公共的

**meaningful** [ˈmiːnɪŋfl]  adj. 重大的

**abroad** [əˈbrɔːd]  adv. 在国外

## 情景实例 *Scene Example*

　　某公司将在春节期间放假 20 天，为了避免客户流失，于是发函告知客户春节放假安排和紧急联系电话。

### 英

Please be informed that we will be closed from Feb. 5 to Feb. 25 due to Chinese Lunar New Year Public Holiday.

All the inquiries and orders placed after Feb. 5 will be processed and replied back after Feb. 25.

We apologize for the inconvenience, and your understanding is greatly appreciated.

If you are in urgent needs and have to contact us during the holiday, please dial our switchboard at (000)0000–0000.

We look forward to serving you again soon. May the year 2020 be meaningful and prosperous as ever for you!

### 中

请注意，由于农历春节假期，我们公司将于 2 月 5 日至 2 月 25 日期间停业。

所有 2 月 5 日后的询盘和订单将在 2 月 25 日后处理并回复。

我们对给你带来的不便表示歉意，非常感谢你的理解。

如果你有急事，并需要在假日期间与我们联系，请拨打我们的总机（000）0000-0000。

我们期待不久能再次为你服务。愿你 2020 年充满意义，欣欣向荣！

## Unit 6　通知复工
### Notice on Returning to Work

　　在度过一个漫长的假期之后，外贸业务员需要给客户发函，通知对方公司和工厂已经重新开工。

## 常用词汇　Vocabulary

### 1. ongoing　adj. 进行的；不断发展的

【双语例句】

The vitality of our entire team from originates the ongoing study.

我们的活力源于整个团队的不断学习。

【用法解析】

相关短语有"ongoing operation（经常业务）""ongoing project（正在实施的项目）"和"ongoing interface（前向接口）"等。

### 2. materials　n. 材料；原料

【双语例句】

The high cost of raw materials keeps prices high.

原料费用昂贵使得产品价格居高不下。

【用法解析】

　　"material"的基本意思是"材料，原料"，泛指"建筑材料，化肥原料，战略物资，原材料"时，用复数形式"materials"。

## 基本词汇 *Basic Words*

**joyful** [ˈdʒɔɪfl]  adj. 高兴的

**normal** [ˈnɔːrml]  n. 常态

**wonder** [ˈwʌndər]  v. 想知道

**festival** [ˈfestɪvl]  n. 节；节日

**provide** [prəˈvaɪd]  v. 提供

## 情景实例 *Scene Example*

　　在度过春节之后，某公司已重新开工。于是外贸业务员发函通知客户，并询问节前相关订单事项。

## 英

How are you? Happy Chinese Lunar New Year. I hope this joyful festival would bring you happiness as well.

We are back to work today and everything is back to normal. Production is ongoing. Since we have prepared raw materials before the holiday, we now can easily run up to 3,000 pcs within this month.We can stably and easily provide CT101 if you need now.

We wonder whether you have stocked CT101 products before our new year holiday or whether your products arrived at your warehouse at this moment? If you urgently require CT101 products, please don't hesitate to contact us. We will forward our new prices for your reference right now.

By the way, if you need them now, we can arrange the shipment in early March.

## 中

你好吗？农历新年快乐。我希望这个快乐的节日也能给你带来快乐。

我们今天已经重新开始工作，一切都恢复如常，生产也在进行之中。由于在放假前，我们已经准备好了原材料，本月我们的产量可以轻松达到 3 000 件。如果你现在需要，我们可以稳定地提供 CT101 产品。

在新年假期前，你们是否储存了足够的 CT101 产品，或者此刻产品是否运达你的仓库？如果你迫切需要 CT101 产品，请随时与我们联系。我们将立即报最新价格，供你方参考。

顺便提一下，如果你方现在需要的话，我们可以安排在 3 月初装运。

## PART 2 问候函电 Greetings Letter

### Unit 1　圣诞节问候
### Christmas Greetings

　　圣诞节在每年的 12 月 25 日，是西方传统节日，一般欧美地区的客户都会过这个节日，届时可以致以问候。

## 常用词汇　Vocabulary

### 1. prosperity　n. 繁荣；兴旺

【双语例句】

I wished you the life of happiness and prosperity.

我祝你生活幸福，万事如意。

【用法解析】

相关短语有"continuous prosperity（持续繁荣）""economic prosperity（繁荣经济）"和"borrowed prosperity（虚假繁荣）"等。

### 2. allegiance　n. 忠诚；效忠

【双语例句】

His allegiance has never been questioned.

他的忠心从未受到质疑。

【用法解析】

相关短语有"pledge allegiance to（发誓效忠于）""give allegiance to（忠诚于）"
和"natural allegiance（对祖国的忠诚）"等。

## 基本词汇 *Basic Words*

**Christmas** [ˈkrɪsməs]　n. 圣诞节

**peak** [piːk]　n. 顶峰；高峰

**occasion** [əˈkeɪʒn]　n. 时机

**express** [ɪkˈspres]　v. 表示；表达

**treasure** [ˈtreʒər]　v. 珍视

## 情景实例 *Scene Example*

在圣诞节来临之际，广州贸易有限公司的外贸业务员发函给客户，祝福
对方圣诞节快乐，并感激对方的支持。

**英**

On behalf of the management of Guangzhou Trading Co., Ltd., we would
like to wish you and your whole family a Merry Christmas. May this season
of festival bring you true happiness, success, and prosperity!

We would like to express our sincere thanks for your contribution to the
development of our company as our loyal customer. Reaching the peak
of development was of course not possible for us without our customers'
support. We will always treasure your allegiance and trust in our products
and management. May our professional relationship strengthen on the great
occasion of Christmas.

Merry Christmas once again! Have a great time with your loved ones.

**中**

我们谨代表广州贸易有限公司的管理层，祝你和你的家人圣诞快乐。愿这个节日
带给你真正的幸福、成功和繁荣！

作为我们的忠实客户，我们真诚地感谢你为我们公司的发展做出了贡献。如果没有后方客户的支持，我们当然不可能达到发展的高峰。我们将永远珍惜你对我们产品和管理的拥护和信任。愿这次圣诞节能加强我们的合作关系。

再次祝圣诞快乐！愿你与你所爱的人度过美好的时光。

**PART 2** *问候函电 Greetings Letter*

## Unit 2 新年祝愿
### New Year Greetings

由于新年有除旧迎新的意义，因此在这一天发函给客户祝福的同时，还可以感谢对方一整年的支持，并展望未来的合作。

## 常用词汇 *Vocabulary*

### 1. draw to 逼近，接近

【双语例句】

The 20th century is drawing to an end.

20世纪即将结束。

【用法解析】

相关短语有"draw to a halt（减缓）""draw to a head（达到顶点）"和"draw to a close（告终）"等。

### 2. in terms of 就…而言；在…方面

【双语例句】

In term of money, he's quite rich, but not in term of happiness.

就钱来说他很富有，但就幸福来说就不然了。

## 【用法解析】

相关短语有以下这些："think in terms of imagines（形象思维）" "judge sth in terms of（以…来判断）" 和 "expresses something in terms of（以…来表达）" 等。

## 基本词汇 *Basic Words*

**faith** [feɪθ]  n. 信任

**gratitude** [ˈɡrætɪtuːd]  n. 感激之情

**anticipate** [ænˈtɪsɪpeɪt]  v. 预料

**fiscal** [ˈfɪskl]  adj. 财政的

**peace** [piːs]  n. 和平

**abundant** [əˈbʌndənt]  adj. 大量的

## 情景实例 *Scene Example*

在新年临近时，某公司发函给客户，表达一年来对客户支持的感谢，明年将继续努力，祝福对方新年快乐。

## 英

As this year draws to a close, we would like to wish you a Happy New Year and thank you for your patronage over the years. Our company would not have been this successful had it not been for the support that we have been provided with by you.

Throughout the whole year of 2020, you maintained your faith in us for which we are very grateful. As gratitude for your loyalty, we would like to offer you a 10% discount for the next order. This is our way to showing you that your support means the world to us.

We look forward to more mutual benefits in this coming year . We will do our best to keep our service standards in the next financial year. We wish you peace, happiness and abundant good health in the new year.

As always, we value your feedback. Please feel free to contact us at any time.

**中**

随着今年接近尾声，我们谨祝你方新年快乐，并感谢你方多年来的惠顾。如果没有你们提供的支持，我们公司是不会如此成功的。

2020 年，你方一直对我们有信心，对此我们非常感激。为感谢你方的忠诚，下一个订单我们愿给你方 10% 的折扣。这样做是因为我们想表达，你们的支持就是我们的全部。

我们期待着新的一年将带来更多的互惠互利。在下一财政年，我们将尽最大努力保持我们的服务水平。祝你们在新的一年里平安、幸福和身体健康。

一如既往，我们重视你方的反馈。请随时联络我。

---

**PART 2** 问候函电 *Greetings Letter*

## Unit 3 感恩节问候
### Thanksgiving Greetings

感恩节是美国和加拿大的节日，在这一天发函感恩美国和加拿大客户的支持，是让他们记住你的好时机。

---

**常用词汇** *Vocabulary*

### 1. joyous adj. 充满快乐的；使人高兴的

【双语例句】

Many blessings on this most joyous of days.
在这喜庆的日子里有太多的祝福。

【用法解析】

相关短语有 "Joyous Garden（怡园）" "joyous childhood（欢乐的童年）" 和 "joyous mood（欢乐气氛）" 等。

## 2. persistence　n. 坚持；毅力

【双语例句】

Persistence is one of your greatest assets in life.

努力不懈、坚持到底，是人生最大的资产。

【用法解析】

相关短语有"persistence testing( 持久测试 )""persistence tendency( 持续性趋势 )"
和"persistence effects（持续效应）"等。

### 基本词汇　*Basic Words*

**amazing** [əˈmeɪzɪŋ]　adj. 令人惊喜的　　　**sense** [sens]　n. 感觉

**humor** [ˈhjuːmər]　n. 幽默　　　**especially** [ɪˈspeʃəli]　adv. 尤其

**holiday** [ˈhɑːledeɪ]　n. 假期

### 情景实例　*Scene Example*

　　在感恩节这一天，广州贸易有限公司外贸业务员向客户发函，感谢对方
一直以来的支持，并祝其感恩节快乐。

**英**

On behalf of all of us at Guangzhou Trading Co., Ltd., I wish you a lovely
Thanksgiving and a joyous holiday season.

In this time of gratitude, I want to express my appreciation to you. Working
with you over the past two years has been an amazing opportunity. I
appreciate your high standards, persistence and the fine sense of humor.

For our company, we are thanking you for being part of our growing
business. We value your patronage and appreciate your confidence in
us. Counting you among our customers is something for which we are
especially grateful.

Again, Happy Thanksgiving and enjoy!

## 中

我代表广州贸易有限公司全体员工，祝你度过一个愉快的感恩节和充满快乐的假期。

在这个表达感激的日子，我想表达我对你方的感激。在过去的两年里和你方合作，是我的幸运。我欣赏你方的高标准，坚持不懈以及良好的幽默感。

对于我们公司，我们感谢你为我们日益增长的业务所做的贡献。我们珍视你的惠顾，感谢你对我们的信任。你成为我们的客户，对此我们特别感激。

再次祝你感恩节快乐！

**Tips 节日问候注意事项**

对于节日问候来说，寄送电子贺卡也是不错的选择。对于如万圣节、复活节及各国国庆节等规模较小的节日，只需要在日常往来邮件的末尾加入一句祝语即可。

## PART 3 其他函电 Other Letter

## Unit 1 自动回复函
## Automatic Response Letter

对于工作情况有小变动，而又不需要专门通知的情况，外贸业务员可以设置自动回复函，以通知当前情况，并告知代班者。

## 常用词汇 Vocabulary

### 1. assist  v. 帮助；协助

【双语例句】

I have too much work and no one assists me.

我工作太多，又没人协助我。

【用法解析】

"assist" 是正式用语，它的原意是 "与…站在一起"，现代英语中主要作 "帮助，促进"，指帮助者处于次要或从属的地位。相关短语有 "assist at（作陪，在场帮忙）" "assist in（在…上给予协助）" 和 "assist with（帮助，照料）" 等。

## 2. tag   n. 标签；附属物  vt. 标记；附加

【双语例句】

Let's tag the disk now or else we'll forget which is which.

我们先给这些磁盘贴上标签吧，不然我们就记不清哪个是哪个了。

【用法解析】

相关短语有 "tag goods（给商品贴标签）" "tag as（把…称作）" 和 "attach a tag（贴标签）" 等。

### 基本词汇 *Basic Words*

during [ˈdʊrɪŋ]  prep. 在…期间

helpdesk [help'desk]  n. 服务台

hand [hænd]  v. 交；递；给

concern [kənˈsɜːrn]  n. 忧虑

respond [rɪˈspɑːn]  v. 回应

### 情景实例 *Scene Example*

某公司外贸业务员因事请假 5 天，在此期间工作将由丽莎代班。在离开前，他设置了自动回复函。

**英**

I will be out of the office starting from February 8 and will not return until February 13.

I wanted to assure you that I have handed off all important information to

Lisa(lisa@abc.com) while I am away. Should you have any questions or need anything during this time, please feel free to contact her and she will do her best to assist you.

For any other concerns, please contact our Helpdesk at (000)000-0000.

Any correspondence (email or phone calls) will be responded to within 2 to 3 days when I return. Please kindly tag confidential messages as such.

Thank you in advance.

**中**

我将从 2 月 8 日起离开办公室，直到 2 月 13 日才回来。

我想向你保证，我不在的时候，已经把所有重要的工作交给了丽莎（lisa@abc. com）。在这段时间，如果你有任何问题或需要，请随时与她联系，她会尽力帮助你。

任何其他问题，请联系我们的客服（000）000-0000。

任何来往通信（电子邮件或电话）都将在我返回后 2 ~ 3 天回复。请标注机密信息。

提前谢谢你。

## PART 3 其他函电 Other Letter

### Unit 2 请求客户推荐
### Requesting a Recommendation from Customers

如果外贸公司与知名企业合作，那么利用对方的名气进行宣传是一种有效的营销策略。这时就需要发函请求对方书写推荐语，或同意己方使用对方的名气进行宣传。

## 常用词汇 *Vocabulary*

### 1. highlight　vt. 强调；照亮；使突出 n. 加亮区；闪光点

【双语例句】

Can you give me the highlight of your resume?

谈谈你简历上有些什么值得特别关注的吗？

The ball was the highlight of the London season.

舞会是伦敦社交活动时期的高潮。

【用法解析】

相关短语有 "the highlight of（亮点）" "highlight the problem（突出问题）"
和 "highlight the importance（显得很突出）" 等。

### 2. recommendation　n. 推荐；建议

【双语例句】

I got the job on the strength of your recommendation.

承蒙足下推荐，我已获得这份工作。

【用法解析】

相关短语有 "follow sb's recommendations（听从某人的劝告）" "write sb a
recommendation（给某人写一封推荐信）" "through recommendation of sb（通
过某人的推荐）" 和 "a letter of recommendation（推荐信）" 等。

## 基本词汇 *Basic Words*

**company** [ˈkʌmpəni]　n. 公司　　　**smooth** [smuːð]　v. 使平坦

**run** [rʌn]　v. 管理；经营　　　　**link** [lɪŋk]　n. 连接

**include** [ɪnˈkluːd]　v. 包括

## 情景实例　*Scene Example*

　　某公司与知名企业合作良好，因此发函请求对方书写推荐语，以便己方能够借此进行营销。

**英**

Further to our recent telephone conversation, please find below further details of our reference request. I appreciate the time you are taking to write this reference for our company.

As you are a much valued and long standing customer, I would like to use your recommendation as a reference for customers who visit our company website. It would be appreciated if a few points could be included within the reference. If you could highlight.

1. The benefits of our business relationship.

2. How long have you cooperated with our company?

3. How have our products helped with the smooth running of your company?

As previously mentioned, we will place a link in your reference that can be used to direct customers to your company website. If you have any questions please feel free to telephone to or email me.

I look forward to reading the reference and the benefits it will bring to both of our companies.

**中**

继我们最近的电话交谈之后，关于我方请求你方写推荐语的进一步详情，请参阅以下内容。感谢你方花费时间为我们公司写推荐语。

鉴于你方是我们非常重要及长期合作的客户，我们想使用你方推荐语，作为浏览我们公司网站的客户的参考。如果在推荐语中可以包含以下几点，我们将不胜感激。希望能够重点强调。

1. 和我们做生意的好处。

2. 和我们公司合作了多久。

3. 我们的产品如何帮助你的公司顺利运行。

如前所述,我们将在你方推荐语中放置一个可将客户引导至你方公司网站的链接。

如果你有任何问题,请随时打电话或给我发电子邮件。

我期待着阅读你方的推荐语及因此给我们两家公司带来的好处。

## PART 3 其他函电 Other Letter

### Unit 3 生病慰问函 Getting Well Letter

如果客户生病或受伤,那么向其发送一封慰问函是必要的。一方面表达对他的关心和慰问,另一方面说明工作正常运作,让他不必担心。

## 常用词汇 Vocabulary

### 1. require v. 要求;需要;命令;规定

【双语例句】

Please call if you require assistance.

如果需要帮忙,请打电话。

【用法解析】

相关短语有"require time(需要时间)""be required by law(法律要求)""require from(向…要求)""require sth. for sth.(为某物需要…)"和"require of(要求…)"等。

### 2. recovery n. 恢复;痊愈;复原;重获

【双语例句】

He is well on his way to recovery.

他正在顺利恢复。

【用法解析】

相关短语有"complete recovery（完全恢复）""economic recovery（经济复苏）""recovery from（从…中恢复过来）"和"a speedy recovery to health（迅速恢复健康）"等。

## 基本词汇 *Basic Words*

**accident** [ˈæksɪdənt]   n. 事故

**manage** [ˈmænɪdʒ]   v. 支撑

**comfort** [ˈkʌmfərt]   v. 安慰；抚慰

**week** [wiːk]   n. 周；星期

**through** [θruː]   adv. 通过

**pray** [preɪ]   v. 祈祷

## 情景实例 *Scene Example*

得知客户受伤需在家静养，外贸业务员发函表示关心和慰问，并说明工作正常运行，请对方安心休息。

**英**

I came to know about your accident and feel very sorry about that. I know that you are required to rest at home for a week or two.

We hope that you recover fast and manage through. Please take this comfort in knowing that we are taking care of your business, you just take care of yourself. Get well soon.

Also, please let me know if you need anything. I will be very happy to help anyway.

Praying for your good health and speedy recovery.

**中**

得知你发生了事故，我们感到非常抱歉。我知道你需要在家休息一两个星期。

我们希望你能尽快恢复过来。请放心，我们会处理好你的业务，你只需要照顾好自己。早点好起来。

还有，如果你有什么需要，请告诉我。无论什么都非常乐意帮助你。

祈祷你身体健康，早日康复。

---

**PART 3 其他函电 *Other Letter***

## *Unit 4* 赠送礼物
### *Gift Giving*

在商务合作中，给客户送一些小礼物表示一下心意是在所难免的。对于公司来说，在重大纪念日可以赠送客户礼物。对于个人来说，在客户生日时送上一份礼物，能够巩固双方的关系。

## 常用词汇 *Vocabulary*

### 1. associate　vt. 联想；联合 n. 伙伴；同事；同伴

【双语例句】

Mr. Miller is a business associate of our company.

米勒先生是我们公司的生意伙伴。

【用法解析】

"associate" 通常指在友好平等的基础上进行联合或交往，用作名词意思是"伙伴，同事"，尤指由于共同的职业、地位或生意而经常联系的人，也指有共同利害关系或目的而经常保持联系的同事或伙伴。

### 2. gesture　n. 手势；姿势；姿态 v. 做手势表达；作姿态

【双语例句】

His resignation was merely a gesture.

他的辞职只是一种表示而已。

【用法解析】

相关短语有"make a gesture（做姿态，做手势）""speak by gesture（用手势示意）""diplomatic gesture（外交姿态）""with a gesture of（摆出一副…的姿态）""gesture of friendship（友好的表示）"和"gesture at sb.（向某人示意）"。

## 3. collaboration　n. 合作；通敌

【双语例句】

The two companies are working in close collaboration each other.
这两家公司密切合作。

【用法解析】

相关短语有"close collaboration（密切合作）""permanent and efficient collaboration（持久有效的合作）"和"collaboration with（与…合作，与…勾结）"等。

## 4. convey　vt. 表达；传达；运输；转移

【双语例句】

I find it hard to convey my feelings in word.
我觉得难以用言语表达我的感情。

【用法解析】

相关短语有"convey emotions（传达感情）""convey thank to（向…转达谢意）"和"convey in words（用言语表达）"等。

### 基本词汇　*Basic Words*

**decade** [ˈdekeɪd] n. 十年

**wholesaler** [ˈhoʊlseɪlər] n. 批发商

**event** [ɪˈvent] n. 重要事情

**track** [træk] v. 跟踪；追踪

**anniversary** [ˌænɪˈvɜːrsəri] n. 周年纪念日

## 情景实例 | *Scene Example*

## 1. 代表公司

在公司成立 10 周年某供应商发函给合作客户，为感谢客户多年来的支持，决定赠送小礼物。

**英**

We would like to sincerely thank our clients who have been associated with us from the time when we started our venture of manufacturing Car Seat covers and selling original Car Accessories. We are extremely glad to share that we have our 10th Anniversary next week.

Yes! We complete a decade of a successful run as a leading wholesaler of Car Accessories and Seat covers in the whole of China market. On the 21st of this month, we will celebrate our anniversary.

On this occasion, we have decided to gift all our clients, a free Apple Air pods. Please accept this as a token of appreciation from our Company. We would like to share our happiness with all our clients and this gift is a small gesture in this direction.

We hope to have a wonderful collaboration in future too and expect to have the opportunity to have much more milestones as such in our journey.

**中**

我们真诚地感谢我们的客户，从我们开始生产汽车座套和销售原装汽车配件以来，就一直与我们合作。我们很高兴地宣布，下个星期就是我们的 10 周年纪念日了。

是的！作为中国市场领先的汽车配件和座椅盖批发商，我们已经成功运营了 10 年。本月 21 日，我们将庆祝周年纪念日。

这一次，我们决定免费赠送所有客户，一个苹果 Air pods 耳机。请接受我们的心意。我们愿与所有的客户分享我们的快乐，送这份礼物给你们是我一点小小的心意。

我们希望将来也能继续这样合作，并希望在我们的前进路途中，有机会达成更多这样的里程碑。

## 2. 代表个人

在客户生日之际，为了巩固客户关系，某外贸业务员发函祝福对方生日快乐，并表示礼物已寄送。

**英**

Please accept my warm gift on the occasion of your 40th birthday. I know that a birthday when you turn 40 is an important event in any person's life.

I hope this Pen Set will bring happiness and joy into your life. My gift conveys my heartiest greetings on this occasion and also expresses my wish that your life after 40 is full of happiness and joyful events.

It has been sent out by DHL express with the tracking number 0000. I hope you will like the little token of my friendship. I have chosen to express my gratitude at having a friend like you.

I wish you the best this year and every year of your life.

**中**

在你 40 岁生日之际，请接受我的温馨礼物。我知道，在任何人的一生中，过 40 岁生日都是一件大事。

我希望这份钢笔套装能给你的生活带来幸福和欢乐。我的礼物表达了我衷心的问候，同时也表达了我的祝愿，希望你 40 岁之后的生活充满了幸福和快乐。

礼物已由 DHL 快递发出，快递单号是 0000。我希望你会喜欢这份象征友谊的小礼物，它代表了我对有一个像你这样的朋友的感激之情。

祝你今年和今后的每一年都无比美好。

---

**PART 3** 其他函电 *Other Letter*

**Unit 5** 升职祝贺
**Promotion Congratulations**

在职场中，升职加薪是值得庆贺的喜事。当得知客户升职时，则应第一时间表示祝贺，并表示对未来合作更有信心。

## 常用词汇 *Vocabulary*

### 1. utilize   vt. 利用；使用

【双语例句】

It is to be hoped that in her new position, her talents will be better utilized than before.

希望在新的岗位上，她的才干能够比以往得到更好地发挥。

【用法解析】

"utilize"在英式英语中也可拼作"utilise"。相关短语有"utilize solar power（利用太阳能）""utilize fully（充分利用）""utilize as（用作）"和"utilize for（用于某目的）"等。

### 2. strengthen   v. 加强；变坚固

【双语例句】

Every effort was made to strengthen unity.

大家尽力加强团结。

【用法解析】

"strengthen"的基本意思是使某物牢固，用于具体物质时，可指结构、强度的增强；也可用于抽象事物，如权势、效力、影响和体制的增强；用于人既可指体力、精力和抵抗力的增强，也可指勇气、意志和道德等的增强或提升。

## 基本词汇 *Basic Words*

**double** [ˈdʌbl]  v. （使）加倍　　　　　　**effort** [ˈefərt]  n. 努力

**personal** [ˈpɜːrsənl]  adj. 个人的　　　　**couple** [ˈkʌpl]   n. 几个人；几件事物

**hard** [hɑːrd]  adj. 艰苦的

## 情景实例 *Scene Example*

在外贸交易中，为了加深与合作企业或具体的合作人之间的关系，某供应商向其合作的销售公司的业务负责人发去函电，祝贺对方被提升为地区销售经理，并表示希望以后有更多的合作机会。

**英**

It was with great pleasure that I heard of your promotion to District Sales Manager. I am sure you will utilize your power in growing further and achieving success.

I am happy for your achievement and you truly deserve it as you have really worked hard from past couple of years. I know from personal experience, for the last three years, you have doubled your company's sales through your own efforts.

I am sure as District Sales Manager of the company you will make the company one of the best in the market in sales. I take this opportunity to look forward to working closely and strengthen the cooperation between our companies.

Congratulations once again and all the best for your future!

**中**

我很高兴得知你被提升为地区销售经理，我相信你会发挥你的能力进一步发展并取得成功。

我为你的成就感到高兴，你真的当之无愧，因为你从过去几年来一直为此努力工作。据我个人所知，在过去的 3 年里，你通过自己的努力把公司的销售额翻了一番。

我敢肯定，作为该公司的地区销售经理，你将使公司成为市场上销售表现最好的公司之一。借此机会，我期待着我们公司之间的合作更加紧密。

再次祝贺你，祝你未来一切顺利！

# 读 者 意 见 反 馈 表

亲爱的读者：

感谢您对中国铁道出版社有限公司的支持，您的建议是我们不断改进工作的信息来源，您的需求是我们不断开拓创新的基础。为了更好地服务读者，出版更多的精品图书，希望您能在百忙之中抽出时间填写这份意见反馈表发给我们。随书纸制表格请在填好后剪下寄到：北京市西城区右安门西街8号中国铁道出版社有限公司大众出版中心 张亚慧 收（邮编：100054）。或者采用传真（010–63549458）方式发送。此外，读者也可以直接通过电子邮件把意见反馈给我们，E-mail地址是：lampard@vip.163.com。我们将选出意见中肯的热心读者，赠送本社的其他图书作为奖励。同时，我们将充分考虑您的意见和建议，并尽可能地给您满意的答复。谢谢！

-------------------------------------------------------------------

所购书名：_____

个人资料：

姓名：_____ 性别：_____ 年龄：_____ 文化程度：_____

职业：_____ 电话：_____ E-mail：_____

通信地址：_____ 邮编：_____

-------------------------------------------------------------------

您是如何得知本书的：

□书店宣传 □网络宣传 □展会促销 □出版社图书目录 □老师指定 □杂志、报纸等的介绍 □别人推荐
□其他（请指明）

您从何处得到本书的：

□书店 □邮购 □商场、超市等卖场 □图书销售的网站 □培训学校 □其他

影响您购买本书的因素（可多选）：

□内容实用 □价格合理 □装帧设计精美 □带多媒体教学光盘 □优惠促销 □书评广告 □出版社知名度
□作者名气 □工作、生活和学习的需要 □其他

您对本书封面设计的满意程度：

□很满意 □比较满意 □一般 □不满意 □改进建议

您对本书的总体满意程度：

从文字的角度 □很满意 □比较满意 □一般 □不满意
从技术的角度 □很满意 □比较满意 □一般 □不满意

您希望书中图的比例是多少：

□少量的图片辅以大量的文字 □图文比例相当 □大量的图片辅以少量的文字

您希望本书的定价是多少：


本书最令您满意的是：

1.

2.

您在使用本书时遇到哪些困难：

1.

2.

您希望本书在哪些方面进行改进：

1.

2.

您需要购买哪些方面的图书？对我社现有图书有什么好的建议？


您更喜欢阅读哪些类型和层次的理财类书籍（可多选）？

□入门类 □精通类 □综合类 □问答类 □图解类 □查询手册类

您在学习计算机的过程中有什么困难？


您的其他要求：